CONFESSIONS

Saint Augustine

Rewritten and Updated by
Dr. Tom Gill

Bridge-Logos

Gainesville, Florida 32614 USA

Confessions—Saint Augustine
Rewritten and Updated by Dr. Tom Gill
Copyright ©2003 by Bridge-Logos

Printed in the United States of America. All rights reserved.
Library of Congress Catalog Card Number: Pending
International Standard Book Number: 0-88270-948-8

All biblical quotations unless otherwise noted are from the New King James Version. Copyright, 1979, 1980, 1982 by Thomas Nelson, Inc. Used by permission. Used by Permission.

Scripture quotations marked NIV are from the Holy Bible, New International Version. Copyright © 1973, 1978, 1984, International Bible Society. Used by Permission.

Published by:
Bridge-Logos
PO Box 141630
Gainesville, FL 32614
www.bridgelogos.com

Editor: Dr. Tom Gill
Cover Design: Andy Toman
Interior Text Design/Layout: Cathleen Kwas

Acknowledgment

It's with deep gratitude that we acknowledge the work of Dr. Albert C. Outler, who translated *Confessions* from Latin to English and published the work in the 1950's. This manuscript is newly edited from that original translation.

Table of Contents

INTRODUCTION

Meet Saint Augustine

Aurelius Augustinus, better known as Augustine, was born in 354 A.D. to a devoutly Christian mother and pagan father (who later accepted Christ). Raised in the city of Tagaste in North Africa, he was educated and taught in Carthage, traveled to Rome, lived in Milan, and returned to Africa where he served as Bishop of Hippo.

Augustine stands as the last of the early church fathers, and the first of the medieval fathers of Western Christianity. An insatiable quest for truth drove Augustine to explore the belief systems of the day, including the philosophers. Trained as a lawyer, his mind thrived on unraveling complex theories and doctrines. His eloquence was legendary, and his writings influenced the early church, standing second only to the apostle Paul in their impact on Christianity.

Augustine's sexual appetite drove him to seek pleasure where he could find it, but also plagued his conscience. He never married, but had a son out of wedlock to a mistress he cared for fondly. A marriage was arranged for Augustine, but his conversion to Christianity and subsequent vow of chastity prevented it from taking place. Nevertheless, he struggled with the desires of his flesh and fought to quench the fires of passion that burned, sometimes uncontrollably, with in him.

Augustine's hunger for religious knowledge led him through many twisting trails of heresy, including, Manichaeism and Neoplatonism. Augustine finally turned completely to God in 386 A.D. when he heard a child say, "take, read" a copy of Paul's letter to the Romans. He died serving as Bishop of Hippo in North Africa in 430 A.D.

Confessions is the autobiography of Augustine, and presents a moving and profound record of a human soul and its struggles. This is the most widely read of all his works that not only tells the story of Augustine's struggle in the faith, but also his love for the Master. It speaks to the heart of humanity about human weakness, human frailty, human depravity, and the human need for a holy God. *Confessions* is an exercise in self-knowledge and true humility in the atmosphere of grace and reconciliation.

Many of the doctrines presented in *Confessions* reflect those of the Roman Catholic Church, of which Augustine became a bishop. However, because of his extensive study of Greek philosophy, many of the thoughts of Augustine are expressed in the language of the philosophers.

Confessions is an autobiography, and some of Augustine's "theology" had not yet been fully developed when it was written. That's why this work isn't presented as a book of theology. Some Christians may disagree with some things written here, others will agree fully. Nevertheless, this is Augustine's story—it's what he wanted to write about subjects of interest to him.

However, as you read Augustine's story, you'll see yourself. Though the era is long past, the cities far distant, and man long dead, his story lives on. The center of his story lives on as well— Jesus Christ.

Augustine's quest to discover true faith and true "religion" is not unlike the journey undertaken by countless souls today. With candid self-disclosure, Augustine reveals the inner struggle he faced in bridling his sexual passions, and the heated battle to conquer his haughty pride. Take heart, you wandering one; God's love pursues you, no matter where you are—just ask Augustine!

The relentless pursuit of truth can only lead to the Source of truth—the Eternal God of heaven. As you read these pages, focus your eyes on Him. Doing so will enable you to see through the empty words of the philosophies of men, past the heresies of false religion, and beyond even the beauty of creation. You'll be led to very feet of Jesus where you, too, will discover the Truth of truth. You'll also experience forgiveness, find wholeness, bask in unconditional love, and will be cleansed from any and all impurity.

"Confession is good for the soul." the old saying goes. It's true—Augustine discovered it, and you will too.

My prayer is that you will be blessed as you read these pages, and that you'll find the Truth as Augustine did.

—Tom Gill, Ph.D.

Augustine's Testimony Concerning The Confessions

Clarifications and Corrections (427 A.D.)

My *Confessions*, in thirteen books, praise the righteous and good God as they speak either of my evil or good, and they are meant to excite men's minds and affections toward Him. At least as far as I am concerned, this is what they did for me when they were being written and they still do so when they are read. What some people think of them is their own affair, but I know that they have given pleasure to many of my brethren and still do.

The first through the tenth book were written about myself; the other three about Holy Scripture from what is written there, *In the beginning God created the heavens and the earth*,[1] even as far as the reference to the Sabbath rest.[2]

When I confessed my soul's misery over the death of a friend in Book four, I said that our soul had somehow been made one out of two souls: "But it may have been that I was afraid to die, lest he should then die wholly whom I had so greatly loved" (Ch. 6). This now seems to be more a trivial declamation than a serious confession, although this inept expression may be tempered somewhat by the "may have been" which I added.

I said in Book 13 that, "The firmament was made between the higher waters (superior) and the lower waters (inferior)." This was without sufficient thought. Whatever the case, the matter is very obscure.

Preserved By God (428 A.D.)

Which of my shorter works has been more widely known or given greater pleasure than the [thirteen] books of my *Confessions*? Though I published them long before the Pelagian heresy had even begun to be, it is plain that in them I said to my God, again and again, "Give what You command and command what You will." When a certain brother of mine repeated these words in the presence of Pelagius at Rome, he could not bear them and so vigorously contradicted my friend that they nearly came to a quarrel. Now what, indeed, does God command, first and foremost except that we believe in Him? This faith He Himself gives, so it is well said to God, "Give what You command."

Moreover, these same books contain the account of my conversion. God turned me to the very faith that I was seeking to destroy with a vile verbal assault.[3] Do you remember how the narration shows that I was given as a gift to the faithful and daily tears of my mother, who had been promised that I should not perish? I certainly declared there that God by His grace turns the will of men to the true faith when they are not only averse to it, but opposed to it as well. As for the other ways in which I sought God's aid in my growth in perseverance, you either know or can review them as you wish.

Letter to Darius (429 A.D.)

Thus, my son, take the books of my *Confessions* and use them as a good man should—not superficially, but as a Christian in Christian charity. Here see me as I am and do not praise me for more than I am. Here believe nothing else about me than my own testimony. Here observe what I have been in myself and through myself. And if something in me pleases you, here praise God with me—Him whom I desire to be praised on my account and not myself. "It is He who has made us, and not we ourselves."[4] He who made us remade us because we were lost. As, then, you find me in these pages, pray for me that I shall not fail but that I may go on to be perfected. Pray for me, my son, pray for me!

BOOK ONE

The Mysterious Pilgrimage of Grace

Using prayer and grateful praise to God, Augustine seeks to trace the mysterious pilgrimage of grace that his life has followed. Lingering in God's presence and basking in God's omnipotent grace, Augustine seeks to recall his infancy and childhood experiences in school. All to the praise and glory of God.

Chapter 1 – I Will Seek You O Lord

"Great is the Lord, and greatly to be praised;"[5] "Great is our Lord and mighty in power; His understanding is infinite."[6] Man desires to praise You, for he is a part of Your creation. He carries his mortality with him and bears the evidence of his sin, the proof that You resist the proud. Still man desires to praise You, this man who is only a small part of Your creation. You have prompted him that he should delight to praise You, for You have made man for Yourself and restless is the human heart until it comes to rest in You.

Grant me, O Lord, to know and understand whether first to call upon You or to praise You, whether first to know You or to appeal to You. But who can summon You without knowing You? For he who does not know You may call upon You as someone You are not.

It may be that we should call upon You, God, so that we may come to know You. But "how then shall they call on Him in whom they have not believed? And how shall they believe in Him of whom they have not heard? And how shall they hear without a preacher?"[7] "Those who seek Him will praise the LORD,"[8] for those who seek Him will find Him,[9] and finding Him, will praise Him.

I will seek You, O Lord, and call upon You. I call upon You, O Lord, in my faith, which You have given me, which You breathed in me through the humanity of Your Son and through the ministry of Your preacher.[10]

Chapter 2—How Can I Call Upon You?

How shall I call upon my God, my God and my Lord? For when I call on Him I ask Him to come into me. But what place is there in me into which my God can come? How could God, the God who made both heaven and earth, come into me? Is there anything in me, O Lord my God, that can contain You? Do even the heavens and the earth, which You have made and in which You made me, contain You? Without You nothing would be which now exists. Is it possible that Your design is that whatever exists has some capacity to receive You?

Why, then, do I ask You to come into me, since I also am and could not be if You weren't in me? For I am not, after all, in hell— and yet You are there too, for "If I make my bed in hell, behold, You are there."[11] Therefore I would not exist. I would simply not be at all, unless I exist in You, from whom and by whom and in whom all things are. Even so, Lord, even so. To where do I call You when I am already in You? Or from where would You come into me? Where, beyond heaven and earth, could I go that there my God might come to me, He who said, "I fill heaven and earth"?[12]

Chapter 3—God Fills All Things

God, since You fill the heavens and earth, do they contain You? Or, do You fill and overflow them because they cannot contain You? Where do You pour out what remains of You after heaven and earth are full? Or is there no need that You, who contains all things, should be contained by any, since those things which You fill, You fill by containing them? The vessels, which You fill, do not confine You, because even if they were broken, You would not be poured out. Furthermore, when You are poured out upon us, You are not brought down; we are uplifted instead.

God, You are not scattered; You gather us together. But when You fill all things, do You fill them with Your entire being? Or, since all things together could not contain You altogether, does any one thing contain just a single part? And do all things contain that same part at the same time? Do singulars contain You singly? Do greater things contain more of You, and smaller things less? Or, is it that You are wholly present everywhere, yet in such a way that nothing contains You wholly?

CHAPTER 4—WHAT IS MY GOD?

What is my God? What, I ask, but the Lord God? "For who is Lord but the Lord himself, or who is God besides our God?"[13] O God, You are most...

- High
- Excellent
- Potent
- Omnipotent
- Merciful
- Just
- Secret
- Truly present
- Beautiful
- Strong

Lord God, You are:

- Stable, yet not supported
- Unchangeable, yet changing all things

- Never new, yet never old
- Making all things new, yet bringing old age upon the proud – and they know it not
- Always working, yet ever at rest
- Gathering, yet needing nothing
- Sustaining
- Pervading
- Protecting
- Creating
- Nourishing
- Developing
- Seeking, and yet possessing all things

O God You...

- Love, but without passion
- Are jealous, yet free from care
- Turn away without remorse
- Are angry, yet remain serene

Lord God, You...

- Change Your ways, leaving Your plans unchanged
- Recover what You have never really lost
- Never are in need but still rejoice at Your gains
- Never are greedy, yet demand dividends

Men pay more than is required so that You become a debtor. Yet who can possess anything that does not already belong to You? You owe humanity nothing; yet pay out to them as if in debt to them. Yet when You cancel debts You lose nothing!

O my God, my life, my holy Joy, what is this that I have said? What can anyone say when speaking of You? But woe to those who keep silence, since those who say most are mute.

CHAPTER 5—RESTORE MY SOUL

Who will bring me to rest in You? Who will send You into my heart to overwhelm it so that my sins will be blotted out, that I may embrace You, my only good? What are You to me?

Have mercy that I may speak. Of what significance am I that You command me to love You and are angry and threaten immeasurable misery if I do not? I ask, is the distress insignificant to not love You? Not to me!

By Your mercy, O Lord, my God, tell me what You are to me. "Say to my soul, 'I am your salvation.'"[14] Speak that I may hear. Behold, the ears of my heart are before You, O Lord. Open them and say to my soul, "I am your salvation." I will hasten after the sound of Your voice and will take hold of You. Do not hide Your face from me. Even if it kills me, let me see Your face. If not, I will surely die.

My soul is too narrow for You to inhabit. Enlarge it, I pray. My soul is in ruins. Restore it, O God. I confess and know that there is much about my soul that offends You, but who will cleanse it? To whom can I cry but You? O Lord, "Cleanse me from secret faults..."[15] "Keep me from deliberate sins."[16] "I believed, therefore I spoke..."[17] But You, O Lord, You know. Have I not confessed my transgressions unto You, O my God? Have You put away the iniquity of my heart?[18] I do not contend in judgment with You,[19] who are Truth itself. Nor would I deceive myself, lest my iniquity lie even to itself. Therefore, I do not contend in judgment with You, for "If You, Lord, should mark iniquities, O Lord, who could stand?"[20]

CHAPTER 6—THE CONSOLATION OF GOD'S MERCY

Though I am merely dust and ashes, allow me to speak to Your mercy, O God. Behold, it is to Your mercy that I speak and not to a man who scorns me. Yet perhaps even You might scorn me. Nevertheless, when You turn and attend to me, be merciful unto me.

What do I wish to say, O Lord my God? Where did I come from before this life-in-death, or should I call it death-in-life? Yet the consolations of Your mercy have sustained me from the very beginning. My earthly parents, from whom and in whom You formed me in time told me this, though I have no memory of it myself. They sustained me with suckling milk, though neither my mother nor my nurses filled their own breasts. You, through them, gave me the food of infancy according to Your ordinance and Your bounty, which underlies all things. For it was You who caused me not to want more than You gave, and it was You who gave to those who nourished me the will to give me what You had given to them. And they, by an instinctive affection, were willing to give me what You had abundantly supplied.

It was good for them that my good should come through them, though in truth, it was not from them but by them. For it is from You, O God, that all good things come, including my health. I have since learned this as You made it abundantly clear by all that I have seen You give, both to me and to those around me. For even at the very first I knew how to suck, to lie quiet when I was full, and to cry when in pain—nothing more.

Afterward I began to laugh, first in my sleep and then upon waking. For this I have been told about myself, though I cannot remember it. I believe it for I see the same things in other infants. Then, little by little, I realized where I was and wished to tell my wants to those who might satisfy them, but I could not! For my wants were inside me while my attendants were outside, around me. They could not by any power of theirs come into my soul.

Therefore, I would fling my arms and legs about and cry. I would make the few and feeble gestures that I could, though the signs were not much like what I inwardly desired. Then, when I was not satisfied from either not being understood or because what I got was not good for me, I grew indignant that my elders were not subject to me and that those on whom I actually had no claim did not wait on me as slaves. Therefore, I avenged myself on them by crying. I know that infants are like this; I have myself been able to learn by watching them. Though the infants didn't know me, they have shown me better what I was like than my own nurses who knew me.

My infancy died long ago, but I am still living. You, O Lord, whose life is forever and in whom nothing dies, have been since before the world was. Before all that can be called "before," You were. You are the God and Lord of all Your creatures, and with You abide all the stable causes of all unstable things. You are the unchanging Source of all changeable things, and the Eternal Reason of all non-rational and temporal things.

O merciful God, tell me, a pitiful creature, whether my infancy followed yet an earlier age of my life that had already passed away. Was it such another age that I spent in my mother's womb? For something of that sort has been suggested to me, and I have myself seen pregnant women. But what, O God, my Joy, preceded *that* period of life? Was I, indeed, anywhere, or anybody? No one can explain these things to me, neither father nor mother, experience of others, nor my own memory. Do You laugh at me for asking such things? Or do You command me to praise and confess unto You only what I know?

I give thanks to You, O Lord of heaven and earth. I give praise to You for that first being and my infancy of which I have no memory. For You have granted to man that he should come to self-knowledge through the knowledge of others, and that he should believe many things about himself on the authority of those women who nurtured him. Now, clearly, I had life and being, and as my infancy closed, I was already learning gestures through which my feelings could be communicated to others.

Where could such a creature come from but You, O Lord? Is any man skillful enough to have fashioned himself? Is there any other source from which being and life could flow into us, save this: that You, O Lord, have made us; You, with whom being and life are one, since You are both Supreme Being and Supreme Life together. For You are infinite and in You there is no change nor end to this present day. Though there is a sense in which it ends in You, since all things are in You and there would be no such thing as days passing away unless You sustained them. "Your years never end,"[21] so Your years are an ever-present day. How many of our fathers' days have passed through this, Your day, and have received from it the measure and fashion of being that they had? All the days to come shall so receive and so pass away. "But You are always the same"![22] Furthermore, all the things of tomorrow and the days yet to come, and all of yesterday and the days that are past, You will gather into this, Your day. What is it to me if someone does not understand this? Let him still rejoice and continue to ask, "What is this?" Let him also rejoice and prefer to seek You, even if he fails to find an answer, rather than to seek an answer and not find You!

CHAPTER 7—HAVE I EVER LIVED IN INNOCENCE?

"Hear me, O God! Woe to the sins of men!" When a man cries thus, You show him mercy, for You created the man but not the sin in him. Who brings to remembrance the sins of my infancy? For in Your sight there is none free from sin, not even the infant who has lived but a day upon this earth. Who brings this to my remembrance? Does not each little one, in whom I now observe what I no longer remember of myself? In what ways, in that time, did I sin? Was it that I cried for the breast? If now I should so cry—not for the breast, but for food suitable to my condition—I would be justly laughed at and rebuked. What I did then deserved rebuke but, since I could not understand those who rebuked me, neither custom nor common sense permitted me to be rebuked.

As we grow we root out and cast away from us such childish habits. Yet I have not seen anyone who is wise who cast away the good when trying to purge the bad. Nor was it good, even in that time, to strive to get by crying for what, if it had been given me, would have been hurtful. Likewise, to be bitterly indignant at those who, because they were older—not slaves but free—and wiser than I, would not indulge my capricious desires. Was it a good thing for me to try, by struggling as hard as I could to harm them for not obeying me, even when it would have done me harm to have been obeyed? Thus, the infant's innocence lies in the weakness of his body and not in the infant's mind. I have myself observed a baby to be jealous, though it could not speak. It was livid as it watched another infant at the breast.

Who is ignorant of this? Mothers and nurses cure these things but I know not the remedies used. Nevertheless, is this innocence, when the fountain of milk is flowing fresh and abundant, that another who needs it should not be allowed to share it, even though he requires such nourishment to sustain his life? Yet we look leniently on such things, not because they are not faults, but because they will vanish as the years pass. For, though we allow for such things in an infant, the same things would not be patiently tolerated in an adult.

Therefore, O Lord my God, You command me to praise You, the One who breathed life into the infant. You gave him a body furnished with senses, shaped with limbs, beautified with form, and endowed with all vital energies for his well being and health. You command me to praise You for these things, to give thanks unto the Lord, and to sing praise unto his name, O Most High.[23] For You are God, omnipotent and good, even if You had done no more than these things, which no other but You can do. You alone made all things fair and ordered everything according to Your law.

I am unwilling to dwell on this part of my life of which, O Lord, I have no remembrance, about which I must trust the word of others and what I can surmise from observing other infants, even if such guesses are trustworthy. For it lies in the deep murk of my forgetfulness and so is like the period that I passed in my mother's womb. But if "I was conceived in iniquity, and in sin my mother nourished me in her womb,"[24] where, I pray, O my God, or when was I, Your servant, ever innocent? Nevertheless, I must pass over that period, for what can I do with a time from which I can recall no memories?

CHAPTER 8—LEARNING TO COMMUNICATE

Did I not, then, as I grew out of infancy, come next to boyhood? Or rather did it not come to me and succeed my infancy? My infancy did not go away, for where would it go? It was simply no longer present. I was no longer an infant who was unable to speak, but a chattering boy. I remember this and have since observed how I learned to talk. Those around me did not teach me words by rote, as they taught me my letters afterward.

When I was unable to verbalize what I wished to say, I used whimpering sounds, grunts and various gestures of my limbs to reinforce my demands. I repeated the sounds already stored in my memory by the mind, which You, O my God, had given me. Then, when those around me called an object by name and pointed it out while they spoke, I saw it and realized that the thing they wished to indicate was called by the name they spoke. What they meant was made plain by the gestures of their bodies, a kind of natural language common to all humanity, which expresses itself through changes of countenance, glances of the eye, gestures and intonations which indicate a disposition and attitude—either to seek or to possess, to reject or to avoid.

So it was that by frequently hearing words in different phrases, I gradually identified the objects that the words stood for and, having formed my mouth to repeat these sounds, was able to express my will. Thus I exchanged with those around me the verbal sounds by which we express our wishes and I advanced deeper into the stormy fellowship of human life. All the while, I was depending upon the authority of my parents and the will of my elders.

CHAPTER 9—EDUCATION THROUGH PAINFUL SUBMISSION

O my God! What miseries and mockeries I experienced when it was impressed on me that obedience to my teachers was necessary if I desired to flourish in this world and become an effective communicator, which would gain honor for me among men and deceitful riches! To this end I was sent to school to obtain an education, the value of which I didn't know, wretch that I was.

When I was slow to learn, I was beaten, because those who had previously completed the same course of study deemed this praiseworthy. They had set the precedent for the sorrowful road on which I was compelled to travel, multiplying labor and sorrow upon the sons of Adam.

About this time, O Lord, I observed men praying to You. I learned from them, according to my capacity to understand, to regard You as some great Being, who, though not visible to our senses, was able to hear and help us. Thus as a boy I began to pray to You, my Help and my Refuge, and in calling on You, shattered the bonds of my tongue. Small as I was, I earnestly prayed that I might not be beaten at school. You did not answer my prayer – for that would have been giving me over to my folly – my elders and even my parents, who wished me no ill, treated the wounds of my beating as a joke, though they were great and grievous to me.

O Lord, is there anyone with a spirit so great and who clings to You with such steadfast affection that he is endowed with so great a courage that he regards with indifference the instruments of torture from which people everywhere fervently pray to be spared? Or is there a kind of dullness that has the same effect? Can they ridicule those who so greatly fear these torments, just as my parents were amused at the torments with which our teachers punished us boys? For we were no less afraid of our pains, nor did we implore You less to escape them. Nevertheless, we were sinning by writing, reading or studying less than our assigned lessons.

For I did not, O Lord, lack memory or capacity; by Your will I possessed enough for my age. However, my mind was consumed with play, and those who were doing the same things themselves punished me for this. However, the idleness of our elders is called business while those same elders punish the idleness of boys, though it is quite similar. Sadly, no one pities either the boys or the men. Will any common sense observer agree that I was rightly punished as a boy for playing ball simply because this hindered me from learning more quickly those lessons, which, as a man, I could engage in more shameful games? Did the one by whom I was beaten do anything different? When this teacher was proven wrong in a small controversy with a fellow teacher, he was more tormented by anger and envy than I was when beaten by a playmate in a ball game.

CHAPTER 10—THE PASSION OF PLAY

Yet I sinned, O Lord my God, Ruler and Creator of all natural things. I sinned in acting against the instructions of my parents and those of my teachers. For this education they wished me to acquire, regardless of their motives, I might have put to good use afterward.

I disobeyed them, not because I had chosen a better way, but from a sheer love of play. I loved the vanity of victory, and I loved to have my ears tickled with flattery, which made them itch even more ardently. A similar curiosity glowed more and more in my eyes for the shows and sports of my elders. Yet those who put on these shows were held in such high repute that nearly all of them desired the same for their children. Therefore, they were willing to have their children beaten if the games of childhood kept them from the studies assigned them.

O Lord, look down on these things with mercy and deliver us who now call upon You. Likewise, deliver those who do not call upon You, that they may cry out and be set free.

CHAPTER 11—THE BAPTISM OF REGENERATION DELAYED

As a boy I had heard of the promise of eternal life through the humility of the Lord our God, who came down to visit us in our pride. I was signed with the sign of His cross, and was seasoned with His salt even from the womb of my mother, who greatly trusted in the Lord. You saw, O Lord, how once when I was a child, I was suddenly seized with stomach pains and was at the point of death. You saw this, O my God, for even then You were my keeper. You witnessed with what agitation and faith I solicited from the piety of my mother and from Your Church (which is the mother of us all) the baptism of Your Christ, my Lord and my God.

However, my mother was very perplexed. With a heart pure in Your faith, she earnestly prayed for my eternal salvation. Had I not quickly recovered, she would have immediately provided for my initiation and baptism, confessing You, O Lord Jesus, for the forgiveness of sins. However, my baptism was deferred because it was clear that I would live. I could then be further polluted because the guilt caused by sins committed after baptism would be still greater and more perilous.

At that time, I "believed" along with my mother and the entire household, with the exception of my father. He did not overrule the influence of my mother's piety in me, nor did he prevent my believing in Christ, although he had not yet believed in Him. For it was her desire, O my God, that I should acknowledge You as my Father rather than him. You aided her in overcoming her husband, to whom she yielded obedience. In this way she also yielded obedience to You, who so commands.

O my God, I ask You, if it is Your will, to what good end my baptism was deferred at that time? Was it really for my good that the reins on me were slackened to encourage me in sin? Or, were they not slackened? If not, then why is it still droned into our ears on all sides, "Let him alone; let him do as he pleases, for he is not yet baptized"?

In the matter of bodily health, no one says, "Let him alone; let him be wounded even more, for he is not yet cured"! How much better, then, would it have been for me to be cured at once! Then, through the diligent care of friends and myself, my soul's restored health would have been kept safe in Your keeping, who gave it in the first place! This would have been far better, in truth. But how many and great the waves of temptation which appeared to hang over me as I grew out of childhood! My mother foresaw these, and she preferred that the unformed clay should be risked to them rather than the clay molded after Christ's image.[25]

CHAPTER 12—GOD'S PROVIDENCE – MY BLESSING

This time of childhood—which was far less dreadful for me than my adolescence—had for me no love of learning and I hated to be driven to it. Yet I was driven to it just the same. It was good for me even though I did not do it well, for I would not have learned had I not been forced to it. No man does well against his will, even if what he does is a good thing.

Those who forced me did not do well either, the good that was done in me came from You, my God. For these masters did not care about how I would use what they forced me to learn. They took it for granted that my learning was to satisfy the selfish desires of a rich beggar and to fulfill a shameful glory. But You, Lord, by whom the hairs of my head are numbered, used for my good the error of all who pushed me on to study. Nevertheless, my error in not being willing to learn You used for my punishment. And I, though so small a boy yet so great a sinner, was not punished unjustly. Therefore, by the instrumentality of those who did not do well, You did well for me, and by my own sin You justly punished me. For it is even as You have ordained, that every selfish affection brings on its own punishment.

CHAPTER 13—A QUEST FOR UNDERSTANDING

What is the root of my strong dislike of Greek literature, which I studied from my boyhood? To this day I have not fully understood the cause. I loved to study Latin, not just the fundamentals, but the grammar as well. I considered the beginner's lessons in reading, writing, and reckoning no less a burden and pain than Greek.

However, from where did this disdain of Greek studies come? Was if from the sin and vanity of this life? For I am nothing more than "A breath that passes away and does not come again."[26] I assure you, those first lessons were better because they were more certain. Through them I acquired, and still retain, the power of reading what I find written and writing for myself what I will. However, in the other subjects I was compelled to learn about the wanderings of a certain Aeneas, while oblivious of my own wanderings. I was required to weep for Dido who was dead. She had killed herself for love. This I did with no regard of my own wretched condition and that I was dying myself. Nevertheless, You, O God, were my life in the midst of these things.

For what can be more wretched than the wretch who has no pity upon himself? The miserable one who sheds tears over Dido, dead for the love of Aeneas, but who sheds no tears for his own death in not loving You, O God? You are the light of my heart, the bread of my soul's inner mouth, the power that links together my mind with my inmost thoughts.

I did not love You, and thus committed fornication against You.[27] Those around me who were also sinning encouraged me, saying, "Well done! Well done!" The friendships of this world are fornication against You, O God, and the "Well done! Well done!" is cried until one feels compelled to show himself a man in this way.

I shed no tears for my own condition, though I wept for Dido who "sought death at the sword's point."[28] Having forsaken You, I was seeking the lowest rung of Your creation; earth sinking back to earth again. Yet had I been forbidden to read these poems, I would have grieved that I was not allowed to read what grieved me. This sort of madness is considered more honorable and more fruitful learning than the beginner's course in which I learned to read and write.

Nevertheless, O my God, cry unto my soul and let Your truth say to me: "Not so, not so! That first learning was far better." For, obviously, I would rather forget the wanderings of Aeneas, and all such things, than forget how to write and read.

Still, there hangs a veil over the entrance of the grammar school. This is not so much the sign of a covering for a mystery as a curtain for error. Let those I no longer fear exclaim against me while I confess to You, my God, what my soul desires. Let me find some rest, for in blaming my own evil ways I may come to love Your holy ways.

O, God, do not allow those who buy and sell the baubles of literature cry out against me. For if, as the poet says, I ask them if it is true that Aeneas once came to Carthage, the unlearned will reply that they do not know and the learned will deny that it is true. But if I ask with what letters the name Aeneas is written, all who can read will answer correctly in accordance with the conventional understanding of men.

Furthermore, if I ask which would cause the greatest inconvenience in our life if it were forgotten: reading and writing, or these poetical fictions, who does not see what everyone would answer who had not entirely lost his own memory? Therefore, as a boy I erred when I preferred those fruitless studies to these more profitable ones, or rather loved the one and hated the other. "One and one are two, two and two are four": this was then a truly hateful song to me. But the wooden horse full of its armed soldiers, and the holocaust of Troy, and the spectral image of Creusa were all a most delightful though empty show![29]

Why then, did I dislike Greek learning, which was full of such tales? For Homer was skillful in creating stories of exciting fantasy, yet when I was a boy, he was most disagreeable to me. I believe that Virgil would have the same effect on Greek boys as Homer did on me if they were forced to learn him. The tedium of learning a foreign language mingled bitterness into the sweetness of those Grecian myths. I didn't understand a word of the language, yet I was threatened with cruel punishments to learn it.

As an infant I knew no Latin, but acquired it without any fear or tormenting. I was merely alert to the coaxing of my nurses, the jokes of those who smiled on me, and the sportiveness of those who toyed with me. Indeed, I learned all this without being pressured with punishment, but because my own heart urged me on. I learned from those who talked to me and into whose ears I could speak whatever I could fashion.

From this it is sufficiently clear that a free curiosity is more effective in learning than a discipline based on fear. Nevertheless, by Your ordinance O God, discipline is given to restrain the excesses of freedom. This ranges from the cane of the schoolmaster to the trials of the martyr, which has the effect of mingling a wholesome bitterness while calling us back to You from the poisonous pleasures that first drew us from You.

Chapter 14—God, Use What I Have Learned

Hear my prayer, O Lord. Prevent my soul from fainting under Your discipline. Let me not faint in confessing Your mercies, whereby You saved me from all my wicked ways. Keep me strong till You become sweet to me beyond all the allure of the world that I used to pursue. Let me come to love You wholly, and grasp Your hand with my whole heart that You may deliver me from every temptation, even unto the last.

Thus, O Lord, my King and my God, may all things useful that I learned as a boy now be offered in Your service. Let it be for Your service that I now speak and write and think. For when I was learning vain things, You imposed Your discipline upon me and You have forgiven my sin of delighting in those vanities. I learned many useful things in those studies, but these same things may have been learned in ways not so self-seeking. Surely that is the safe way for youths to walk.

CHAPTER 15—ABANDONING THE
TRUTH TO LAY HOLD OF A FABLE

Woe unto you, O torrent of human custom! Who will stay your course? When will you ever run dry? How long will you carry the sons of Eve down into that vast and hideous ocean, which even those who have the Tree (for an ark)[30] can scarcely pass over? Do I not read in you the stories of Jove the god of thunder and the adulterer?[31] How could he be both? But so it says, and the façade of thunder served as a cloak for him to play at real adultery.

Nevertheless, which of our renowned professors will give hearing to a man trained in their own schools who cries out saying: "These were Homer's fictions; he transfers things human to the gods. I could have wished that he would transfer divine things to us."[32] But it would have been more true if he said, "These are, indeed, his fictions, but he attributed divine attributes to sinful men, that crimes might not be accounted crimes, and that whoever committed such crimes might appear to imitate the celestial gods and not abandoned men."

O torrent of hell, masses of humanity are cast into you, and they pay tuition for learning all these things! Much is made of it when this goes on in the universities under the support of laws which give a salary over and above the fees. All the while you beat against your rocky shore and roar: "Here words may be learned. Here you can attain the eloquence which is so necessary to persuade people to your way of thinking and so helpful in unfolding your opinions." Truly, they seem to argue that we should never have understood the words, "golden shower," "bosom," "intrigue," "highest heavens," and more if Terence had not introduced a good-for-nothing youth upon the stage, setting up a picture of Jove as his example of lewdness and telling the tale:

Of Jove's descending in a golden shower
Into Danae's bosom...
With a woman to intrigue.

See how he excites himself to lust, as if by a heavenly authority, when he says:

Great Jove,
Who shakes the highest heavens with his thunder;
Shall I, poor mortal man, not do the same?
I've done it, and with all my heart, I'm glad.[33]

These words are not learned one bit easier because of this vileness, but through them the depravity is more boldly perpetrated. I do not blame the words, for they are, as it were, choice and precious vessels, but I do deplore the wine of error that was poured out to us by teachers already drunk. Unless we also drank we were beaten without the liberty of appeal to a sober judge. Nonetheless, O my God, in whose presence I can now with security recall this, I learned these things willingly and with delight, and for it I was called a boy of good promise.

CHAPTER 16—MISUSED TALENT

Bear with me, O my God while I speak of Your gifts, the talents you gave me and of the follies on which I wasted them. I was given a lesson that sufficiently disturbed my soul, for in it there was both hope of praise and fear of shame or a beating. The assignment was that I should recite the words of Juno, as she raged and sorrowed that she could not,

Bar off Italy
/ From all the approaches of the Teucrian king.[34]

I had learned that Juno never uttered these words. Yet I was compelled to stray in the footsteps of these fictitious poems and turn into prose what the poet had said in verse. In the recitation, the boy who most strikingly reproduced the passions of anger and sorrow according to the "character" of the persons presented, and who clothed it all in the most suitable language won the most applause. O my true Life, my God, what is it to me now that my acting was applauded above that of many of my classmates and fellow students? Actually, was it not all merely smoke and wind? Was there nothing else on which I could have exercised my wit and tongue?

Your praise, O Lord, might have strengthened the weakness of my heart by Your Scriptures. Then it would not have been dragged away by these empty trifles as shameful prey to the spirits of the air. For there is more than one way in which men sacrifice to the fallen angels.

CHAPTER 17—HUMILITY IN CHILDHOOD

When men were held up to me as models, it was no wonder that I was carried toward vanity and estranged from You, O my God. These men, when relating a deed of theirs, though not in itself evil, were covered with confusion if found guilty of barbaric behavior or impropriety. Nevertheless, they could boast about their own immorality and be applauded for it, so long as they did it with an ornate oration of well-chosen words.

You see this all, O Lord, and keep silent. O God, You are "longsuffering and abundant in mercy and truth."[35] Will You keep silent forever? Even now You draw from that vast deep the soul that seeks You and thirsts after Your delight, whose "heart said to You, 'Your face, LORD, I will seek.'"[36] For I was far from Your face in the dark shadows of passion.

It is not by our feet, nor by change of place, that we either turn from You or return to You. That younger son did not charter horses or chariots, or ships, fly away on visible wings, or journey by walking so that in the far country he might wantonly waste all that You gave him when he set out.[37] A kind Father when You gave, and kinder still when he returned destitute! To be wanton, that is to say, to be darkened in heart, this is to be far from Your face.

Look upon us, O Lord God, and in Your mercy patiently observe how diligently the sons of men adhere to the conventional rules of letters and syllables, taught them by those who learned beforehand, while they neglect the eternal rules of everlasting salvation taught by You. They carry it so far that if he who practices or teaches the established rules of pronunciation should speak without properly aspirating the first syllable of "*human*" and thus make it a "*uman*" being, he will offend men more than if he, a human being, were to *hate* another human being contrary to Your commandments! It's as if he should feel that there is an enemy who could be more destructive to himself than that hatred which incites him against his fellow man; or that he could destroy him whom he hates more completely than he destroys his own soul by this same hatred. Obviously, there is no knowledge of letters more instinctive than the writing of conscience against doing unto another what one would not have done to himself.

How mysterious You are, who "dwells in the heavens"[38] in silence. You are the only great God, who by an unwearied law hurls down the penalty of blindness to unlawful desire! When a man seeking the reputation of eloquence stands before a human judge, surrounded by a thronging multitude, and verbally barrages his enemy with fierce hatred, he takes utmost care that his tongue does not slip in a grammatical error.

These were the customs in which I was thrust as an unhappy boy. In this arena I was more fearful of making a verbal faux pas than envying those who had not. These things I declare and confess to You, my God. I was applauded by those whom I thought it my duty to please. I was blind to the depth of iniquity wherein I was cast away from Your eyes.

O Lord, in Your eyes, what was more wicked than I? For I displeased even my own kind and with endless lies deceived my tutor, my masters and parents. This sprang from a love of play, a craving for the frivolous, a stage-stricken restlessness to imitate what I saw in these shows.

I stole from my parents' storehouse and table, often driven by gluttony, and other times simply to have something to trade with other boys in exchange for their trinkets, which they were prepared to sell though they liked them as well as I. Moreover, in this kind of play, I often sought dishonest victories, being myself conquered by the selfish desire for superiority.

What was I so unwilling to endure, and what was it that I so violently censured when I caught anyone, except the very things I did to others? However, when I was myself detected and censured, I preferred to quarrel rather than to yield. Is this the innocence of childhood? It is not, O Lord, it is not. I entreat Your mercy, O my God, for these same sins as we grow older are transferred from tutors and masters. They pass from father to son, mother to daughter, and generation to generation. They flow then upward to magistrates and kings, to lands and to slaves, just as the rod is succeeded by more severe punishment. You, O our King, approved as a symbol of humility, the fact of humility in childhood by saying, "Of such is the Kingdom of Heaven."[39]

CHAPTER 18—MY BEING COMES FROM GOD

O Lord, You are most excellent and most good. You are the Architect and Governor of the universe. Thanks would be due to You, O God, even if You had not willed that I should survive my boyhood. For I existed even then; I lived and felt, and was concerned about my own well-being, a trace of that mysterious unity from whence I had my being.[40]

By my inner sense, I kept watch over the integrity of my outer senses, and even in these small things and my thoughts about them as well, I learned to take pleasure in truth. I was averse to being deceived. I had a vigorous memory and was gifted with the power of speech. I was softened by friendship and shunned sorrow, meanness and ignorance. Is not such an animated creature as this wonderful and praiseworthy?

However, all these are gifts of my God; I did not give them to myself. Moreover, they are good and together constitute myself. Good, then, is He that made me. He is my God and before Him I will rejoice exceedingly for every good gift, which even as a boy, I had.

Nevertheless, herein lay my sin. It was not in God, but in His creatures (myself and the rest) that I sought pleasure, honor, and truth. Therefore, I fell into sorrow, trouble, and error. Thanks to You, my joy, my pride, my confidence, my God for Your gifts. But do You preserve them in me? If You do, then those things which You have given me will be developed and perfected. Then, I will be with You, because my very being comes from You.

BOOK TWO

Trapped in Sinful Self

Augustine looks back on his sixteenth year and the indelible mark left by idleness, lust, and the mischief of adolescence. His recollection of stealing some pears leads to a deep probing of the motives and aims of sinful behavior:— "I became to myself a wasteland."

Chapter 1–Memories of Past Wickedness

I wish now to review my past wickedness and the carnal corruptions of my soul—not because I still love them, but that I may love You more, O my God. For the love of Your love I do this as I recall in the bitterness of self-examination my wicked ways, that You may grow ever sweeter to me, You who are sweetness without deception! You are sweetness, happy and assured! You gathered me up out of those fragments in which I was torn to pieces, while I turned away from You, O Unity, and lost myself among "the many."[41] For as I became a youth, I longed to be satisfied with worldly things, and I dared to grow wild in a succession of shallow loves. I wasted away and became corrupt in Your eyes, but was still pleasing to my own. Furthermore, I was eager to please the eyes of others.

Chapter 2–Wrestling with Puberty

What was it that delighted me except to love and to be loved? Still I did not stay on the bright path of friendship, the moderate way of the love of mind to mind. Instead, the steamy mists of passion rose from the flaming lusts of my flesh. Fanned by the hot imagination of puberty, lust so obscured and overcast my heart that I was unable to distinguish pure affection from unholy desire. Both boiled in confusion within me, dragging my unstable youth down over the cliffs of impure desires and plunging me into a gulf of indecency.

O God, Your anger had come upon me, and I knew it not. I had been deafened by the incessant rattling of the chains of my mortality, the punishment for my soul's pride. I wandered farther from You, and You permitted me to do so. I was tossed to and fro, so wasted and poured out that I ran in frenzy after illicit sexual encounters. Yet You held Your peace, O my tardy Joy! You still held Your peace while I wandered even farther from You into other yet more empty fields of sorrow. I sank ever deeper in proud dejection and restless idleness.

If only someone had been there to regulate my disorder and turn to my profit the fleeting beauties of the things around me. Someone to fix a boundary to their sweetness so that the tides of my youth might have spent themselves upon the shore of marriage! Then, I may have been tranquilized and satisfied with having children as Your law prescribes. O Lord, You form the offspring of our death and are able also with a tender hand to blunt the thorns whichthorns, which were excluded from Your paradise![42] Your omnipotence is not far from us even when we are far from You.

Now, on the other hand, I might have paid more attention to the voice from the clouds: "Nevertheless such will have trouble in the flesh, but I would spare you,"[43] and, "It is good for a man not to touch a woman,"[44] and, "He who is unmarried cares for the things of the Lord—how he may please the Lord. But he who is married cares about the things of the world—how he may please *his* wife."[45] I should have listened more attentively to these words, and then having been "made a eunuch for the Kingdom of Heaven's sake,"[46] I would have expected Your embraces with greater happiness.

Nevertheless, fool that I was, I foamed as the sea in my wickedness and forsaking You, followed the rushing of my own tide only to burst out of all Your boundaries. However, I did not escape

Your discipline. For what mortal can ever escape? You were always by me, mercifully angry and flavoring all my unlawful pleasures with bitter discontent so that I might seek pleasures free from discontent. But where could I find such pleasure except in You, O Lord. Only in You can I find true pleasure, You who teaches usteach us by sorrow, who wounds us to heal us, and kills us that we may not die apart from You.

Where was I, O God, and how far was I exiled from the delights of Your house in that sixteenth year of my life? How far astray had I gone when the madness of lust held full sway in me, that madness that leads to human shamelessness though forbidden by Your laws? Meanwhile, my family took no steps by marriage to save me from ruin. Their only care was that I learn how to make a powerful speech and become a persuasive orator.

CHAPTER 3–SUBMITTING TO THE PASSIONS OF ADOLESCENCE

During my sixteenth year, my studies were interrupted. I had returned from Madaura, a neighboring city[47] where I had gone to study grammar and public speaking, while money for a term at Carthage was being gathered for me. This project was more a matter of my father's ambition than of his means, for he was a poor citizen of Tagaste.

To whom am I narrating all of this? Not to You, O my God, but to my own kind in Your presence—to that small part of the human race who may chance to come upon these writings. And to what end? In that I, and all who read them, may understand the great depths from which we are to cry unto You.[48] For what is more surely heard in Your ear than a confessing heart and a faithful life?

My father was commended and praised by others because he went far beyond his means to supply me with the necessary expenses for a journey to a far land in the interest of myhis education. Few citizens, even those with more wealth did not do as much for their own children. Still, this same father did not trouble himself at all as to how I was progressing toward You, God, nor how pure I was. All that mattered was that I become skillful in speaking. Sadly, it did not matter how barren I was to Your cultivation, O God. You are the one true and good Lord of my heart, which is Your field.[49]

I lived with my parents during my sixteenth year, having a break from school for a time. This idleness was imposed upon me by my parents' lack of finances to keep me in school. Therefore, the thorny bushes of lust grew out of control in my head, and there was nobody to root them out. In fact, one day my father saw me showing the outward signs of adolescence at the baths, and perceiving that I was becoming a man, joyfully told my mother as if he were already looking forward to grandchildren. He began reveling in that drunkenness of the world that ignores You, its Creator, only to fall in love with the creature instead. This is the intoxication of the invisible wine of a perverted will, which turns and bows down to immorality.

However, in my mother's heart, You had already begun to build Your temple and the foundation of Your holy habitation, whereas my father was only recently converted and still learning the basics of the Christian faith. Therefore, mother was startled with holy fear and trembling, for though I had not yet been baptized, she feared the shameful walk of those who turn their backs toward You and not their faces.

O God, my soul is in anguish! Do I dare affirm that You held Your peace while I wandered farther away from You? Did You really remain silent? Then whose words were they but Yours that my mother, Your faithful handmaid, spoke into my ears? None of them, however, sank into my heart to change my behavior. As I remember, she disapproved of and warned me privately with great concern, "not to have sex outside of marriage; but above all, never defile another man's wife."

My mother's appeals seemed to be but womanish counsels, which I would have blushed to obey. Yet they were from You, O God, and I knew it not. I thought that You were silent and that it was only she who spoke. Yet it was through her that You did not keep silence toward me. Furthermore, in rejecting her counsel I was rejecting You. Yes, —I, her son, "the son of Your handmaid, Your servant."[50]

However, I did not realize this and rushed headlong with such blindness that I was embarrassed to be less shameless than my friends. Especially when I heard them boasting of their disgraceful exploits and glorying all the more as their depravity worsened. Moreover, I took pleasure in such exploits, not for the sake of pleasure only, but for the praise I received as well. I made myself out worse than I was so that I would not go lacking for praise. Furthermore, when I had not sinned as the worst in the group, I would say that I had even though I had not, so as not to appear contemptible because I was more innocent than they. I did not want to be lessened in their esteem because I was more pure.

Behold with what companions I walked the streets of Babylon! I rolled in its mire and lounged about on it, as if on a bed of spices and precious ointments. My invisible enemy was drawing me closer to the very center of that city so I could be worn down and seduced, for I was easy to seduce. My mother had already fled out of the midst of Babylon[51] and was progressing, though slowly, toward its outskirts. For in counseling me to purity, she did not bear in mind what her husband had told her about me. Although she knew that my passions were even then destructive and dangerous for the future, she did not think the bonds of matrimonial affection could restrain them if they could not be completely quenched. She took no heed of this, for she was afraid that a wife would prove to be a hindrance and burden to my hopes.

The hopes of my mother for me were not of the world to come, but the hope of learning, which both my parents were so anxious that I acquire. My father was anxious because he had little or no thought of You and only vain thoughts for me. Mother was anxious because she thought that the usual course of study would be of no hindrance and would actually help in my eventual return to You. This much I assume as I remember the temperaments of my parents.

Meantime, the reins of discipline were slackened on me, so that without the restraint of discipline, I did what I wanted to do, even to the point of debauchery. In all this there was that fog of unbridled lust and passion that obscured the brightness of Your truth. O my God! My iniquity bulged out, as it were, with fatness![52]

Chapter 4—The Bitterness of Forbidden Fruit

Theft is punished by Your law, O Lord, and the law written in men's hearts. This law cannot be erased, even by ingrained wickedness. For what thief will tolerate another thief stealing from him? Even a rich thief will not tolerate a poor thief driven to theft by want. Yet I had a desire to commit robbery, and did so. I was compelled to it by neither hunger nor poverty, but through rebellion against morality and a strong impulse to iniquity. What I stole was something I already had in sufficient quantity, and of much better quality. I had no desire to enjoy what I had stolen, but to enjoy the theft and the sin itself.

Close to the vineyard of my parents was a pear tree, heavy with fruit. These pears were tempting only for stealing, not for their color or flavor. Late one night, after roaming the streets in search of mischief—as was our bad habit—a group of us went to shake and rob this tree. We carried off a huge load of pears, and after barely tasting some, fed the rest to the hogs. We had no intention of eating the pears, but to simply steal them. This act pleased us all because it was forbidden.

Such was my heart, O God, upon which You took pity even in that bottomless pit. O God, let my heart confess to You what it was seeking when I was being shamefully deceitful, having no inducement to evil but the evil itself. It was against the law and I loved it. I loved my own undoing. I loved my error, not that for which I erred but the error itself. As a depraved soul, I was falling away from security in You to destruction, seeking nothing from shameful behavior but shame itself.

Chapter 5—The Fading Luster of Earthly Goods

Beautiful bodies are alluring, as is gold and silver and all things that God created. The sense of touch has its own power to please, as do the other senses in their own way. Worldly honor also has its own glory, as do the powers to command and to overcome, although from these the desire for revenge springs up. Nevertheless, in seeking pleasure from the alluring things of God's creation or the sensuality of human life, we must not depart from You, O Lord, nor deviate from Your law.

The life that we live here has its own peculiar attractiveness, an allure all its own, especially in its harmony with the rest of creation. The bond of human friendship has a sweetness of its own, binding many souls together as one. Yet because of these things we value, sin is committed. We have an inordinate preference for these goods of a lower order while neglecting the better and the higher good. We neglect You, Lord God—Your truth and Your law.

While these inferior things we value have their delights, none are equal to You. For in You, O God, the righteous delight and You are the sweetness of the upright in heart.

Therefore, when we inquire why a crime was committed, we do not accept the explanation unless it appears there was the desire to obtain some of those inferior things or a fear of losing them. For truly they are beautiful and desirable, though in comparison with the superior, heavenly goods they are dismal and loathsome.

A man has murdered another man. What was his motive? Either the murderer desired the dead man's wife or property (for he would simply steal to support himself), or else he was afraid of losing something of value to him. Or, having been injured, the fires of revenge burned within him.

Would a man commit murder without a motive? Would one delight simply in the act of murdering another? Who would believe such a thing? Even that savage and brutal man, Catiline, of whom it was said was gratuitously wicked and cruel, has a motive assigned to his deeds. "Lest through idleness," he says, "hand or heart should grow inactive,."[53] But to what purpose? That having once taken possession of the city through his wickedness, he might gain honor, empire, and wealth. This would exempt him from fear of the law, from the financial difficulty of supplying for his family, and from the consciousness of his own depravity. Therefore, it seems that even Catiline did not love his own lawlessness. Something else gave him the motive for his crimes.

CHAPTER 6—HOW VAIN THE HONOR OF AMBITION

What was in me that desired theft?. How could I, miserable wretch that I was at sixteen, nourish that awful deed of darkness?

The deed was not beautiful; : it was theft. But how could I analyze the deed? The pears that we stole were appealing to the eye because they were Your creation, O Beauty beyond compare. God, You are Creator of all. You are the highest good and my only true good.

Those pears were truly pleasant to the sight, but it was not for them that my miserable soul lusted, because I had more than enough pears that were better. I stole them simply that I might steal, for having stolen them I threw them away. Therefore, my sole gratification was my own sin, which I was pleased to enjoy. If any one of these pears entered my mouth, the only good flavor was from my sin in eating it. And now, O Lord my God, I ask what it was in that theft of mine that caused me such delight; for behold it had no beauty of its own. And certainly not the sort of beauty that exists in justice and wisdom, nor such as is in the mind, memory, senses, and the life of man. It was not the kind of beauty as is the glory and beauty of the stars in their courses, nor the beauty of the earth, or of the sea, teeming with spawning life and replacing in birth that which dies and decays. Indeed, it did not even have that false and shadowy beauty that accompanies the deceptions of vice.

We see pride ourselves in wearing the mask of high-spirit-edness, though only You, God, are high above all. Ambition seeks honor and glory, whereas only You should be honored above all and glorified forever. The powerful man seeks to be feared, because of his cruelty, but who ought really to be feared but God alone? What can be forced away or withdrawn out of God's power? By whom, what, when or where?

Promiscuity claims the name of love as an enticement. However, nothing is more enticing than Your love, nor is anything loved more healthfully than Your truth, which is bright and beautiful above all. Curiosity prompts a desire for knowledge, but only You know all things supremely. Indeed, ignorance and foolishness themselves go masked under the names of simplicity and innocence, yet there is no being that has true simplicity like You, and none is innocent like You. Therefore, it is by a sinner's own deeds that he is harmed.

Laziness pretends to yearn for rest, but what sure rest is there except in the Lord? Luxury would gladly be called plenty and abundance, but You are the fullness and unfailing abundance of unfading joy. Promiscuity presents a show of liberality, but You are the most lavish giver of all things good. Covetousness desires to possess much, but You are already the possessor of all things. Envy contends that its aim is for excellence, but what is as excellent as You? Anger seeks revenge, but who avenges more justly than You? Fear shrinks back as sudden change threatens the way things are and fear is wary for its own security, but what can happen that is unfamiliar or sudden to You, O God? Or who can deprive You of what You love? Where is there unshaken security except with You? Grief longs for those delightful things we've lost because it wills to have nothing taken from it, just as nothing can be taken from You.

The soul commits infidelity when turned from You.[54] What it seeks apart from You, it cannot find pure and untainted until it returns to You. This is how things imitate You, though in a perverted manner, when they separate themselves far from You and raise themselves up against You. Nevertheless, even in this act of perverse imitation, they acknowledge You to be the Creator of all nature and recognize that there is no place where they can altogether separate themselves from You.

What was it, then, that I loved in that theft of the pears? How was I imitating my Lord, even in a corrupt and perverted way? Did I wish, if only by gesture, to rebel against Your law—though I had no power to actually do it—so that, even as a captive, I might produce a sort of counterfeit liberty. By doing with impunity things that were forbidden, was I seeking a deluded sense of omnipotence? O God! Behold this servant of Yours, fleeing from his Lord and following a shadow! O rottenness! O monstrousness of life and abyss of death! Could I find pleasure only in what was unlawful, and only because it was unlawful?

Chapter 7 – God's Mercy Freely Given

"What shall I render to the Lord"[55] for the fact that while my memory recalls these things my soul no longer fears them? I love You, O Lord; I thank You and confess Your name, because You have put away from me such wicked and evil deeds. To Your grace and mercy I attribute the fact that You have melted away my sin as if it were ice. To Your grace also I attribute whatsoever of evil I did *not* commit—for what might I not have done, loving sin as I did, just for the sake of sinning? Lord, I confess all the sins that now have been forgiven me, both those which I willfully committed and those which, by Your providence, I did not commit.

What man is there who, when reflecting upon his own depravity, dares to attribute his purity and innocence to his own powers? Would he do so that he should love God less—as if he were in less need of Your mercy in which You forgive the transgressions of those that return to You? As for that man who, when called by You obeyed Your voice and shunned those things which he reads here about me, let him not despise me. The same Physician by whose aid he did not fall sick, or rather was less sick than I, has healed me. For this, let him love You all the more since he sees me restored from such great wickedness by the same Savior by whom he sees himself preserved from the same.

CHAPTER 8—THE PARADOX OF SIN

What profit did such a wretched one as I receive from those things that now cause me shame, especially from that theft that I loved only for the theft's sake? The theft itself was nothing, but I was all the more wretched in that I loved it so. Yet by myself, I would not have done it. I remember how I felt at the time and know I could not have done it alone. I loved it then because of the companionship of my accomplices with whom I did it. Therefore, I did not love the theft alone. Nevertheless, it was only the theft that I loved, for the companionship was nothing.

What is this paradox? Who can explain it to me but God? It is He who illumines my heart and searches out its dark corners. What is it that has prompted my mind to inquire about it, to discuss and reflect upon all this? For had I at that time loved the pears that I stole and wished to enjoy them, I might have done so alone. Likewise, if I could have been satisfied with the mere act of theft that served my pleasure. I did not need to have that itching of my own passions inflamed by the encouragement of my accomplices. However, the pleasure I received came not from the pears, but from the crime itself, enhanced by the companionship of my fellow sinners.

CHAPTER 9—THE SEDUCTION OF FRIENDSHIP

By what passion, then, was I motivated? It was undoubtedly depraved and a great misfortune for me to feel it. Nevertheless, what was it? "Who can understand his errors?"[56]

We laughed because our hearts were tickled at the thought of deceiving the owners. They had no idea what we were doing and would have strenuously objected had they known! But, why did I find such delight in doing what I would not have done alone? Is it that no one readily laughs alone? Sometimes when people are alone, a fit of laughter will overcome them when something very funny happens or comes to mind. However, alone I would not have stolen. Alone I could not have stolen at all.

O my God, the review of the secrets of my soul is laid bare before You. I would not have committed that theft by myself. My pleasure was in not what I stole but, the act of stealing. I would not have enjoyed doing it alone, in fact I would not have done it! Friendship is a strange seducer of the soul. It hungers for mischief from the impulses of amusement and selfishness, it craves another's loss with no desire for one's own profit or revenge, so that when they say, "Let's go, let's do it," we are embarrassed not to be shameless.

Chapter 10—I Became to Myself a Wasteland

Who can unravel such twisted and tangled knots? It is unclean. I hate to reflect upon it. I hate to look on it. However, I do long for You, O Righteousness and Innocence, so beautiful and appealing to all virtuous eyes. I long for You, Lord, with insatiable gratitude. With You alone is perfect rest and unchanging life. He who enters into You enters into the joy of his Lord.[57] He will have no fear and will achieve excellence in the Excellent.

I fell away from You, O my God, and in my youth I wandered too far from You, my true support. I became to myself a wasteland

BOOK THREE

Infatuated by Philosophical Pursuit

Augustine recounts his days as a student in Carthage where he discovered "Hortensius" by Cicero, which sparked an interestedt in philosophy. He talks of his infatuation with the Manichean heresy. Finally, Augustinehe tells of his mother's dream that prophesied his return to faith in God.

CHAPTER 1—OFF TO CARTHAGE IN SEARCH OF...

I came to Carthage, a caldron of unholy loves that seethed and bubbled all around me. I was not yet in love, but was in love with love. Love, for me, was a hidden hunger, and I hated myself for not feeling a more intense sense of hunger. I was looking for something to love, for I was in love with loving. I hated security and a smooth way, free from snares. Within me I lacked that inner food which is You, my God, though that lack caused me no hunger. Therefore, I remained with no appetite for incorruptible food, not because I was already filled with it, but because the emptier I became the more I loathed it. Because of this my soul was unhealthy. It was full of sores, stretching itself forth, itching to be scratched by scraping on the things of the senses.[58] Yet, if these things had no soul, they would certainly not inspire our love.

To love and to be loved was sweet to me, and became all the more sweet when I gained the enjoyment of the body of the person I loved. Thus I polluted the spring of friendship with the filth of unholy sexual desire and dimmed its luster with the slime of lust. Yet, foul and unclean as I was, I still craved, in self-seeking grandeur, to be thought of as elegant and sophisticated. And I did fall rashly into the love I was longing for. My God, my mercy, with how much bitterness did You, out of Your infinite goodness, flavor that sweetness for me!! For I was not only beloved but also secretly reached the climax of enjoyment. However, I was joyfully bound with troublesome tics, so that I could be pummeled with the burning iron rods of jealousy, suspicion, fear, anger, and strife.

Chapter 2—The Empty Compassion of Fantasy

I was also captivated with stage plays. They were full of the images of my own miseries and added fuel to my own fire.

Why does a man enjoy being made sad by viewing mournful and tragic scenes, which he himself could not endure by any means? Yet, as a spectator, he wishes to experience from them a sense of grief, and out of this very sense of grief derive his pleasure. What is this but abject madness?

A spectator is greatly affected the more his imagination is involved in these stories. Now, if he would suffer these agonies himself, he would call it "misery," but when he suffers with another, it is "compassion." What kind of compassion arises from viewing fictitious and make-believe suffering? The spectator is not expected to aid the sufferer but merely to grieve for him, and the more he grieves the more he applauds the actor. If the misfortunes of the characters, whether historical or entirely imaginary, are represented and do not touch the feelings of the spectator, he goes away disgusted and complaining. However, if his feelings are deeply touched, he sits through it attentively, and sheds tears of joy.

Tears and sorrow are loved. Surely everyone desires to be joyful. No one is willingly miserable. However, actors are paid to appear miserable so that we, the audience, can revel in their sorrows. Without them we would have nothing to pity.

Beware of Uncleanness

This compassion springs from that same vein of worldly friendship we explored earlier. But where does this compassion go? Where does it flow? Why does it empty into that huge seething flood of despicable lusts where it is changed beyond recognition, being diverted and corrupted from its heavenly purity? Shall compassion be renounced? By no means! Let us love the sorrows of others, but beware of uncleanness.

Under Your protection, O God, Guard my soul from uncleanness. Thank God, I have not yet ceased to have compassion. However, during those days in the theaters I sympathized with lovers when they sinfully enjoyed one another, though this was done fictitiously in the play. When they lost one another, I grieved with them, as if pitying them, and yet had delight in both grief and pity.

Today, I feel more compassion for one who delights in his wickedness than for one who counts himself unfortunate because he failed to get some harmful pleasure, or suffers the loss of some unholy bliss. This is surely the truer compassion, but the sorrow I feel in it has no delight for me. Though one that grieves with the unhappy should be commended for his work of love, the one with the power of real compassion would still prefer that there be nothing to grieve about. For if good will were to be ill will, which it cannot be, only then could he who is truly and sincerely compassionate wish that there were some unhappy people so that he might share their misery with them.

Some grief may then be justified, but none of it loved. Thus it is that You act, O Lord God, for You love souls far more purely than we do and are more incorruptibly compassionate, though never wounded by sorrow. "Who is sufficient for these things?"[59]

Nevertheless, at that time in my wretchedness, I loved to grieve and sought things to grieve about! Another man's misery moved me to tears. Even though it was the performance of an actor, it pleased me and held a strange attraction for me. Therefore, it came as no surprise that I, an unhappy sheep straying from Your flock and impatient with Your care, became infected with a foul disease. This is the reason for my love of grief: that I would not be examined too thoroughly (for I hated to suffer the very things I loved to watch). It was the sort of grief that came from hearing those fantasies and affected only the surface of my emotion. Still, just as if they had been poisoned fingernails, their scratching was followed by inflammation, swelling, infection, and decay. Such was my life! But was it life, O my God?

Chapter 3—Inventing Mischief

Nevertheless, Your faithful mercy hovered over me from afar. The pursuit of sin and impurity wore me out. I was bent on following my blasphemous curiosity, which, having deserted You, began to drag me down into the treacherous abyss and into the beguiling obedience of devils. To these I made offerings of my wicked deeds.

Yet in all this Your judgment did not fail to reach me. Even while Your solemn rites were being celebrated inside the walls of Your church, I dared to desire and plan a project whichproject, which merited death as its fruit. For this You chastised me with grievous punishment, but nothing in comparison to my sin. O God, You are my greatest mercy. My God, You are my refuge from the terrible dangers in which I wandered in rebellion, drifting farther from You, loving my own ways and not Yours, loving a homeless person's liberty!

Those studies I pursued were generally deemed respectable and were aimed at distinction in the courts of law. To excel, I had to be crafty and to earn praise I needed ready wit. Such is the blindness of men that they even glory in their blindness. By this time I had become a master in the School of Law. I rejoiced proudly in this honor and became inflated with arrogance. Still I was relatively sedate, as You know O Lord, and had no share in the destruction of "The Wreckers."[60] This stupid and diabolical name was regarded as the very badge of gallantry among those with whom I lived, though with a sort of ashamed embarrassment that I was not as they were.

Nevertheless, I lived with them, and at times I was delighted with their friendship, even when I abhorred their acts (that is, their "wrecking") in which they insolently attacked the modesty of strangers, tormenting them by uncalled-for jeers, gratifying their mischievous delight. Nothing could more nearly resemble the actions of devils than these fellows. By what name, therefore, could they be more aptly called than "wreckers"? They were themselves wrecked first, and altogether turned upside down. They were secretly mocked at and seduced by the deceiving spirits, in the very acts by which they amused themselves in jeering and horseplay at the expense of others.

CHAPTER 4—CAPTIVATED BY PHILOSOPHY

It was during in that unstable period of my life and among such as hooligans as these, that I studied the art of articulate speech. I was eager to excel in eloquence, though my desire sprang from the reprehensible and conceited motive of delighting my human arrogance.

Following the customary course of study I came upon a certain book of Cicero's, whose language, though not his heart, nearly all admire. This particular book contains an exhortation to philosophy and was called *Hortensius*.[61]

Reading Cicero's book changed my attitude completely and turned my prayers toward You, O Lord; it gave me new hope and new desires. Suddenly every self-serving hope became worthless to me. With incredible warmth of heart I yearned for the immortality of wisdom and began my journey to return unto You.

I did not use Cicero's book to further sharpen my tongue. I was nineteen and my father had been dead for two years.[62] Therefore, my mother was providing the money for my study of law. What captured me in the book was not its style but its substance.

How eager I became, my God, to flee from earthly things to You, though I didn't know how You were then dealing with me. For with You is wisdom. Greeks call the love of wisdom "philosophy," and it was with this love Cicero's book inflamed me. Some use philosophy to seduce others, using it to color and adorn their own errors. NThough nearly all who did this, in Cicero's time and earlier, are censored and identified out in his book.

Therefore, we must pay heed to this constructive admonition of Your Spirit, spoken by Your good and upright servant: "Beware lest anyone cheat you through philosophy and empty deceit, according to the tradition of men, according to the basic principles of the world, and not according to Christ. For in Him dwells all the fullness of the Godhead bodily."[63] As You know, O Light of my heart, at that time, the words of the apostle were unknown to me. Therefore, I was delighted with Cicero's exhortation, at least enough to be stimulated by it.

I was enkindled and inflamed to love, to seek, to obtain, to hold, and to embrace, not this or that sect, but wisdom itself wherever it might be. Only one thing dampened my enthusiasm: that the name of Christ was not in it. For this name—by Your mercy, O Lord—the name of my Savior, Your Son, had my tender heart had spiritually absorbed and deeply treasured even with my mother's milk. Therefore, whatever lacked that name, no matter how scholarly, polished, and truthful, did not take complete hold of me.

CHAPTER 5—MY INTRODUCTION TO THE HOLY SCRIPTURES

I decided, then, to enter into serious study of the Holy Scriptures so I could learn what they were. When I did, I saw something not comprehended by the proud and not disclosed to children, something lowly in the hearing but uplifting in the doing, something veiled in mystery. Yet I was still unwilling to submit to what the Scriptures revealed or to follow its steps. For then I felt quite different from what I do now.

Nevertheless, when I turned toward the Scriptures, they appeared to me to be quite unworthy to be compared with the dignity of Tully.[64] My inflated pride was repelled by their style, and I was unable to penetrate their inner meaning with the sharpness of my wit. Truly, the Scriptures were of a sort to aid the growth of little ones, but I refused to be a little one. Swollen with pride, I looked upon myself as fully-grown.

CHAPTER 6—THE DARKNESS OF DECEIT

My pride caused me to fall among men who were delirious in their pride. They were carnal and eloquent, leading many astray. Their mouths were the snares of the devil, and set a trap consisting of a mixture of the use of Your name and the names of our Lord Jesus Christ and of the Holy Spirit.[65] These Holy names streamed out of their mouths, but only as sound and the empty clatter of their tongue because their heart was empty of truth.

Still they cried, "Truth, Truth," and were forever speaking the word to me. But truth itself was not in them. They spoke falsely not only of You, who is Truth, but also about the basic elements of this world, Your creation. Indeed, I should have passed by the philosophers themselves even when they were speaking truth concerning Your creatures; . tThis for the sake of Your love, O Highest Good, and my Father; O Beauty of all things beautiful.

O Truth, Truth, the very core of my soul longed for You even when the Manicheans sounded out Your name using various methods and prolific writing. Sadly, it was only a sound! While I starved for You, the food they served to me in Your stead was the sun and moon and Your beautiful works, but still only Your works and not You.

This empty philosophy served not even Your first work. For Your spiritual works came before this material creation, celestial and shining though it is. is. I was hungering and thirsting, not even after those first works of Yours, but after You, the Truth "with whom is no variableness, neither shadow of turning."[66]

Malnourished On Empty Philosophies

Nevertheless, these teachers of falsehood continued to serve me dishes of glowing fantasy. Truly, it would have been better to have loved the very sun, which is at least true to our sight, than those illusions of theirs which theirs, which deceive the mind through the eye. However, because I believed these illusions to be from You I fed on them. You were not in these heresies, O God, so I did not taste You as You are, nor was I nourished by them, but was exhausted.

Food in dreams looks the same as real food, but with no nourishment because it exists only in a dream. Likewise, the heresies of the Manicheans were in no way like You, Lord, as You have revealed Yourself. They were simply far-fetched and false. By comparison, the actual things that we see with our eyes, both in the heavens and on the earth, are far more certain. These created bodies are perceived by beasts and birds, as well as by human beings and are more certain than what is imagined about them. The Manicheans formed far-fetched ideas about these objects, and then went on to create in their imagination other greater and infinite bodies, which have no existence. With such worthless food was I then fed, and yet was not fed.

Nevertheless, my Lord, whom I longed for so that I might be strong, the celestial bodies (stars and planets) seen in the heavens and those earthly bodies that are here are not You. Though You created them, You do not esteem them among Your greatest works. How far, then, are You from those fantasies of mine, fantasies of bodies which have no real being at all! The images of those bodies that actually exist are far more certain than my fantasies, and the bodies themselves are more certain than the images, yet even these are not You. Furthermore, You are not the soul, which is the life of bodies, though the life of the body is clearly better than the body itself. But You are the life of souls, the life of lives, having life in Yourself, and never changing. You are the Life of my soul.[67]

In Search of Wisdom

O Lord, where were You then. How far away from You was I? Though I was wandering far from You, You prevented me from eating the same empty pods as those swine.[68] Far better were the tales of the storytellers and poets than these snares of the Manicheans! Verses, poems and "the flying Medea"[69] are still more profitable than the "five elements" of these men with their various colors, answering to "the five caves of darkness"[70]—none of which exist and yet in which they slay the one who believes in them. Verses and poems can be turned into food for the mind, for though I sang about "the flying Medea," I never believed it, but those heresies of the Manicheans I did believe. In wretched despair and misery I was dragged down to "the depths of hell,"[71] toiling and fuming because of my lack of the truth, even when I was seeking after You, my God!

To You, my God, I plead guilty, for You had mercy on me when I had not yet confessed. I sought after You following the guidance of my physical senses, not according to the understanding of my mind—which You willed should surpass the animals. You were more inward to me than the most inward part of me, yet higher than my highest reach.

In my search for wisdom, I came upon the brazen woman in Solomon's obscure parable, who devoid of good sense, sits at the door of her house and says, "Stolen waters are sweet, and bread eaten in secret is pleasant."[72] She seduced me, because she found my soul outside its own door, dwelling on the sensations of my flesh and pondering the trash I had devoured with my physical senses alone.

CHAPTER 7—THE PARADOX OF RIGHTEOUSNESS

I was ignorant of the reality of true Being. So I was cleverly persuaded to agree with these foolish deceivers when they put their questions to me:

"Where does evil originate?"

"Does God have a body?" "

"Does God have hair and fingernails?"

"Are the patriarchs to be esteemed righteous, even though they had many wives at one time, killed men, and sacrificed living creatures?"

I was greatly disturbed over these things in my ignorance and though I was retreating from the truth, it appeared to me that I was going toward it. I did not yet know that evil was nothing but a deprivation of good and that it has no being.[73] How could I have seen this when my vision went no farther than physical objects, and the reach of my mind no further than apparitions? I did not know that God is a spirit who has no parts extended in length and breadth, whose being has no mass. God can not have mass, for every mass is less in a part than in a whole, and if it be an infinite mass it must be less in parts that are limited by a certain space than in its infinity. Mass cannot be wholly everywhere as Spirit is, as God is. I was entirely ignorant as to what that principle is within us by which we are like God, and which is rightly said in Scripture to be made "after God's image."

I also did not know that true inner righteousness, which does not judge according to custom but by the measure of the most perfect law of God Almighty, adapts to the traditions of various places and times. This, though the law itself is the same always and everywhere, not one thing in one place and another in another. By this inner righteousness, Abraham, Isaac, Jacob, Moses, David, and all the others commended by the mouth of God were righteous, and were judged unrighteous only by foolish men judging by human standards.

These same foolish men based their judgment of the entire human race on the narrow norms of their own traditions. It's as if a man in an armory, not knowing what piece goes on what part of the body, should put leg armor on his head and a helmet on his shin, then complain because they do not fit. Or as if, on some holiday when afternoon business was forbidden, one were to grumble at not being allowed to go on selling as it had been lawful for him to do in the morning. Or, again, as if, in a house, a man sees a servant handle something that the butler is not permitted to touch, or when something is done behind a stable that would be prohibited in a dining room. Then a person should be indignant that in one house and one family the same things are not allowed to every member of the household. Such is the case with those who cannot bear to hear that something was lawful for righteous men in former times that is not so now. Or that God, for certain temporal reasons, commanded one thing then to them and another now to these, yet both would be serving the same righteous will.

Justice Presides Over Time

It becomes important to see that in one man, one day, and one house, different things are fit for different members, and a thing that was formerly lawful may after a time become unlawful. Likewise, something allowed or commanded in one place is justly prohibited and punished in another.

Therefore, is justice variable and changeable? No. However, the times over which she presides are not all alike because they are different times. But men, whose days upon the earth are few, cannot by their own perception harmonize the causes of former ages and other nations. These men have no experience with these other nations and time, and it would be folly to compare them to that which they do have experience. Although in one and the same body, or day, or family, they can readily see that what is suitable for each member, season, part, and person may differ. To the one they take exception; to the other they submit.

These things I did not know then, nor had I observed their importance. They met my eyes on every side, and I did not see. I composed poems, in which I was not free to place a foot just anywhere, but in one meter one way, and in another meter another way, nor even in any one verse was the same foot allowed in all places. Yet the art by which I composed did not have different principles for each of these different cases, but used the same law throughout. Still I did not see how, by that righteousness to which good and holy men submitted, all those things that God had commanded were gathered in a far more excellent and sublime way, into one moral order. I also didn't understand how righteousness did not vary in any essential respect, though it did not in varying times prescribe all things at once but, rather, distributed and prescribed what was proper for each. Therefore, being blind, I blamed those pious fathers, not only for making use of present things as God had commanded and inspired them to do, but also for foreshadowing things to come, as God revealed it to them.

Chapter 8—The Abomination of Rebellion

Can it ever, at any time or place, be unrighteous for a man to love God with all his heart, soul, and mind, and his neighbor as himself?[74] Offenses against nature are everywhere, and they should be detested at all times and the offenders punished. Such offenses, for example, were those committed by the Sodomites. Even if all nations committed them, they should all be judged guilty of the crime according to the divine law.

God did not create man to abuse one another. The fellowship that should exist between God and humanity is violated any time the nature of that which God created is polluted by perverted lust. These offenses against morality are to be avoided according to the design of God.

The Sovereign Rule of God

Behavior that is agreed upon by men, or upheld by tradition and confirmed by custom or law in any city or nation, may not be violated at the lawless whim of anyone, whether citizen or stranger. For any part that is not consistent with its whole is improper. However, when God commands something contrary to the customs or laws of a nation, even though they have never done it before, it must be done. Likewise, if God's edict has been interrupted, it must be restored, or if it has never been established, it must be established.

It is lawful for the king who reigns over a kingdom to command that which neither he nor anyone before him had commanded. If it cannot be determined to be detrimental to the public interest to obey him—though in truth, it would be detrimental if he were not obeyed since obedience to royalty is a general law of society—then how much more should we unhesitatingly obey God, the Governor of all His creatures! For, just as among the authorities in human society, the greater authority is obeyed before the lesser. So also must God be obeyed above all.

This applies equally to deeds of violence where there is a real desire to harm another, either by humiliating treatment or by injury. Either of these may be done for reasons of revenge, as one enemy against another, or in order to obtain some advantage over another, as in the case of the highwayman and the traveler. Likewise, they may be done in order to avoid some other evil, as in the case of one who fears another, or through envy as, for example, an unfortunate man harming a happy one just because he is happy. These violent deeds may also be done by a prosperous man against someone he fears will become equal to him or whose equality he resents. Violence may even be done for the mere pleasure of enjoying another man's pain, as in the case of spectators of gladiatorial shows or people who deride and poke fun at others.

These forms of iniquity find their source in the lust of the flesh, the lust of the eye, and the lust for power.[75] Sometimes there is just one, sometimes two together or sometimes all at once. Thus we live, committing sin against the Three and the Seven—that harp of ten strings—Your Decalogue [the Ten Commandments], O God most high and most sweet.[76]

How can vile sin harm You, O God, who cannot be defiled? How can deeds of violence harm You who cannot be harmed? Still You punish these sins which men commit against themselves because, even when they sin against You, they are also sinning against their own souls. Iniquity gives itself the lie, either by corrupting or by perverting that nature which You have made and ordained. This is done by immoderate use of lawful things, by lustful desire for things forbidden as "against nature." Men are guilty of sin by raging with heart and voice against You, rebelling against You by "kicking against the goads."[77] They are guilty when they cast aside respect for human society and take audacious delight in conspiracies and feuds according to their private likes and dislikes.

This is what happens whenever You are forsaken, O Fountain of Life, the one and true Creator and Ruler of the universe. This is what happens when through self-willed pride a part is loved under the false assumption that it is the whole. Therefore, we must return to You in humility and let You purge from us our evil ways. Be merciful to those who confess their sins to You, hear the groaning of the prisoners, and loosen us from the fetters which we have forged for ourselves. This You will do, provided we do not rise up against You in the arrogance of a false freedom, for thus we lose all through craving more and by loving our own good more than You, the common good of all.

CHAPTER 9—THE SOVEREIGNTY OF GOD

However, among all these vices, crimes and countless iniquities, there are also sins that are committed by men who are, on the whole, making progress toward the good. When these are judged rightly and after the rule of perfection, the sins are censored but the men are to be commended because they show the hope of bearing fruit, like the green shoot of the growing corn. There are some deeds that resemble vice and crime and yet are not sin because they don't offend You, Lord God, or social custom. For example, when suitable reserves for hard times are provided, we cannot judge that this is done merely from a hoarding impulse. Or, again, when constituted authority, for the sake of correction, punishes behavior, we cannot judge that it is done merely out of a desire to inflict pain. Thus, many deeds that are disapproved of in man's sight may be approved by Your testimony.

Many a man who is praised by others is also condemned, because frequently the deed itself, the mind of the doer, and the hidden circumstance of the situation are at odds. However, when You, Lord, contrary to human expectation, command something unusual or not thought of before, who doubts but that it should be done, for only the righteous obeys You? Indeed, You may command something that You have previously forbidden and conceal the reason for Your command at that particular time. Furthermore, You can do this even though it is contrary to the ordinance of some society of men![78]

Blessed are those who know what You command. For all things done by those who obey You either demonstrate something necessary at that particular time or foreshadow things to come.

Chapter 10—Manichean Heresies

I was ignorant of all this, and so I mocked those holy servants and prophets of Yours. Yet what did I gain by mocking them except to be mocked by You? Little by little, I was senselessly led into heresies that caused me to believe that a fig tree wept when it was plucked and that the sap of the mother tree were tear drops.as tears. Notwithstanding this, if a fig was plucked, not by its own wickedness, but a man's wickedness, some Manichean "saint" might eat it, digest it in his stomach, and breathe it out again in the form of angels!

Indeed, in his prayers this "saint" would assuredly groan and sigh forth particles of God, although these particles of the most high and true God would have remained bound in that fig unless they had been set free by the teeth and belly of some "elect saint"![79]

Wretch that I was, I believed that more mercy was to be shown to the fruits of the earth than unto human beings for whom these fruits were created. For, if a hungry person, who was not a Manichean, should beg for any food, the morsel that we gave to him would seem condemned, as it were, to capital punishment.

CHAPTER 11—THE RIGHTEOUS PRAYERS OF MY MOTHER PREVAILED

Nevertheless, O God, You "stretched out Your hand from above"[80] and drew my soul out of the profound darkness of Manicheism, because my mother, Your faithful one, wept to You on my behalf more than most mothers weep after the bodily deaths of their children. For by the light of faith and the Spirit she received from You, she saw that I was dead. You heard her, O Lord, and did not reject her tears as they poured down and watered the earth under her wherever she prayed. Yes, Lord, You truly did heed her prayers.

What other source but You could there be for the dream by which You consoled her? Because of it, she permitted me to live with her and have my meals at the table she had begun to avoid while fasting in prayer. She allowed this even though she hated and detested the blasphemy of my error.

Mother's Dream

In her dream, she saw herself standing on a sort of wooden rule. She saw a bright youth approaching, who was joyous and smiling at her while she was grieving and bowed down with sorrow. However, when he asked her the cause of her sorrow and daily weeping (not to learn from her, but to teach her, as is customary in visions), she answered that it was my soul's doom she was lamenting. The youth told her to rest contentedly and to see that where she was, I was there as well. Then she looked she saw me standing near her on the same rule.

Where could this vision have come from unless it was that Your ears were inclined toward her heart? O You Omnipotent Good, You care for every one of us as if You cared for the individual only. You care for all as if they were but one!

When mother told me of this vision, I tried to put this meaning on it: "that she should not despair of being someday what I was." Immediately she replied, "No. F; for it was not told to me that 'where he is, there you shall be' but instead 'where you are, there he will be.'" I confess my remembrance of this to You, O Lord, as far as I can recall it, and I have often mentioned it. Your answer was given through my watchful mother who was not disturbed by my false interpretation, but immediately saw what should have been seen. Until she told me, I certainly had not seen it, and this answer moved me more deeply than the dream itself. Still, that dream served as a consolation for her present anguish, revealing the joy that was to come to that pious woman.

Nearly nine years passed in which I wallowed in the mud of that deep pit of heresy and in the darkness of falsehood, striving often to rise, but being all the more severely knocked down. Through all of that, my mother, a chaste, pious, and sober widow was now more buoyed up with hope, though no less zealous in her weeping and mourning. She did not cease to bewail my case before You, in all the hours she spent in prayer. Her prayers entered Your presence, and yet You allowed me still to tumble and toss around in that darkness.

CHAPTER 12—YOUR WORD TO MY MOTHER

Meanwhile, Lord, You gave mother yet another answer, as I recall. (I'm passing over many things as I hasten on to that which more strongly impels me to confess to You, and many things I have simply forgotten.) However, You gave her another answer, by a priest of Yours, a certain bishop reared in Your Church and well versed in Your books.

Mother begged this bishop to talk with me and refute my errors. She wanted him to help me to unlearn evil and to learn the good, for he liked to do this when he found people ready to receive. Prudently, he refused, as I afterward realized. He knew that I was still un-teachable because I was infatuated with the novelty of that [Manichean] heresy. He also knew that I had already silenced many inexperienced persons with difficult questions. "Let him alone for a time," he said, "only pray to God for him. He will of his own accord, by reading, come to discover what an awful error it is and how great its deception."

The bishop went on to tell mother at the same time how he himself, as a boy, had been given over to the Manicheans by his misguided mother. He had not only read but had even copied nearly all their books. Yet he had come to see, without external argument or proof from anyone, how much that sect was to be shunned, and he had shunned it. When he said this, my mother was not satisfied, but begged him with tears to see and talk with me. Finally the bishop, a little vexed at her persistence, exclaimed, "Go your way; as you live, it cannot be that the son of these tears should perish." As she often told me afterward, she accepted this answer as though it were a voice from heaven.

BOOK FOUR

Captured by the Manichaen Heresy

This book contains the story of Augustine's years among the Manicheans. It also includes his recollection of teaching in his hometown, Tagaste, entering into a relationship with a mistress, the attractions of astrology, and the tragic loss of a friend, all of which leads to an analysis of grief and the brevity of life. Augustine also reports on his first book, "De pulchro et apto," his introduction to Aristotle's "Categories" and other books of philosophy and theology, which he easily mastered, though with little profit.

CHAPTER 1—NINE YEARS OF FRUITLESS STRIVING

During the nine years between my nineteenth and my twenty-eighth years, I went astray and led others astray. I was deceived and deceived others in various lustful projects, at times publicly by the teaching of what is called "the liberal arts," and other times secretly under the false guise of religion. In the one, I was proud of myself while in the other, superstitious. However, I was filled with pride in all!

I actively sought the fleeting glitz of popular fame in my public life. Doing so, I went after theatrical applause by entering poetic contests. I was striving for the straw wreaths of fame and recognition in the theatre, all to fulfill my insatiable desires.

I was seeking in my private life to be purged from the corruption of pride by taking food to those who were called "elect" and "holy." In the laboratory of their stomachs, this food was supposed to turn into angels and gods so that they could set us free. I pursued these projects with my friends who were deceived along with me and by me.

O God! Let the proud laugh at me, laugh at me and those who have not yet been stricken for salvation's sake and smitten by You.. Nevertheless, I confess my shame to Your glory. Bear with me I pray, and give me the grace to retrace in my present memory the devious ways of my past errors and so be able to "offer to God thanksgiving."[81] For what am I to myself without You but a guide to my own downfall? Or what am I, even at the best, but one nourished on Your milk and feeding on You, O Food that never perishes?[82] What indeed is any man, seeing that he is but a man? Therefore, let the strong and the mighty laugh, but let us who are "poor and needy"[83] confess to You.

Chapter 2—On an Encounter with a Magician

I taught the art of legal debate during those years. Conquered by the desire for gain, I offered my speaking skills for sale to be used to subdue others. Nevertheless, O Lord, You know that I really preferred to teach honest scholars (or what were esteemed as such). You also know, Lord, that using no tricks of speech, I taught these scholars the tricks of speech, not to be used against the life of the innocent, but to attempt to save the life of the guilty. O God, You viewed me from afar, stumbling on that slippery path, yet sending out brief flashes of honesty amid much smoke. I guided those who were steeped in self-importance and sought after lying,[84] myself being their companion.

During those years I had a mistress to whom I was not married. She was a woman I had discovered in my wayward passion, void as it was of understanding, yet she was the only one. I remained faithful to her and with her discovered through experience the great difference between the restraint of the marriage bond, entered into with the intent of having children, and the agreement of lustful love, where children are born against the parents' will—although once born compel their love.

I remember once, when I decided to compete for a theatrical prize, some magician—I don't remember him now—asked me what I would give him to be certain to win. I detested and loathed such ungodly practices[85] and answered "that, even if the garland were of imperishable gold, I still would not permit a fly to be killed to win it for me." This man would have killed living creatures in his sacrifices, and by those offerings would have invited demons to help me.

I refused this evil, but not out of a pure love of You, O God of my heart, for I didn't know how to love You. At that time, I didn't know how to regard anything beyond physical pleasure. A soul commits indecency against You by sighing after such idleness and trusting in false things "to feed on the winds."[86] Nevertheless, I would not have sacrifices offered to devils on my behalf, though I was myself still offering them sacrifices of a sort by my own [Manichean] superstition. For what does it mean "to feed on the winds" but to feed on the devils—that is, in our wanderings to become their sport and mockery?

CHAPTER 3—ASTROLOGY

However, without scruples I consulted other impostors, whom they call "astrologers." They used no sacrifices and invoked the aid of no spirit for their divinations. Nevertheless, true Christian integrity must reject and condemn their art as well.

I find it good to confess to You and to pray, "LORD, be merciful to me; Heal my soul, for I have sinned against You."[87] I ask not to abuse Your goodness as a license to sin, but to remember the words of the Lord, "See, you have been made well. Sin no more, lest a worse thing come upon you."[88]

This wholesome advice of Your Scriptures the astrologers labor to destroy by saying, "The cause of your sin is inevitably fixed in the heavens" or, "This is the doing of Venus, or of Saturn, or of Mars." All this so that a man, who is only flesh and blood, and filled with proud corruption, may regard himself as blameless, while the Creator and Ruler of all heaven and the stars must bear the blame of our ills and misfortunes. Who is this Creator but You, O God, the sweetness and wellspring of righteousness, who renders to every man according to his works and does not despise "a broken and a contrite heart"?[89]

At that time, there was a wise man that was very skillful and quite famous in medicine.[90] He was proconsul then, and with his own hand placed on my distempered head the crown I had won in a debate. However, he did not do this as a physician. For only You, "who resists the proud and gives grace to the humble,"[91] can heal this distemper. Did You fail me in that old man, or withhold Your healing from my soul?

Good Advice From a Wise Friend

When I became better acquainted with this wise one, I listened with rapt attention, eager to apprehend his words. Though he spoke in simple language, his conversation abounded with exuberance, life, and sincerity. He recognized from the way I talked that I was interested in the books of horoscope casters. But in a kind and fatherly way, he advised me to discard them and not to spend myself on these deceptions. He encouraged me instead, to expend my energy and effort in more useful things.

My wise friend told me that in his earlier years, he had studied the astrologers' art with the idea of earning his living by it as a profession. Since he already understood Hippocrates, he was fully qualified to understand this as well. However, he gave it up and followed medicine for the simple reason that he had discovered astrology was utterly false and, as a man of honest character, was unwilling to gain his living by deceiving people. "But you," he said, "have the profession of rhetoric [legal debate] to support yourself. You are following this delusion by your own free will and not of necessity. Therefore, you ought to believe me all the more, since I worked at it to learn the art perfectly to gain my living by it."

When I asked my friend to account for the fact that many true things are foretold by astrology, he answered me, reasonably enough, that the force of chance, diffused through the entire order of nature brought these things about. For when a man, by accident, opens the pages of some poet (who sang and intended something far different) a verse oftentimes turns out to be wondrously appropriate to the reader's present business. "It is not to be wondered at," he continued, "if out of the human mind, by some higher instinct which does not know what goes on within itself, an answer should be arrived at by chance and not art, which would fit both the business and the action of the inquirer."

Alas, either by him or through him, You, my Lord, were looking after me. Furthermore, You fixed all this in my memory so that afterward I might search it out for myself. Nevertheless, at that time, neither the proconsul nor my most dear Nebridius, a splendid and most cautious youth who scoffed at the whole business of divination, could persuade me to give it up. The authority of the astrological authors influenced me more than those close to me did. At that time, I had encountered no sound evidence that could prove to me without a doubt, that what had been foretold by the masters of astrology came from accident or chance, and not from the art of their stargazing.

CHAPTER 4—THE DEATH OF MY DEAR FRIEND

When I first began to teach legal debate in my hometown, I had a very dear friend about my age that was an associate of mine in the same field. Like me, he was just then rising up into the flower of youth. He had grown up with me from childhood and we had been both schoolmates and playmates. However, he was not then my friend, nor indeed ever became my friend in the true sense of the word. There is no true friendship except between those God binds together and that cling to Him by "the love of God [that] has been poured out in our hearts by the Holy Spirit who was given to us."[92]

Nevertheless, it was a sweet friendship, ripened by the zeal of common studies. Moreover, I had turned him away from the true faith, which he had not soundly and thoroughly mastered as a youth, and pointed him toward the superstitious and harmful fables that my mother mourned in me. This man went with me as I wandered off in error, and we became so close my soul could not exist without him. However, You were close behind us fugitives. You are at once a God of vengeance and a Fountain of mercies, turning us to Yourself by ways that make us marvel. You took my friend out of this life less than a year after our friendship began. His companionship was sweeter to me than all the sweetness of my life up till then.

Who can show forth all Your praise[93] for that which he has experienced in himself alone? What was it that You did at that time, O my God? The depths of Your judgments are unsearchable! My friend was extremely ill with a fever and for a long time lay unconscious in a death sweat. Everyone feared that he would not recover, so without his knowledge he was baptized.

Immersed in the Darkness of Grief

I cared little about my friend's baptism at the time, presuming that his soul would retain what it had taken from me rather than what was done to his unconscious body. However, things turned out far differently, for he was revived and restored! Immediately, as soon as I could talk to him—I did this as soon as he was able, for I never left him because we were so close—I tried to joke with him about his baptism, supposing that he would joke about it as well because his mind and senses were inactive. But he recoiled from me as if I were his enemy, and with a remarkable and unexpected freedom, he admonished me that if I desired to continue as his friend, I must cease to say such things.

Confounded and confused, I hid my feelings till my friend was fully recovered and strong enough for me to deal with him as I wished. But he was snatched away from my madness, so that with You he might be preserved from my folly. A few days later, while I was away, the fever returned and he died.

My heart was completely darkened by this sorrow and everywhere I looked I saw death. My home was a torture room, and my father's house a strange unhappiness. All the things I had done with my friend became a frightful torment now that he was gone. My eyes sought him everywhere, but did not see him. I hated all the places we loved because he was not in them. They could not call out to me saying, "Look, he is coming," as they did when he was alive and only absent.

I became a difficult mystery to myself, and I asked my soul why she was so downcast and why this upset me so deeply.[94] My soul knew not how to answer me. If I said, "Hope in God,"[95] my soul disobeyed me. This was proper, because that dear friend my soul had lost was just a man, though seemingly truer and better than the imagined deity in whom my soul was ordered to place hope. Nothing but tears was sweet to me and so tears took my friend's place in my heart's desire.

Chapter 5—Sweet Fruit from the Bitterness of Life

These things are past now, O Lord, and time has healed the wound. Let me learn from You, who is Truth, and put the ear of my heart to Your mouth so You can tell me why weeping is so sweet to the unhappy. Have You, though omnipresent, dismissed our miseries from Your concern? You abide in Yourself while we are faced with trial after trial. Yet unless we weep in Your ears, there would be no hope for us remaining.

How is it that such sweet fruit is plucked from the bitterness of life, and from groans, tears, sighs, and mourning? Is it the hope that You will hear us that sweetens it? This is true in the case of prayer, for in a prayer there is a desire to approach You. But is it also the case in grief for a lost love, and in the kind of sorrow that had overwhelmed me? For I had neither a hope of his coming back to life, nor in all my tears did I seek that return.it. I simply grieved and wept, for I was miserable and had lost my joy. Or is weeping a bitter thing that gives us pleasure because of our dislike of the things we once enjoyed, and this only as long as we can't bear them?

Chapter 6—Wearisome to Live, Fearful to Die

Why do I speak of these things? Now is not the time to ask such questions, but rather to confess to You. I was wretched. Every soul that is fettered in the friendship of mortal things is wretched. It is torn to pieces when it loses them, and then realizes the misery which it had even before it lost them. That is how it was at that time with me. I wept bitterly and found rest in bitterness.

I was wretched, and yet still held that wretched life dearer than my friend. Though I willingly would have changed it, I was less willing to lose it than to have lost him. Indeed, I doubt whether I was willing to lose it at all, even for him. Unless it is fiction, it's like the friendship of Orestes and Pylades.[96] They would have gladly died for one another, or both together, because not to love together was worse than death to them. Nevertheless, a strange kind of feeling had come over me that was quite different from this. Now it was wearisome to live and fearsome to die. I suppose that the more I loved my friend, the more I hated and feared the cruel enemy of death that had robbed me of him. I even imagined that death would suddenly annihilate all men, since it had had such a power over him. This is how I remember it was with me.

Look into my heart, O God! Look deep within me and see, for I remember it well, O my Hope who cleanses me from the uncleanness of such affections, directing my eyes toward You while plucking my feet out of the snare. I marveled that other mortals went on living since my friend, whom I had loved as if he would never die, was now dead. I marveled all the more that I, who had been a second self to him, could go on living when he was dead. Someone spoke rightly of his friend as being "his soul's other half."[97] Likewise, I felt that my soul and his soul were but one soul in two bodies. Consequently, my life was now a horror to me because I did not want to live as a half self. It may have been that I was afraid to die, lest he, whom I had so greatly loved, should then die completely.

CHAPTER 7—MY RETURN TO CARTHAGE

Such madness, not knowing how to love others as they should be loved! O foolish man that I was, enduring in such rebellion the reward of every man! So I worried, sighed, wept, tormented myself, and neither rested nor sought counsel. I was dragging around my torn and bloody soul.

My soul was impatient of my dragging it around, and yet I could find no place to lay it down. Not in pleasant groves, nor in sport or song, not in fragrant gardens, nor in magnificent banquets, nor in the pleasures of the bed or the couch, not even in books or poetry did my soul find rest.

Everything looked gloomy in my grief, even the very light itself. That which was not what my friend was, had become repulsive and hateful, except my groans and tears, for in those alone I found a little rest. However, when my soul would stop weeping, a heavy burden of misery weighed me down. I should have surrendered this up to You, O Lord, for You to lighten and to carry. This I knew, but was neither willing nor able to do so, especially because my thoughts of You were not true but only an empty fantasy. Thus error was my god. If I tried to cast off my burden on this fantasy that it might find rest there, it sank through the vacuum and came rushing down again upon me.

Therefore, I remained to myself. I was closed up like an unhappy lodging where I could neither stay nor leave. Besides, where could my heart flee from my heart? Where could I flee from myself? Where could I go and not follow myself? Yet I did flee from my familiar surroundings so that my eyes would look for him less in places where they were not accustomed to seeing him. That is why I left the town of Tagaste and returned to Carthage.

Chapter 8—Overcoming Grief

Time never lapses, nor does it glide at leisure through our sense perceptions. It does strange things in the mind. Time came and went from day to day, and by coming and going it brought to my mind other ideas and memories. Little by little they patched me up again with pleasures I had known earlier, and my sorrow yielded a bit to them.

Nevertheless, after the sorrow of the death of my friend, other sorrows followed. That first sorrow had so easily penetrated me to the quick, because I had poured out my soul onto the dust by loving a man as if he would never die, but who had died anyway. What revived and refreshed me more than anything else was the consolation of other friends, with whom I went onjoined lovingin loving the things I loved instead of You. This was a monstrous fable and a tedious lie. It corrupted my soul by its adulterous rubbing on my soul's "itching ears."[98] That fable would not die to me as often as one of my friends died.

Other things in our companionship took strong hold of my mind as well. Together we would...

visit, and talk, joke and indulge in courteous debates. We would read pleasant books, spend time together, and engage in serious discussions. At times we would differ without arguing, and through these infrequent dissensions add zest to our more frequent agreements. Each of us would teach and be taught at times, sometimes teach, sometimes be taught. And when we were absent, we would long impatiently for one another, and then welcome one another of them home with joy.

These tokens of friendship and more, spring spontaneously from the hearts of those who love and are loved in return. They are demonstrated by a look, a word, an expression on the face and a thousand more gestures, and served as fuel to melt our souls together. Thus, out of the many we were made one.

CHAPTER 9—THE BLESSEDNESS OF LOVE

This, and more, is what we love in our friends. We love it so much that a man's conscience accuses itself if he does not love one who loves him, or respond in love to love, while seeking nothing from the other but the evidence of his love. This is the source of our moaning in grief and the feeling of death in the living, because of the loss of the life of the dying. It ushers in the gloom of sorrow, the steeping of the heart in tears, and turns all sweetness into bitterness.

Blessed is he who loves You, God, and who loves his friend in You. Blessed is he who loves his enemy also, for Your sake, for he alone loses none dear to him, if all are dear in Him who cannot be lost. Who is this but our God that created heaven and earth, and filled them because He created them by filling them up? None loses You but he who leaves You. However, where can one go when he leaves You? Where can he flee but from You, well pleased to have offended You? Where would this one not find Your law fulfilled in his own punishment? "Your law is truth"[99] and You are Truth.

CHAPTER 10—THE EBB AND FLOW OF BEAUTIFUL THINGS

"Restore us, O God; Cause Your face to shine, And we shall be saved!"[100] Unless turned toward You, wherever the soul of man turns itself it is enmeshed in sorrows, even though it is surrounded by beautiful things outside You and outside of itself. Lovely things would simply not be unless they were from You. They come to be and then pass away. By coming, these lovely things begin to be and grow toward perfection. Then, when perfect, they begin to grow old and perish, and though all may not grow old, all still perish. Therefore, when they rise and grow toward being, the more rapidly they grow to maturity, and then the more rapidly they hasten back toward nonexistence. This is the way of things.

This is the place You have given to all things in creation. They are part of things that do not all exist at the same time, but by passing away and succeeding each other all make up the universe, of which they are all parts. For example, our speech is accomplished by sounds, each of which has meaning. However, a meaning is not complete unless one word passes away after it has sounded its part so that the next word may follow.

Let my soul praise You, in all these things, O God, Creator of all. However, prevent my soul from being stuck to these things by the glue of love through the senses of my body. For they go where they were meant to go, that they might exist no longer. They tear the soul with deadly desires because she longs to be and yet loves to rest secure in the created things she loves. But in these things there is no resting place to be found. They do not remain, but flee away.

Who can follow these things with the physical senses? Who can grasp them, even when they are present? Physical senses are slow because they are physical and bear in themselves their own limitations. Physical senses are quite sufficient for what they were made to do, but are not sufficient to prevent things from running their course. For in Your word, by which they were created, their appointed boundaries are established, "From there—to here!"

CHAPTER 11—GROWING WEARY OF DECEIT

Don't be foolish, O my soul, and don't let the clamor of self-importance deafen the ear of your heart. Be attentive. The Word Himself calls you to return, and with Him [Jesus] is a place of unperturbed rest where love is not forsaken unless it first forsakes. These things must pass away so that others may come to take their place. Then, even this lowest level of unity [the physical universe] may be made complete in all its parts.

"But do I ever pass away?" asks the Word of God. Fix your habitation in Him. O my soul, commit whatever you have to Him. At long last you are growing weary of deceit. Commit to truth whatever you have received from the truth and you will lose nothing. What is decayed will flourish again. Your diseases will be healed. Your perishable parts will be reshaped and renovated, and made whole again within you. Furthermore, these perishable things will not carry you with them down to where they go when they perish, but will stand and abide before God—who abides and continues forever—along with you.

O my perverse soul. Why do you go on following your flesh? Instead, let it be converted so it will follow you. Whatever you feel through the flesh is but partial. You do not know the whole, of which sensations are but parts, yet the parts delight you. If my physical senses had been able to comprehend the whole, you would want whatever exists in the present time to also pass away so that the whole might please you more.

As a part of your punishment, you received only a portion of the whole as you own territory. For what we speak, you hear through physical sensation, yet you do not wish that the syllables remained. Instead, you wish them to fly past so that others may follow them, and the whole be heard. Thus it always is, that when any single thing is composed of many parts that do not coexist simultaneously, the whole gives more delight than the parts ever could when perceived separately.

However, far better than all this is He who made it all. He is our God and He does not pass away, for there is nothing to take His place.

CHAPTER 12—TURN YOUR HEART TO GOD

If physical objects please you, praise God for them. However, you must turn your love back to their Creator, lest you displease Him in those things that please you. If souls please you, let them be loved in God, for in themselves they are changeable, but in Him are firmly established. Without Him, souls would simply cease to exist. Let them be loved, then, in Him, and bring to Him along with yourself as many souls as you can. Say to them:

Let us love God, for He created all these. He is not far away from them, for He did not create them, and then go away. They are of Him and in Him. Listen, wherever truth is known, He is there. He is within the inmost heart, yet the heart has wandered away from Him.

Return to your heart, O you transgressors, and hold fast to Him who made you. Stand with Him and you shall stand fast. Rest in Him and you shall be at rest. Where do you go along these rugged paths? What is your destination? The good that you love is from Him, and because it is also for Him, it is both good and pleasant. But it will rightly be turned to bitterness if whatever comes from Him is not rightly loved and if He is deserted for the love of the creature.

Why then will you wander farther and farther in these difficult and toilsome ways? There is no rest where you seek it. Seek what you seek, but remember that it will not be found where you seek it. You seek for a blessed life in the land of death, but it is not there. For how can there be a blessed life where life itself is not?

Jesus is the Source of Life

Our very Life, J [Jesus,] came down to earth and bore our death, killing it with the very abundance of hHis own life. Thundering, He called us to return to Him into that secret place from which He came to us. He came first into the Virgin's womb, where the human creature, our mortal flesh, was joined to Him that it might become immortal. He also came "as a bridegroom coming out of his chamber, rejoicing as a strong man to run a race."[101] He did not delay, but ran through the world, crying out by words, deeds, death, life, descent, and ascension, crying aloud to us to return unto Him. He then departed from our sight that we might return to our hearts and find Him there. For though He left us, He is here!

Jesus could not linger with us long, yet He did not leave us. He went back to the place that He had never left, for "the world was made through Him."[102] In this world He was, and into this world He came to save sinners. To Him my soul confesses, and He heals it, because it had sinned against Him. O sons of men, how long will you be so slow of heart? Even now after Life itself has come down to you, will you not ascend and live? But where will you climb if you are already on a pinnacle and have set your mouth against the heavens? First come down that you may climb up, climb up to God. For you have fallen by trying to climb against Him. Tell this to the souls you love that they may weep in the valley of tears. Then, bring them along with you to God. For it's by His Spirit that you speak to them, if you burn with the fire of love as you speak.

Chapter 13—The Beauty of Harmony

These things I did not understand at that time, and so I loved those inferior beauties. All the while, I was sinking down to the very depths. I said to my friends:

> Do we love anything but the beautiful? What then is the beautiful? Furthermore, what is beauty? What is it that allures and unites us to the things we love, for unless there were a grace and beauty in them, they could not possibly attract us to them?

As I reflected on this, I saw that in the objects themselves there is a kind of beauty that comes from their forming. This was an entirely different kind of beauty that came from mutual fitness— like the harmony of one part of the body with rest of the body, or a shoe with a foot, etc. This idea sprang up in my mind out of my inmost heart, and I wrote some books, two or three, I think, entitled *On the Beautiful and the Fitting*.[103] You know them, O

Lord, though they have escaped my memory. I no longer have them; somehow they have been mislaid.

Chapter 14—My Infatuation with Hierius

What was it, O Lord my God, that prompted me to dedicate these books to the Roman lawyer, Hierius? He was a man I did not know by sight but whom I admired for his reputation of learning. He was famous for his eloquent speaking, and also for some words of his that I had heard which had pleased me. However, he pleased me more because he pleased others. They praised him highly, amazed that a Syrian, who had first studied Greek oration, could become such a skillful a Latin orator and so well versed in philosophy. Thus a man wwe hadve never seen wasis commended and loved.

Love like this does not come into the heart of the hearer from the lips of him who sings the other's praise. Instead, one catches the spark of love from one who loves. This is why we love someone who is praised when the one praising him expresses it from a sincere heart. That is, when he loves the one he is praising.

Discerning Love and Admiration

I admired men based on the judgment of others, not Yours, O my God, in whom no man is deceived. But why is it that the feelings I had for such men was not like my feelings toward the renowned charioteer, or the great gladiatorial hunter, famed far and wide and popular with the crowds? Actually, I admired the orator in a different and more serious fashion, as I wanted to be admired. For I did not want them to praise and love me as actors were praised and loved, although I praise and love them too. I would prefer being unknown than to be known in that way, or even being hated rather than loved that way.

How are these various influences and different kinds of love distributed within one soul? What is it that I am in love with in another, which if I did not hate, I should neither detest nor cast away from myself, seeing that we are equally men? It doesn't follow that because the good horse is admired by a man who would not be that horse, even if he could, the same kind of admiration should be given to an actor who shares our nature. Do I then love that in a man, which I, as a man, would hate to be? Man is himself a great deep. You number his very hairs, O Lord, and they do not fall to the ground without You. Yet the hairs of his head are more readily numbered than are his affections and the movements of his heart.

The lawyer whom I so greatly admired was the kind of man I wanted to be. However, my pride was the primary motivation, so I "was carried about with every wind."[104] Through it all, You, Lord, were secretly piloting me. This is my confident confession to You: I know that I loved Hierius more because of the love of those who praised him than for what they praised him for. However, if these same people had criticized him, saying the same things about him but with scorn and disapproval, I would never have been moved to admire him. Yet his qualities would not have been different, nor would he have been different, only the opinions of the spectators would be different.

This is where the helpless soul that is not sustained by the stability of truth lies powerless! Just as the breezes of speech blow from the breast of the narrow-minded, so also the soul is tossed this way and that, driven forward and backward. Light then becomes obscured and the truth is not visible. Yet, the truth is there, right in front of us.

To me, it was important that this man I revered know of both my literary work and my enthusiasm to learn. If he approved of them, I would be even more fonder of him, but if he disapproved, my prideful heart, devoid of Your steadfastness, would have been offended. Therefore, I meditated on the problem "of the beautiful and the fitting" and dedicated my essay about it to him. I admired it, though no one else joined me in doing so.

CHAPTER 15—PROBING THE MYSTERY OF LIFE

I completely missed the fact that the main point in these great issues, which concerned [concerning the nature of beauty,] is found in Your craftsmanship, O Omnipotent One, "who alone does wondrous things."[105] Therefore, in my mind I sifted through the physical creation, defining and distinguishing as "beautiful" that which is so in itself, and as "fit" that which is beautiful in relation to some other thing. I supported this argument by the examples I had so distinguished.

Then I turned my attention to the nature of the mind. However, the false opinions that I held concerning spiritual things prevented me from seeing the truth. Still, the very power of truth forced itself upon me, so I turned my throbbing soul away from things with no physical substance to qualities of line, color and shape. Then, because I could not perceive these with my mind, I concluded that I could not perceive my mind.

Since I loved the peace found in virtue and hated the discord which is in vice, I determined that the unity found there is in virtue and the discord is in vice. Furthermore, I determined that unity consisted of the rational soul, the nature of truth, and the highest good. But I imagined that in the disunity there was some kind of substance of irrational life, and some kind of entity in the supreme evil. This evil I thought was not only a substance but real life as well, yet I did not believe that it came from You, O my God, from whom are all things.

The first I called a Monad, as if it were a soul without sex. The other I called a Dyad, which revealed itself in anger, deeds of violence, and deeds of passion and lust. Nevertheless, I didn't know what I was talking about. I didn't understand nor had I been taught that evil is not a substance at all, and that our souls are is not that supreme and unchangeable good.

Just as in violent acts, if the emotion of the soul that births the violent impulse is depraved, it asserts itself in a rude and divisive manner. This is also true in acts of passion if the affection of the soul that gives rise to carnal desires is unrestrained. Likewise, errors and false opinions contaminate life if the rational soul itself is depraved. That's how it was with me. I was ignorant about my soul, and didn't know that it was not the essence of truth. I also didn't know that my soul needed to be enlightened by another light in order to partake of the truth. "For You will light my lamp; The LORD my God will enlighten my darkness."[106] "And of his fullness have we all received,"[107] for "That was the true Light which gives light to every man coming into the world."[108] For in You "there is no variation or shadow of turning."[109]

Pursuing the Vanity and Futility of Philosophy

Therefore, I pushed on toward You, and was pressed back by You that I might know the taste of death, for "You resist the proud."[110] What greater pride could there be for me than to assert myself to be that nature which You are? This was insane! I was subject to change. This was perfectly clear to me because my very longing to become wise arose out of a wish to change from worse to better. Nevertheless, I chose to think of You as changeable rather than think I was not as You are.

For this reason I was thrust back. You resisted my fickle pride. So I went on imagining physical forms. Since I was flesh, I accused the flesh. Since I was "a breath that passes away,"[111] I chose not return to You but instead went wandering on toward that which has no being—neither in You, in me, nor in the body. These theories were not created for me by Your truth, but were conceived by my own prideful self and sensory notions.

I used to flippantly ask Your faithful children, my own fellow citizens from whom I stood unconsciously exiled, "Why, then, does the soul, which God created, sin?" However, I would not allow anyone to ask me, "Does God sin?" I preferred to contend that Your unchangeable substance was involved in error through necessity rather than admit that my own changeable substance had gone astray. My soul, of its own free will, had fallen into error as its punishment.

I was about twenty-six or twenty-seven when I wrote those books, analyzing and reflecting upon those sensory images, which clamored in the ears of my heart. I was straining to hear Your inward melody, O sweet Truth, pondering on "the beautiful and the fitting." I longed to stay and hear You and to rejoice greatly at "the Bridegroom's voice."[112] Yet I could not. The clamor of my own errors pushed me away from You, and the weight of my own pride was sinking me ever lower. You did not "make me hear joy and gladness," nor did my bones rejoice.[113] They were not yet humbled.

Reveling in Aristotle

What did it profit me that, when I was scarcely twenty years old, a book of Aristotle's entitled *The Ten Categories*[114] fell into my hands? I took hold of the very title as something great and divine since my law professor at Carthage, and others who had reputations for learning, always referred to it with such intellectual pride. I read it by myself and understood it. What did it mean that when I discussed it with others, they said that even with the assistance of tutors— who not only explained it, but drew many diagrams in the sand—they scarcely understood it and could tell me no more about it than I knew from reading it by myself?

This book spoke plainly to me about substances, like a man, for example. It went on to speak of the qualities of that substance, such as its...

Shape,
Kind,
Stature,
Family relationship,
Status,
Birthdate,
And also,
Whether the man, as a substance, he was ...
Sitting or standing,
Wearing shoes,
Was armed,
Was doing anything or perhaps
Having something done to him.

These innumerable things are either classified under categories like the examples above, or under the chief category of substance.

What did this profit me, since it actually hindered me when I imagined that whatever existed was comprehended within those ten categories? I tried to interpret them, O my God, so that I could understand You according to this formula. According to this, Your wonderful and unchangeable unity could be understood as subjected to Your own magnitude or beauty, as if they existed in

You as their Subject—as they do in physical bodies—whereas You are Your own magnitude and beauty.

A body is not great or fair because it is a body. Even if it were less great or less beautiful, it would still be a body. However, my conception of You was false and not true. It was a figment of my own misery, not the stable ground of Your blessedness. For You had commanded, and it was carried out in me, that the earth should bring forth briars and thorns for me, and that with heavy labor I should earn my bread.[115]

My Useless Pursuit of Human Wisdom

What did it profit me that I could read and understand all the books I could get in the so-called "liberal arts," when I was actually a worthless slave of wicked lust? I took delight in them, not knowing the real source of what it was in them that was true and certain. For I had my back toward the light, and my face toward the things on which the light falls. Therefore, my face was not illuminated, but was constantly in the dark.

Whatever was written in any of the fields of law or logic, geometry, music, or arithmetic, I could understand with little difficulty and without human the instruction. Of another man. All this You know, O Lord my God, because both quickness in understanding and acuteness in insight are Your gifts. Yet for such gifts I gave no thanks to You. Therefore, my abilities served not my profit but rather my loss, since I went about trying to bring so large a part of my substance under my own power. I did not store up my strength for You, but went away from You into the far country to prostitute my gifts on ungodly appetites.[116]

What did these abilities profit me if I did not put them to good use? I did not realize that these subjects were difficult to understand, even by the studious and intelligent. It wasn't not until I tried to explain them to others that I discovered that even the most proficient among them were too slow in following my teaching.

What did this profit me, since I still supposed that You, O Lord God, the Truth, were a bright and vast body and that I was a particle of that body? O, such perversity gone wild! But so it was with me. I don't blush to confess Your mercies to me in Your presence, O my God. O, or to call upon You any more than I didn't blush when I openly declared my blasphemies before men, howling like a dog against You.

What good was it for me that my nimble wit could run through those studies and disentangle all those knotty volumes? What gain was it that I could understand with no help from a human teacher, since all the while I was sinning hatefully and with such disrespect for the righteous faith? What kind of burden was it for Your little ones to have a far slower wit, since they did not use it to depart from You, and since they remained in the nest of Your Church to safely grow and nourish their wings of love with the food of a sound faith?

Praise God's Faithfulness

O Lord our God, defend us. Support us under the shadow of Your wings. Let us hope.[117] You will bear us up when we are little and when we are old, You will carry us. Our stability, when it is in You, is stable, but when in us, is unstable. Our good lives forever with You, but when we turn from You in rebellion, we sink into perversion.

Let us now, O Lord, return that we be not overturned. With You our good lives without blemish, for our good is You alone. We need not fear that there is no place to which to return because we fell away from You. For, in our absence, our home, which is Your eternity, does not fall away.

BOOK FIVE

Intrigued by Christianity and Bishop Ambrose

Augustine faces a year of decision. He is in Carthage when Faustus visits, but quickly becomes disenchanted as a solid demonstration of the truth of Manichean doctrine proves to be fleeting. Choosing to leave Carthage and its troubles behind, he sets out for Rome. His hopes again dashed, Augustine applies for a teaching position at Milan. There he meets Ambrose, an impressive witness to Augustine for Catholic Christianity. This introduces him to allegorical interpretation of Scripture, causing Augustine to begin studying Christianity at the most basic level.

Chapter 1—My Soul Praises You, O God

Lord God, accept this sacrifice of my confessions from the hand of my tongue. You formed it and have prompted it to praise Your name. Heal all my bones and let them say, "LORD, who is like You?"[118] It is not that one who confesses to You instructs You as to what goes on within him. The closed heart does not prevent Your seeing into it, nor does the hardness of a heart hold back Your hands. For You can soften the heart at will, either by mercy or in vengeance, "and there is nothing hidden from Your heat."[119]

Let my soul praise You, that it may love You. Let it confess Your mercies to You, that it may praise You. Your entire creation praises You without ceasing: The spirit of man, by his own lips, with his voice lifted up to You as well as animals and lifeless things by the mouths of those who meditate upon them.

This is how our souls climb out of their weariness toward You and lean on those things which You have created. We pass through them to You, Lord God, who created them in a marvelous way. With You, there is refreshment and true strength.

Chapter 2—Draw the Unrighteous Back unto You

The restless and unrighteous depart and flee away from You, God. Nevertheless, You see them, and Your eye pierces through the shadows in which they run. Though, they live in a world of beauty they are themselves most foul. How have they harmed You? Or in what way have they discredited Your power, which is just and perfect in its rule even to the last item in creation? Indeed, where could they flee when they run from Your presence? Would You be unable to find them? They fled so they wouldn't see You, the One who saw them, lest they be blinded and stumble into You.

You forsake nothing that You have made. The unrighteous stumble against You, and are justly plagued. Fleeing from Your gentleness, they collide with Your justice and fall on their own rough paths. For in truth they do not know that You are everywhere, that no place contains You, and that only You are near— even to those who go farthest from You. Therefore, let them turn back and seek You, because even if they have abandoned You, their Creator, You have not abandoned them, Your creatures.

Let the unrighteous turn back and seek You. Then they will see that You are already there, in the hearts of those who confess to You. Let them cast themselves upon You, and weep on Your bosom after all their weary wanderings. Then, You will gently wipe away their tears[120] causing them to weep even more, yet rejoicing in their weeping, since You, O Lord, are not a man of flesh and blood. You are the Lord, who can remake all that You have previously made and can comfort them.

Where was I when I was seeking You? There You were, before me. However, I had gone away—even from myself—and could not find myself, much less You.

Chapter 3—Twenty-nine Years Old and Deceived

Now I will lay bare in the sight of God the twenty-ninth year of my life. A certain bishop of the Manicheans, Faustus by name, had just come to Carthage. He proved to be a great snare of the devil, and he entangled many through the charm of his eloquence. Even though I found his eloquence admirable, I was beginning to distinguish the charm of words from the truth of things I was eager to learn. Furthermore, I did not consider the dish as much as I did the kind of meat that their famous Faustus served me. His fame had run before him, as one highly skilled in an honorable profession and unsurpassed in the liberal arts.

I had already filled my mind with numerous doctrines of the philosophers, so I began to compare them to the tedious fables of the Manicheans. It struck me that probability was on the side of the philosophers. Their power reached far enough to enable them to form a fair judgment of the world, even though they had not discovered the sovereign Lord of it all. For You are great, O Lord, and You have respect unto the lowly, but the proud You know afar off.[121] You only draw near to those who have a contrite heart and You can't be found by the proud, even if in the skill of their reasoning they number the stars and the sands, map out the constellations, and trace the courses of the planets.

The mind and the intelligence that You gave the philosophers is what enabled them to investigate these things. Yes. They have discovered much, even predicting many years in advance the day, the hour, and the extent of the eclipses of the sun and moon. Their calculations are accurate and the eclipses happen just as they predict. They have written down the rules they've discovered, which can be used today to calculate the year, month, day, hour of the day, and at what quarter of its light either the moon or the sun will be eclipsed. And it will come to pass just as predicted. Men who are ignorant in these matters marvel and are amazed, while those who understand offer praise and are praised.

The Vanity of Philosophy

Nevertheless, in unholy pride these men pull away from You and forsake Your light. They foretell an eclipse of the sun before it happens, but fail to see their own eclipse, which is even then occurring. They don't ask, as religious men should, what the source of the intelligence is by which they investigate these matters. Moreover, when they discover that You made them, they refuse to submit to You so that You may preserve what You have made. Nor do they offer as sacrifices to You what they have discovered. They slaughter sacrificial fowls, but refuse to slaughter their pride or their curiosity, by which they wander through the unknown paths of the deep like the fishes of the sea. Neither do they curb their own indulgences as they do those of "the beasts of the field,"[122] so that You, O Lord, "a consuming fire,"[123] may burn up their mortal cares and renew them unto immortality.

The philosophers don't know that You created by Your word the things that are and also the men who measure them. That You created the senses by which they perceive what they measure, and the intelligence whereby they discern the patterns of measure. They don't know that Your wisdom isn't a matter of measure.[124] Nevertheless, the Only Begotten has been "made unto us wisdom, and righteousness, and sanctification"[125] and has been numbered among us and has paid tribute to Caesar.[126]

Jesus is the "Way"

The philosophers don't know the "Way" [Jesus] by which they could descend from themselves to Him in order to ascend through Him to Him. They didn't know this "Way," and so they thought themselves exalted to the stars and the shining heavens. Therefore, they fell upon the earth and "their foolish heart was darkened."[127] They see many true things about the creature but they choose not to seek the Truth, the Architect of Creation, with humble integrity and hence do not find Him. Or, if they do find Him, and know that He is God, they refuse to glorify Him as God.

Furthermore, these men are not thankful but become vain in their imagination, and say that they themselves are wise, attributing to themselves what is Yours. At the same time, with the most perverse blindness, they wish to attribute to You their own qualities. In that way they load their lies on You who are the Truth, "and change the glory of the incorruptible God into an image made like corruptible man—and birds and four-footed animals and creeping things."[128] They "exchanged the truth of God for the lie, and worshiped and served the creature rather than the Creator."[129]

Yet I remembered many true sayings of the philosophers about the creation, and I saw the confirmation of their calculations in the orderly sequence of seasons and the visible evidence of the stars. I compared this with the doctrines of Mani, who in his heretical foolishness wrote many books on these subjects. However, I could not discover in them any account of the solstices or the equinoxes, the eclipses of the sun and moon, or anything of the sort that I had learned in the books of secular philosophy. Nevertheless, I was ordered to believe, even when the ideas did not correspond with, or even contradicted, the rational theories established by mathematics and my own eyes.

Chapter 4—The Blessing of Knowing And Acknowledging God

O Lord God of Truth, is any man pleasing to You because he knows these things? No. For surely that man is unhappy who knows these things and doesn't know You. Furthermore, that man is happy who knows You, even though he doesn't know all these things! Moreover, he who knows both You and these things is not the more blessed for his learning. You only are his blessing so long as in knowing You as God, he glorifies You and gives thanks, not becoming proud in his thoughts.

This is like that man who knows how to possess a tree and give thanks to You for the use of it. Though he may not know how tall it is or how wide it spreads, he is better off than the man who can measure it and count all its branches, but neither owns it nor knows or loves its Creator. Likewise, a faithful man who possesses the world's wealth as though he had nothing possesses all things through his union through You, whom all things serve. He is blessed even though he doesn't know the orbit of the Great Bear constellation. It is foolish to doubt that the faithful man is better off than the one who can measure the heavens, number the stars and weigh the elements, but who is forgetful of You. For it is You "who have set in order all things in number, weight, and measure."[130]

Chapter 5—Confronting the Insane Heresies of Mani

Who ordered Mani to write about these things, the knowledge of which is not necessary to godliness? Lord, You have said to man, "Behold, godliness is wisdom"[131] and of this he might have been ignorant however perfectly he may have known these other things. However, since he didn't know even these other things, but still recklessly dared to teach them, it's clear that he had no knowledge of godliness. Even when we have knowledge of this worldly lore, it's foolish to make a *profession* of it when godliness comes from *confession* to You.

Mani strayed from godliness. His show of learning only enabled the truly learned to recognize from his ignorance what they knew. Therefore, he was not worthy to make plain the more difficult matters. He did not aim to be lightly esteemed, but sought to persuade men that the Holy Spirit, the Comforter and Enricher of Your faithful ones, was personally resident in him with full authority. Therefore, when he was caught in blatant errors about the sky, the stars, and the movements of the sun and moon, even though these things do not relate to religious doctrine, the ungodly presumption of the man became clearly evident. He not only taught things about which he was ignorant but also perverted them. He did this with such foolish and insane pride, that he claimed the things he said were the same as if a divine person had spoken them.

I can tolerate the uninformed opinion of a Christian brother who is ignorant of these things or in error concerning them. Nor do I believe that a lack of knowledge as to the form or nature of the material creation can do him much harm, so long as he holds no belief in anything that is unworthy of You, O Lord, the Creator of all. But if he thinks that his secular knowledge pertains to the essence of the doctrine of godliness, or ventures to assert dogmatic opinions in matters in which he is ignorant, therein lies the damage. Nevertheless, even a weakness such as this is tolerated by our Mother Charity in the infancy of our faith, until the new man can grow up "unto a perfect man," and not be "carried away with every wind of doctrine."[132]

However, Mani presumed to be at once the teacher, author, guide, and leader of all whom he could persuade to believe his heresies, so that all who followed him believed that they were following not an ordinary man but Your Holy Spirit! Who would not judge that such insanity, when it once stood convicted of false teaching, should then be abhorred and utterly rejected? But I had not yet decided whether the alternation of day and night, longer and shorter days and nights, eclipses of sun and moon, and whatever else I read about in other books could be explained consistently with his theories. If they could have been explained, doubt would still have remained in my mind about whether the theories were right or wrong. Nevertheless, on the strength of his reputed godliness, I was prepared to rest my faith on his authority.

Chapter 6—My Disappoint With Faustus

For nearly all of the nine years that I listened with unsettled mind to the Manichean teaching, I had, with great eagerness, looked forward to the arrival of Faustus. Every other member of the sect that I had met always referred me to his coming when they were unable to answer the questions I raised. They promised that, in discussion with him, these and even greater difficulties, if I had them, would be quite easily and amply cleared away.

When Faustus finally did come, I found him to be a man of pleasant speech, who spoke of the very same things these other members did, although more fluently and in a more agreeable style. But what profit was there to me in the elegance of my cupbearer, since he could not offer me the more precious drink for which I thirsted? My ears had already had their fill of such stuff, and it seemed no better simply because it was better expressed, nor more true because it was dressed in fancy words. Nor could I think the man's soul necessarily wise because his face was comely and his language eloquent.

Those who commended Faustus to me were incompetent judges. They thought him able and wise because his eloquence delighted them. At the same time, I realized that there is another kind of man, suspicious of even the truth itself if it is expressed in smooth and flowing language. But You, O my God, had already taught me in wonderful and marvelous ways. Therefore, I believed, because it's true, that You taught me, and beside You there is no other teacher of truth wherever truth shines forth.

I had already learned from You, Lord God, that simply because a thing is eloquently expressed it should not be received as necessarily true. Likewise, because a thing is spoken with stammering lips it should not be taken as false. Nor, again is what is spoken necessarily true because it is rudely uttered, nor untrue because the language is brilliant. Wisdom and folly are both are like meats that are wholesome and unwholesome. Likewise, eloquent or simple words are like town-made or rustic vessels. Both kinds of food may be served in either kind of dish.

Seeking Answers but Finding None

The eagerness with which I had so long awaited this man was rewarded by his actions and passion in a debate. I reveled in his fluency and admired the appropriate words with which he clothed his ideas. Therefore, I was delighted to join with others, and even exceed them, in exalting and praising him. Nevertheless, I was annoyed that during his lectures, I was not allowed to ask any of the questions that troubled me and so engage in any kind of discussion with him. I sought an opportunity, when it was not inconvenient for him, to enter into a discussion with my friends and me so I could set before him some of my doubts.

To my astonishment, I discovered at once that Faustus knew nothing of the liberal arts except grammar, and that in only an ordinary way! He had, however, read some of Tully's orations, a very few books of Seneca, some of the poets, and such few books of his own sect that were written in good Latin. With this meager learning and his daily practice in speaking, he had acquired an eloquence that proved the more delightful and enticing because it was under the direction of a ready wit and a sort of native grace.

O Lord my God, You are the Judge of my conscience. Was this as I now recall it? My heart and my memory are laid open before

You. For You were even then guiding me by the secret impulse of Your providence and setting my shameful errors before my face so that I might see and hate them.

Chapter 7—Doubts About Manichean Doctrine Increase

As soon as it became plain to me that Faustus was ignorant in those things that I had believed him distinguished, I began to doubt that he would be able to clarify and explain all the confusing things that troubled me. I realized that such ignorance should not have affected the authenticity of his godliness, if he had not been a Manichean. Though their books are filled with long stories about the sky, the stars, the sun and the moon, I didn't believe Faustus could satisfactorily prove what I so desperately wanted to know: Were the explanations contained in the Manichean books better, or at least as good as the mathematical explanations I had read elsewhere?

When I suggested that these subjects be considered and discussed, Faustus quite modestly declined to undertake the task. He knew that he had no knowledge of these things and was not ashamed to admit it. Faustus was not a talkative person, the likes of whom I had endured so much in the past. These earlier teachers would set out to teach me what I wanted to know, but say nothing. Faustus had a heart, which, if not right toward You, God, was at least not altogether false toward himself. Faustus was not ignorant of his own ignorance, so he chose not to be entangled in any controversy from which he could not withdraw gracefully. For this trait of honesty, I liked him all the more. The modesty of an ingenious mind is a finer thing than the acquisition of the knowledge I desired. I found this to be Faustus' attitude toward all obscure and difficult questions.

Manichean Doctrine Loses Its Appeal

As a result, the zeal with which I had plunged into the Manichean system was checked. Because Faustus, the most famous among them, had been such a disappointment in answering the issues that puzzled me, I grew even more wary of their other teachers. Therefore, I began to work with Faustus in the pursuit of his favorite subject, literature.

At that time, I was teaching as a professor of law among the young Carthaginian students. Then with Faustus I read whatever he wished, or what I judged suitable to be of interest to him. Any endeavor to progress further in Manichean thought came completely to an end through my acquaintance with that man. I did not sever my ties with them immediately, but since I had discovered nothing better, I studied whatever attracted my attention until something more desirable came along.

Ironically, Faustus, who had entrapped so many in this heresy to their death, now began to loosen the snare in which I had been caught. For Your hands, O my God, in the hidden design of Your providence did not desert my soul. Out of the blood of my mother's heart, and through the tears that she poured out day and night, a sacrifice was offered to You for me. You dealt with me, Lord, in marvelous ways. You, O my God, are the One who did it, for "The steps of a *good* man are ordered by the LORD, And He delights in his way."[133] How shall we attain salvation without Your hand remaking what it had already made?

CHAPTER 8—FROM CARTHAGE TO ROME

O God, thus You dealt with me. Therefore, I was decided to go to Rome and teach what I had been teaching at Carthage. I will not hesitate to confess to You how I was persuaded to do this, because in this also, the profound work of Your wisdom and constant mercy must be pondered and acknowledged.

My desire to go to Rome was not due to the higher fees or greater dignity promised by my friends there, though these did figure in my decision. However, my primary motive for going was that I had been told that the students studied more quietly and were easier to control with stern discipline. The students did not impulsively and rudely rush into the classroom of a teacher not their own. In fact, they were not admitted at all without the permission of the teacher.

At Carthage, on the other hand, the students behaved shamefully and were very unruly. They would rush into class rudely, and with wild outbursts disrupt the order that the teacher had established for the good of his pupils. These bold students perpetuated many outrageous deeds that would be punishable by law if they were not sustained by custom. Thus custom makes it plain that such behavior is all the more worthless because it allows men to do what Your eternal law never will allow. They think that their behavior is not punishable, though the very blindness with which they act is their punishment. They suffer far greater harm than they inflict.

The manners that I refused to adopt as a student I was compelled as a teacher to endure in others. Therefore, I was glad to go where such conduct was not allowed.

"You *are* my refuge, my portion in the land of the living."[134] You pressed me into moving away from Carthage for the preservation of my soul. At the same time, You offered me an incentive to go to Rome because of the behavior of students caught in the grip of this death-in-life. I faced insane conduct in the one place and empty promises in the other. Nevertheless, to correct my wandering footsteps, You secretly employed their twisted desires and my own. Those who disturbed my tranquility were blinded by shameful madness while those who lured me to Rome used nothing more than the earth's cunning. I hated the real misery in Carthage so I sought fictitious happiness in Rome.

Bidding My Mother Goodbye

You knew the cause of my going from one country to the other, O God, but didn't disclose it either to me or to my mother. She grieved deeply over my departure and followed me down to the sea. She embraced me tightly, willing to either hold me back or go with me. However, I deceived her by pretending that I had a friend whom I could not leave until he had a favorable wind to set sail. I lied to my persistent mother and escaped.

Nevertheless, Lord, You mercifully pardoned my foolishness and preserved me from the waters of the sea for the water of Your grace. You did this so that when I was purified by Your grace, the fountain of tears from my mother's eyes that daily watered the ground as she prayed would be dried.

Since my mother refused to return without me, I persuaded her, with some difficulty, to spend the night in a place near our ship where there was a shrine in memory of the blessed Cyprian. That night I secretly slipped away while she remained to pray and weep. What was it, O Lord, that she was asking of You in such a flood of tears, but that You would not allow me to sail? Nevertheless, You, took Your own secret counsel and, noting the real point to her desire, didn't grant what she was asking in order to grant to her what she had always sought.

The wind blew and filled our sails, and the shore dropped out of sight. Wild with grief, my mother was there the next morning, and fillinging Your ears with complaints and groans which You disregarded. At the very same time, You used my longings as the means to hasten me toward the fulfillment of all my longing, thus the earthly part of my mother's love was justly purged by the pain of sorrow. Still, like all mothers, though even more than others, she loved to have me with her. She had no idea what joy You were preparing for her through my departure. Not knowing this secret ending, she wept and mourned, and saw in her agony the inheritance of Eve—seeking in sorrow what she had brought forth in sorrow.[135] However, after accusing me of betrayal and cruelty, she still continued to intercede for me to You. Saddened, she returned to her own home and I sailed on to Rome.

Chapter 9—Rescued from Certain Death by Fervent Prayers

When I arrived in Rome, I was extremely ill and very near death. Had I died, I would surely have fallen into hell, burdened by the multitude of grievous sins I had committed against You, myself and others and myself. All of this sin was over and above the fetter of that original sin whereby we all die in Adam. You had forgiven me of none of these things in Christ, neither had Christ abolished by His cross the enmity[136] that I had incurred from You through my sins. How could You abolish sin by the crucifixion of a phantom, which was all I supposed Jesus to be? The death of my soul was as real to me then as the death of His flesh seemed unreal to me. Yet the life of my soul was as false, because it was as unreal as the death of his flesh was real, though at that time I didn't believe it.

My fever increased, and I was on the verge of passing away and perishing. If I had passed away, where would I have gone but into the fiery torment which my misdeeds deserved, measured by the truth of Your rule? My mother knew nothing of this, but went on praying for me though she was far away. And You, present everywhere, heard her cry where she was, and had pity on me where I was so that I regained my health, though I was still rebellious in my sacrilegious heart.

That peril of death did not make me wish to be baptized. I was better off when, as a lad, I requested baptism of my mother's devotion, as I have already related and confessed.[137] I had since increased in dishonor, madly scoffing at all the purposes of Your medicine which would have saved me, sinner though I was, from dieing a double death. However, had my mother's heart been pierced with this wound, it never would have healed.

Persistent Prayers of a Mother's Love

I cannot adequately tell of the love she had for me, or how she continued to travail for me in the spirit with far more anguish than when she bore me in the flesh. Therefore, I cannot conceive how she could have been healed had I died while still in my sins. Where, then, would have all her earnest, frequent, and ceaseless prayers to You been? Nowhere but with You.

Could You, O merciful God, despise the "broken and contrite heart"[138] of that pure and prudent widow? She was so faithful in her giving and so gracious and attentive to Your saints. She never failed to visit church twice a day—morning and evening, not for vain gossiping or old wives' fables, but in order to listen to You in Your sermons, and You to her in her prayers. Could You, by whose gifts she was so inspired, despise and disregard the tears of such a one without coming to her aid? Those tears by which she entreated You were not for gold or silver, and not for any changing or fleeting good, but for the salvation of the soul of her son. By no means, O Lord. It is certain that You were near and were listening and carrying out the plan that You had predetermined should be done.

Far be it from You to have deluded my mother in the visions and answers she had received from You—some of which I have mentioned, and others not—which she kept securely in her faithful heart. She was forever reminding You about them as if they had Your own signature. For You, "because Your mercy endures forever,"[139] have so availed Yourself to those whose debts You have pardoned that You likewise become a debtor by Your promises.

CHAPTER 10—IRRECONCILABLE PROBLEMS WITH MANICHEAN DOCTRINE

Lord God, You restored me from that illness, and healed the son of Your handmaid in his body. You did this that he might live for You and that You might endow him with a better and more certain health.

Nevertheless, at Rome I again joined those deluding and deluded "saints." Not their "hearers" only, such as the man in whose house I had fallen sick, but also with those whom they called "the elect." For it still seemed to me "that it is not we who sin, but some other nature sinned in us." It gratified my pride to be beyond blame, and when *I* did anything wrong not to have to confess that *I* had done wrong—that You might "heal my soul, for I…sinned against You."[140]

I loved to excuse my soul and to accuse something else inside me—I didn't know what, but it wasn't I! Nevertheless, it was I. And it was my sinfulness that had divided me against myself. That sin then was all the more incurable because I did not deem myself a sinner. It was such a deplorable evil, O God Omnipotent, that I would have preferred to have You defeated in me to my destruction, than to be defeated by You to my salvation. You had not yet set a guard upon my mouth and a door around my lips to prevent my heart from turning to evil speech, or to make excuses for sin with men that work iniquity.[141] Therefore, I continued in the company of their "elect."

Hopeless of profiting from that false doctrine, I began to stray away from those points, which I had decided to be content with since I could find nothing better. I was half inclined to believe that the philosophers whom they call "The Academics"[142] were wiser than the rest by saying we ought to doubt everything, and in maintaining that man does not have the power of comprehending any certain truth. Although I had not yet understood their meaning, I was fully persuaded that they thought this way in their daily affairs.

I also began to openly dissuade my host's confidence in the teachings of Mani. Despite this, I was still an intimate friend with more of these folk (Manicheans) than with others who were not of their heresy. I did not defend it with my former passion, but my familiarity with that group (, and there were many of them concealed in Rome at that time),[143] made me slower to seek any other way. This was particularly easy since I had no hope of finding truth in Your Church, Lord, from which they had turned me aside.

Doubts About the Humanity of Jesus

O Lord of heaven and earth, You are Creator of all things both visible and invisible. Nevertheless, it still seemed most improper to believe that You could have the form of human flesh and be bounded by the bodily shape of our limbs. Therefore, when I desired to meditate on my God, I didn't know what to think of but a huge extended body. This was the greatest and almost the sole cause of my unavoidable errors. For that without what had no bodily extension was inexistent didn't exist to me.

Likewise, I believed that evil was a similar kind of substance, and that it had its own hideous and deformed extended body. This body was either in a dense form, which the Manicheans called the earth, or a thin and subtle form, like the substance of air for example, which they imagined as some malignant spirit penetrating that earth. However, because my religious devotion, such as it was, still compelled me to believe that the good God never created any evil substance, I formed the idea of two masses. Each mass opposed the other; both were infinite but with the evil more compact and the good more expansive. From this diseased beginning, other blasphemies followed.

When my mind tried to turn back to the Catholic faith, I was cast down, since the Catholic faith was not what I judged it to be. It seemed to me a greater devotion to regard You, my God—to whom I make confession of Your mercies—as infinite in all respects except one:: wWhere the extended mass of evil stood opposed to You, I was compelled to confess that You are finite rather than think that You could be confined by the form of a human body.

It seemed better to me to believe that no evil had been created by You, for in my ignorance evil appeared not only to be some kind of substance but a physical one at that. This was because I had no conception of mind, except as a subtle body diffused throughout local spaces. This seemed better than to believe that anything could emanate from You which had the character that I considered evil to be in its nature.

I believed that our Savior, Your Only Begotten Son, had been brought forth for our salvation out of the mass of Your bright shining substance. Therefore, I could believe nothing about Him except what I was able to harmonize with these vain imaginations. I thought that such a nature could not be born of the Virgin Mary without being mingled with the flesh, and I could not see how the divine substance, as I had conceived it, could be mingled with the flesh without being contaminated by it. Therefore, I was afraid to believe that Jesus had been born in the flesh, lest I should also be compelled to believe that the flesh had contaminated Him.

Now, will Your spiritual ones smile blandly and lovingly at me if they read these confessions? Nevertheless, such was I.

CHAPTER 11–ELPIDIUS ARGUES FROM THE SCRIPTURES

Furthermore, I thought it impossible to defend the things the Manicheans criticized in Your Scriptures. I thought were impossible to be defended. Nevertheless, I occasionally wanted to discuss various matters with someone well educated in those books to test what he thought of them.

The teaching of Elpidius, who spoke and disputed face to face against the Manicheans, had begun to impress me. I first heard of him when I was at Carthage, and was impressed because his arguments came out of the Scriptures and were not easily overcome. In fact, the answers of the Manicheans appeared feeble to me. One of their feeble answers was not expressed publicly, but only to us in private. They said that unknown persons who desired to incorporate Jewish law into the Christian faith had tampered with the writings of the New Testament. However, they never produced any uncorrupted copies.

Still thinking in physical categories, very much ensnared and to some extent stifled, I was weighed down by the ideas of bodily substance. I gasped under this load for the air of Your truth, but was unable to breathe it pure and undefiled.

Chapter 12—Beset By Dishonesty in Rome

I diligently set about to practice what I came to Rome to do,: teach law. The first task was to gather in my home a few people to whom and through whom I had begun to be known. That's when I began to learn about offenses committed in Rome that I didn't have to bear in Africa. Just as I had been told, those riotous disruptions by young hooligans were not practiced here. Instead, my friends told me that many of the Roman students were unfaithful. They placed little value on loyalty and would conspire together to suddenly transfer to another teacher, all to evade paying their master's fees. My heart hated such people, though not with a "perfect hatred,"[144] for I undoubtedly hated them more because I suffered financially because of their dishonesty.

Such people are lower than low. They commit whoredoms against You, for they love the transitory pleasure of temporal things and the filthy gain which dirties the hand that grabs it. They embrace the fleeting world and scorn You, who abides and invites us to return to You and who pardons the prostituted human soul when it does return to You.

I hate such crooked and perverse men, although I love them if they will receive correction and come to prefer the learning they obtain to money, and above all, to prefer You to such learning. O God, You are the truth and fullness of our positive good, and our most pure peace. However, my desire was more that I would not suffer evil from them than that they would become good for Your sake.

Chapter 13—Bishop Ambrose

Therefore, when the officials of Milan sent a request to the officials in Rome to provide a teacher of law for their city and to send him at the public expense, I applied for the job. I sent my application through the same people who were drunk with the Manichean vanities. I wanted to be free of those folk, though neither they nor I were aware of it at the time. They recommended that the official, Symmachus appoint me after I was proved by audition.

To Milan I came, where I met Ambrose the bishop, famed through the entire world as one of the best of men and Your devoted servant. His eloquent discourses in those times abundantly provided Your people with the flour of Your wheat, the gladness of Your oil, and the sober intoxication of Your wine.[145]

You led me to him without my knowledge, inso that I would be ledmight lead me to You in full knowledge. That man of God received me as a father would, and welcomed my coming, as a good bishop should. I began to love him, though not at first as a teacher of the truth, for I had entirely despaired of finding truth in Your Church, but as a friendly man.

I listened to his preaching intently, though not with the right motive. I was trying to see if his eloquence lived up to his reputation, and whether it flowed fuller or thinner than others said it did. Thus I hung on his words intently, but as to his subject matter, I listened carelessly and contemptuously. I was delighted with the charm of his speech, which was more cultured, though less cheerful and soothing, than Faustus' style. As for subject matter, however, there could be no comparison, for Faustus wandered around in Manichean deceptions, while Bishop Ambrose was teaching salvation most soundly. However, "salvation is far from the wicked,"[146] such as I was then when I stood before him. Yet I was drawing nearer, gradually and unconsciously.

CHAPTER 14—THE ALLEGORICAL INTERPRETATION OF SCRIPTURE

I didn't trouble myself to learn what Ambrose said, but only to hear how he said it. This empty concern was of highest priority with me as long as I felt hopeless of finding a clear path from man to You. Nevertheless, along with the eloquence I prized, there also came into my mind ideas. I ignored them because I couldn't separate them, but while my heart was open to acknowledge the skill with which he spoke, there came with it a gradual awareness of how *truly* he spoke.

First of all, his ideas had already begun to appear defensible to me. The Catholic faith, for which I supposed no defense could be made against the onslaught of the Manicheans, I now realized could be maintained without presumption. This was especially clear after I had heard one or two parts of the Old Testament explained allegorically. When, in the past, I had interpreted them literally, they had "killed" me spiritually.[147] However, when many of these same passages were explained to me allegorically, I blamed my own despair for having believed that no reply could be given to those who hated and scoffed at the Law and the Prophets.

Nevertheless, I didn't see that this was reason enough to follow the Catholic way—just because its learned advocates could answer objections adequately and logically. Nor could I see that what I had held to before should now be condemned, because both sides were equally defensible. The Manichean way did not yet appear to be vanquished, but neither did it seem victorious.

However, I now earnestly set my mind to discover if there was any way possible to prove the Manicheans guilty of falsehood. If I could have conceived of a spiritual substance, all their strongholds would have collapsed and been cast out of my mind. But I could not. Still, concerning the body of this world, nature as a whole— now that I was able to consider and compare such things more and more—I decided that the majority of the philosophers held the more probable views.

Therefore, in what I thought was the method of the Academics, doubting everything and fluctuating between all the options, I came to the conclusion that the Manicheans were to be abandoned. For I judged, even in that period of doubt, that I could not remain in a sect to which I preferred some of the philosophers. However, I refused to commit the cure of my fainting soul to the philosophers because they were without the saving name of Christ. Therefore, I resolved to immerse myself in the Catholic Church, which my parents had previously urged me to do, until something certain appeared that would guide my course.

BOOK SIX

Seeking Truth

*Augustine faces his tumultuous twenties. His
mother, Monica, follows Him to Milan and finds
him engaged in catechism of the Catholic Church.
Augustine and Monica admire Ambrose but find
little help for Augustine regarding his personal
problems. Alypius and Nebridius join him in an
ambitious though confused quest for the happy
life. Augustine continues his fruitless search for
truth, becoming engaged along the way. He
dismisses his first mistress and takes another.*

Chapter 1–Mother Arrives In Milan

O Hope from my youth,[148] where were You to me, and where had You gone away?[149] Have You not created me and made me different from the beasts of the field and the birds of the air? Have You not made me wiser than they? Yet I was wandering about in a dark and slippery way, seeking You outside myself and thus not finding the God of my heart. I had gone down into the depths of the sea and had lost faith, and had despaired of ever finding the truth.

By this time my mother had come to me, having mustered the courage of devotion. She followed me over sea and land, secure in You through all the perils of the journey. Remarkably, in the midst of the dangerous voyage she comforted the sailors! These were men to whom the inexperienced voyagers would go for comfort when alarmed. Fearlessly, she assured them of a safe arrival because she had been assured of it by You in a vision.

Mother found me in deadly peril upon her arrival, despairing of ever finding the truth. When I told her that I was no longer a Manichean, though not yet a Catholic Christian, she didn't jump for joy as I expected. You had already shown her my misery and she had mourned as if I were dead, but You also showed her that I would be raised to You. She had carried me out, as it were, in the coffin of her thoughts, so that You would say to the widow's son, "Young man, I say unto you, arise!"[150] He would then revive and begin to speak, and You would deliver him to his mother.

Mother's heart was not overly exuberant even though she discovered that a great part of what she had prayed daily to You for had already been done. Nor was she concerned that I had not yet fully grasped the truth, because I was rescued from falsehood. She was fully confident that because You had promised her my salvation, You would deliver. Therefore, calmly and with a fully confident heart, she told me that she believed, in Christ, that before she died she would see me a faithful Catholic—and that is all she said. But to You, O Fountain of mercy, she poured out even more frequent prayers and shed even more tears that You would hasten Your aid and enlighten my darkness.

Mother hurried with even more passion to the church and hung upon the words of Ambrose, praying for the fountain of water that springs up into everlasting life.[151] She loved that man as an angel of God, since she knew that it was by him that I had been brought to that wavering state of agitation I was now in. She was fully persuaded I would pass from sickness to health, even though it would be after a sharper convulsion which physicians call "the crisis."

CHAPTER 2—AMBROSE FORBIDS MOTHER'S OFFERINGS TO SAINTS

Mother also brought to certain shrines erected in the memory of the saints, offerings of oatmeal, bread, and wine, as had been her custom in Africa. However, the doorkeepers forbade the practice. As soon as she learned that it was the bishop who had forbidden it, she acquiesced so devoutly and obediently that I marveled at how readily she changed her own customs, rather than question the prohibition.

Wine consumption had not taken possession of mother's spirit, nor did the love of wine stimulate her to hate the truth. When she brought her basket with the festive gifts, she would taste it first herself. However, she would never allow herself more than one little cup of wine, diluted according to her own temperate palate, and that she simply tasted out of courtesy. If there were many shrines of departed saints that needed to be honored in the same way, she carried the same little cup with her to be used everywhere. Carrying it about caused the wine to become very watered down and quite tepid. Nevertheless, she would distribute it by small sips to those around, for she sought to stimulate their devotion, not pleasure.

Bishop Ambrose objected to mother offering wine to others, because he felt that it could cause problems for those already drunk. Therefore, even those who used it in moderation were prevented from doing so. Also, these funereal memorials were very much like some of the superstitious practices of the pagans, so it was fitting for him to object. Therefore, mother willingly abstained from doing it any more.

Instead of a basket filled with fruits of the earth, mother started to bring a heart full of pure petitions to the shrines of the martyrs, and to give all that she could to the poor. That way, the Communion of the Lord's body might be rightly celebrated in those places where, after the example of his Passion, the martyrs had been sacrificed and crowned.

However, it seems to me, O Lord my God—and my heart thinks of it this way in Your sight—that my mother would probably not have given in so easily to the rejection of this custom if it had been forbidden by someone she didn't love as much as Ambrose. For, out of her concern for my salvation, she loved him most dearly. He loved her truly as well, because of her faithful religious life. "Fervent in spirit,"[152] she frequented the church with good works. Ambrose would often burst forth into praise of her when he saw me, congratulating me that I had such a mother.

He did this, little knowing what a son she had in me. I was still a skeptic in all these matters and could not conceive that the way of life could be discovered.

Chapter 3—Disillusioned By Ambrose's Lack of Attention

I had not yet begun to groan in my prayers that You would help me. My mind was wholly intent on knowledge and eager for debate. Ambrose himself I esteemed a happy man, as the world counted happiness, because famous people held him in honor. Only his celibacy appeared to me a painful burden. Nevertheless, I could neither conjecture nor experience the hope he cherished, the struggles he faced against the temptations common to his lofty position, the solace he found in adversity, and the savory joys Your bread possessed for the hidden mouth of his heart when feeding on it.

Ambrose was unaware of my own frustrations and the pit of my danger, because I couldn't request of him what I wanted when I wanted it. Crowds of people with infirmities prevented me from conversing with him because he was so devoted to ministering to their needs. Furthermore, when he was not busy with them, which was never for very long, he was either refreshing his body with necessary food or his mind with reading.

Visitors were not forbidden to enter Ambrose's room, but their arrival was never announced to him. As he read, his eyes glanced over the pages and his heart searched out the sense, but his voice and tongue were silent. Therefore, when we went by to visit we would often see him reading to himself. Then, after we had sat for a long time in silence, for who would dare interrupt one so intent? We would depart, realizing that he was unwilling to be distracted from the little time he had for the refreshing of his mind, free from the clamor of other men's business.

Perhaps Ambrose was fearful that by reading out loud, for the author he was studying expressed himself vaguely, some doubtful and attentive hearer would ask him to expound or discuss some of the more perplexing questions raised. He surely knew that if his time were occupied with others, he couldn't study as much as he desired. An even truer reason for his reading to himself might have been the preserving of his voice, which was very easily weakened. Whatever his motive, in such a man it was doubtless a good one.

Seeking a Moment with Ambrose

Actually, I could find no opportunity to pose the questions I had to that holy oracle of Yours, unless it was a matter which could be dealt with briefly. However, the passion within me required that he give me his full attention so I could pour out my questions to him, but I never had that opportunity. I heard him, indeed, every Lord's Day, "rightly dividing the word of truth"[153] among the people. Therefore, I became all the more convinced that those knots of crafty misrepresentation, knit together against the divine books by deceivers, could be unraveled.

I came to understand that Your spiritual sons, whom You had regenerated through the Catholic Mother (the Church) by grace, didn't understand the statement that man was made after the image of Him that created him.[154] It's as if they believed and imagined that You were contained by a human form, although what the nature of that spiritual substance was I had no clue.

Still rejoicing, I blushed that for so many years I had railed, not against the Catholic faith, but against the fables of fleshly imagination. For I had been both ungodly and rash in that I had condemned by pronouncement what I ought to have learned by inquiry. For You, O Most High are most near, most secret, most present. You are without limits, wholly everywhere, yet nowhere in space, and are not shaped by some physical form.

You created man after Your own image and, see; he dwells in space, both head and feet.

CHAPTER 4—BETWEEN TRUTH AND FICTION

Since I didn't then understand how this image of Yours could subsist, I should have knocked on the door and expressed my doubts. I shouldn't have insultingly opposed it as if I actually believed it. Therefore, my anxiety as to what I could count on as certain gnawed all the more sharply into my soul.

I felt ashamed because during the long time I had been deluded and deceived by the [Manichean] promises of certainties, I had, with childish petulance, chattered about so many uncertainties as if they were certain. That they were falsehoods became apparent to me only afterward. However, I was certain that they were uncertain, and since I had held them as certainly uncertain, I had accused Your Catholic Church with blind contentiousness. I had not yet discovered that the Church taught the truth, but I now knew that it didn't teach what I had so vehemently accused it of teaching.

I was both confounded and converted by this knowledge. I rejoiced, O my God, that the one Church, the body of Your only Son—in which the name of Christ had been sealed upon me as an infant—did not delight in these childish matters. Also, that the Church did not maintain in its sound doctrine any tenet that involved pressing You, the Creator of all, into a space like that of a human body. Any space, no matter how extended and immense, would still be bounded on all sides.

The Scriptures Begin to Come Alive

I was also glad that the old Scriptures of the Law and the Prophets were set before me to read. Though now, I didn't read them with a critical eye like I had in the past. Then, I faulted Your holy ones for thinking one way when they actually didn't.

Furthermore, I listened with delight as Ambrose preached his sermons to the people. He often recommended this text, and offered it as a rule: "The letter kills, but the Spirit gives life."[155] At the same time, he drew aside the veil of mysticism and opened to view the spiritual meaning of what at first seemed to teach perverse doctrine if taken literally.

I found nothing in Ambrose's teachings that offended me, though I could not yet be certain that what he taught was true. I greatly feared falling headlong into error, so all this time I restrained my heart from agreeing to anything. Instead, by hanging in suspense I was being strangled.[156] For my desire was to be as certain of invisible things as I was that seven plus three equals ten. I was not so deranged as to believe that *this* could not be comprehended, but my desire was to have other things as clear as well. This desire persisted whether they were physical objects, which were not present to my senses, or spiritual objects, which I did not know how to conceive of except in physical terms.

If I could have believed, I might have been cured. Then, with the sight of my soul cleared up, I may in some way have been directed toward Your truth, which always abides and fails in nothing. However, just as it happens that a man who has tried a bad physician fears to trust himself with a good one, so it was with the health of my soul, which could not be healed except by believing. But lest it should believe falsehoods, it refused to be cured. I resisted Your hand that prepared the medicine of faith and applied it to the maladies of the entire world, endowing them with such great efficacy.

Chapter 5—The Authority of Scripture

From this time forward, I began to prefer the Catholic doctrine. I felt that with moderation and honesty it commanded things to be believed that were not demonstrated—whether they could be demonstrated, but not to everyone, or whether they could not be demonstrated at all. This was far better than the method of the Manicheans, in which our credulity was mocked by an audacious promise of knowledge and then many fabulous and absurd things were forced upon believers *because* they were incapable of demonstration.

O Lord, little by little, and with a gentle and most merciful hand, by drawing and calming my heart, You persuaded me that, if I took into account the multitude of things I had never seen, nor been present when they were enacted, that unless I believe they existed or were enacted, I could do nothing in this life.[157] This thing included the events of secular history, the numerous reports of places and cities which I had not seen, and relationships with many friends

Finally, I was confronted with the lack of absolute proof about which two people were my parents. This was impossible for me to know other than by hearsay. By bringing all this into my consideration, You persuaded me that it was not the ones who believed Your books—which You have established in all the nations—but those who did not believe them, who were to be blamed. Moreover, those men were not to be listened to who would say,

"How do you know that those Scriptures were imparted to mankind by the Spirit of the one and most true God?" This was the point that was most of all to be believed, because no blasphemous argument like I had read in the books of self-contradicting philosophers could snatch from me the belief that You do exist, and that to You belongs the governance of human affairs. Although *what* You are I still did not know.

The Necessity of Scriptural Authority

This much I believed, some times more strongly than others. But I always believed both that You are, and that You care for us.[158] I was ignorant, though, about what should be thought about Your substance and which way led (back) to You. Human beings are too weak to discover truth by unaided reason, so they need the authority of the Holy Writings. Therefore, I had begun to believe that under no circumstances would You have given such eminent authority to those Scriptures throughout all lands had it not been through them that Your will might be discerned and that You might be sought.

Some of the passages in Scripture that had once seemed absurd and offensive to me had been interpreted through human reasoning. Therefore, I could see that the Scriptures in a whole were to be resolved by the mysteries of spiritual interpretation. The authority of Scripture then, seemed all the more revered and worthy of devout belief. Although Scripture was visible for all to read, it reserved the full majesty of its secret wisdom within its spiritual understanding. While Scripture stooped to everyone in the great plainness of its language and simplicity of style, it still required the close attention of the most serious-minded. This was so that Scripture might receive everyone into its common bosom, and direct some few through its narrow passages toward You. Those directed would be many more than if there had it not been such a lofty authority, which allured multitudes to its bosom by its holy humility.

I continued to reflect upon these things, and You were with me. I sighed, and You heard me. I vacillated, and You guided me. I roamed the broad way of the world, and You didn't desert me.

CHAPTER 6—LESSONS FROM A DRUNKEN BEGGAR

I still eagerly aspired to honors, money, and matrimony, but You mocked me. During the pursuit of these ambitions I endured bitter hardships. However, You demonstrated Your grace by not allowing anything that was not You to grow sweet to me. Look into my heart, O Lord, whose prompting it is that I should recall all this and confess it to You. Let my soul cling to You, since You have freed it from that fast-sticking glue of death.

How wretched my soul was! You irritated its sore wounds so that it might forsake all else and turn to You, and be converted and healed. O God, You are above all, without whom all things would be nothing at all.

How wretched I was then, and how You dealt with me to make me aware of my wretchedness. I recall the day when I was preparing to recite an elaborate praise on the emperor. I was to deliver many a lie in it, and the lying was to be applauded by those who knew I was lying. My heart was agitated with a sense of guilt and it seethed with the fever of my uneasiness. For, while walking along one of the streets of Milan, I saw a poor beggar, with what I believe was a full belly, joking and hilarious.

Sighing, I spoke to the friends around me of the many sorrows that flowed from such madness. I was dragging the burden of my unhappiness under the spur of ambition, and, by dragging it, increasing it at the same time. Despite all our efforts, we still aimed only to attain the very happiness that this beggar had reached before us—and there was a grim chance that we should never attain it! For what he had obtained through a few coins gotten by his begging, I was still scheming for by many a wretched and tortuous turning, namely, the joy of a passing bliss. He had not gained true joy, but at the same time, with all my ambitions, I was seeking one that was even more untrue. Anyhow, he was now joyous and I was anxious. He was free from care, and I was full of alarm.

Seeking True Happiness

Now, if anyone should inquire of me whether I prefer to be merry or anxious, I would reply, "Merry." Again, if I had been asked whether I should prefer to be as the beggar was or as I myself then was, I would have chosen to be myself, though I was beset with cares and alarm. But would not this have been a false choice? Was the contrast valid? Actually, I ought not to prefer myself to him because I happened to be more learned than he was. I derived no great pleasure from my learning, but sought, rather, to please men by its exhibition—and this not to instruct, but only to please. Thus You broke my bones with the rod of Your correction.

Let my soul take its leave of those who say: "It makes a difference as to the object from which a man derives his joy. The beggar rejoiced in drunkenness; you longed to rejoice in glory." What glory, O Lord? The kind that is not in You, for just as his was no true joy, so was mine no true glory, but it turned my head all the more. He would get over his drunkenness that same night, but I had slept with mine many a night and risen again with it, and was to sleep again and rise again with it unknown times more.

It does make a difference as to the object from which a man's joy is gained. I know this is so, and I know that the joy of a faithful hope is incomparably beyond such vanity. Yet, at the same time, this beggar was beyond me, for he truly was the happier man. He was happier not only because he was thoroughly immersed in his mirth while I was torn to pieces with my cares, but because he had gotten his wine by giving good wishes to passers-by, while I followed after the ambition of my pride by lying.

I shared my thoughts with my good companions, and saw how readily they reacted like I did. That is how I found that it went ill with me, and I fretted and doubled that very ill. If any prosperity smiled upon me, I hated to seize it, for almost before I could grasp it, it would fly away.

CHAPTER 7—MY FRIEND, ALYPIUS

Those of us who were living as friends together bemoaned our lot in our common talk. However, I discussed it with Alypius and Nebridius in very familiar terms. Alypius was born in the same town that I was, his parents were of the highest rank there, but he was a bit younger than I. He had studied under me when I first taught in our town, and then afterward at Carthage. He esteemed me highly because I appeared to him good and learned, and I esteemed him for his inborn love of virtue, which was uncommonly marked in a man so young.

In the whirlpool of Carthaginian fashion, where frivolous spectacles are hotly followed, Alypius had been lured into the madness of the gladiatorial games. While he was miserably tossed about in this fad, I was teaching law in a public school. At that time he was not attending my classes because of some ill feeling that had arisen between his father and me. I then discovered his fatal attraction to these bloody games, and was deeply grieved, for he seemed likely to cast away his very great promise, if he had not already done so.

Nevertheless, I had no means of advising Alypius, or any way of reclaiming him from bloodlust through restraint, either by the kindness of a friend or by the authority of a teacher. I imagined that his feelings toward me were the same as his father's, but this turned out to be false. In fact, he disregarded his father's will in the matter and began to be friendly toward me. He would visit my lecture room and listen for a while before departing.

Turning Alypius

It slipped my mind to try and deal with his problem and prevent him from ruining his excellent mind in his blind and headstrong passion for meaningless sport. But You, O Lord, who holds the helm of all that You have created,[159] had not forgotten him who was one day to be numbered among Your sons and a chief minister of Your sacrament.[160] So that his cure would plainly be attributed to You, You brought it about through me completely unawares.

One day, when I was sitting in my accustomed place with my scholars before me, he came in, greeted me, sat down, and fixed his attention on the subject I was discussing. It so happened that I had a passage in hand and, while I was interpreting it, a simile occurred to me taken from the gladiatorial games. It struck me as relevant to make more pleasant and plain the point I was trying to convey by adding a biting gibe at those whom that madness had enthralled.

You know, O God, that I had no thought at the time of curing Alypius of that plague. But he took it to himself and decided that I would not have said it but for his sake. Any other man would have taken offense against me, but this worthy young man saw a reason for being offended at himself, and for loving me even more fervently.

You said it long ago and have written in Your Book, "Rebuke a wise man, and he will love you."[161] Now I had not rebuked Alypius, but You who can make use of everything, both witting and unwitting and in the order which You know to be best, made my heart and tongue into burning coals and used them to cauterize and cure the hopeful mind of Alypius languishing in the pit of despair.

Free From the Plague of Gladiatorial Contest

Let him be silent in Your praise who does not meditate on Your mercy, which rises up in my inmost parts to confess to You. For after that speech Alypius rushed up out of that deep pit into which he had willfully plunged and in which he had been blinded by its miserable pleasures, and he roused his mind with a resolve to moderation. When he had done this, all the filth of the gladiatorial pleasures dropped away from him, and he went to them no more. Then he also prevailed upon his reluctant father to allow him to be my pupil. At the son's urging, the father at last consented.

This is how Alypius began to hear my lectures again and became involved with me in the same superstition—loving the Manicheans' outward display of ascetic discipline—which he believed was true and unfeigned. It was, however, a senseless and seducing self-restraint that ensnared precious souls who were unable as yet to reach the height of true virtue, and who were easily beguiled with the facade of what was only a shadowy and feigned virtue.

CHAPTER 8—ALYPIUS AGAIN ENTRAPPED

Alypius had gone to Rome before me to study law, which was the worldly course his parents urged him to pursue. While there he was carried away again with an incredible passion for the gladiatorial shows. Although he had been utterly opposed to such spectacles and detested them, one day he met by chance a company of his acquaintances and fellow students returning from dinner. With friendly violence, they drew him, resisting and objecting vehemently, into the amphitheater during one of those cruel and murderous shows.

Alypius protested, saying: "Though you drag my body to that place and set me down there, you cannot force me to give my mind or lend my eyes to these shows. Thus I will be absent while present, and so overcome both you and them." When his friends heard this, they dragged him on; probably interested to see whether he would do as he said. When they got to the arena, and had taken what seats they could get, the entire place became a tumult of inhuman frenzy. However, Alypius kept his eyes closed and forbade his mind to pursue such wickedness. Would that he had shut his ears also! For when one of the combatants fell in the fight, a mighty cry from the entire audience stirred him so strongly that he was overcome by curiosity. Still prepared, he thought, to despise and rise superior to the lure no matter what it was, he opened his eyes and was struck with a deeper wound in his soul than what the victim he desired to see received.

Thus Alypius fell more miserably than the one whose fall had raised that mighty clamor that had entered through his ears and unlocked his eyes, making way for the wounding and beating down of his soul. He was more audacious than truly valiant, and was weaker because he depended on his own strength when he ought to have depended on You. For, as soon as he saw the blood, he drank in with it a savage temper and did not turn away. He fixed his eyes on the bloody pastime, unwittingly drinking in the madness, delighted with the wicked contest and drunk with bloodlust.

Alypius was now no longer the same man who came in, but was one of the mobs he came into, a true companion of those who had brought him there. Why need I say more? He looked, he shouted, he was excited, and he took away with him the madness that would stimulate him to come again. Not only with those who first enticed him, but even without them, indeed, dragging in others as well. Yet from all this, with a most powerful and merciful hand, You plucked him out and taught him not to rest his confidence in himself but in You, though not till long after.

Chapter 9—Alypius Falsely Charged

This was all being stored up in Alypius' memory as medicine for the future. So also was another incident when he was still studying under me at Carthage. He was meditating at noonday in the market place on what he had to recite, as scholars usually do for practice, and You allowed him to be arrested as a thief by the police in the market place. I believe, O my God, that You allowed this for no other reason than so this man who was to prove so great in the future would now begin to learn that, in making just decisions, a man should not readily be condemned by other men with reckless naïveté.

As he was walking up and down alone before the judgment seat with his tablets and pen, another young man, one of the scholars who was the real thief, secretly brought a hatchet and, without Alypius seeing him, got in as far as the leaden bars which protected the silversmith shop and began to hack away at the lead gratings. But when the noise of the hatchet was heard the silversmiths below began to call to each other in whispers and sent men to arrest whomsoever they should find.

The thief heard their voices and ran away, leaving his hatchet because he was afraid to be caught with it. Alypius, who had not seen him come in, got a glimpse of him as he went out and noticed that he rushed off in great haste. Being curious to know the reasons, he went up to the place, where he found the hatchet. As he stood wondering and pondering the situation, those that were sent caught him holding the hatchet that had made the noise and startled them. They seized him and dragged him away, gathering the tenants of the market place about them and boasting that they had caught a notorious thief. Thereupon he was led away to appear before the judge.

Recognized by a Friend

However, this was as far as Alypius' lesson was to go. Because immediately, O Lord, You came to the rescue of his innocence, of which You were the sole witness. As he was being led off to prison or punishment, the custodian who had charge of the public buildings met them on the way. The captors were especially glad to meet him because he had more than once suspected them of stealing the goods that had been lost out of the market place. Now, at last, they thought they could convince him it was Alypius that had committed the thefts. However, the custodian had often met Alypius at the house of a certain senator, whose receptions he used to attend. He recognized him at once and, taking his hand, led him away from the crowd and inquired about the cause of all the trouble.

When the custodian learned what had occurred, he commanded the entire threatening mob to follow him, and they came to the house of the young man who had committed the deed. There, before the door, was a slave boy so young that he was not afraid of harming his master by telling the entire story. Furthermore, he had followed his master to the market place.

Alypius recognized him, and whispered to the architect, who showed the boy the hatchet and asked whose it was. "Ours," he answered directly. Upon further questioning, the slave boy disclosed the entire matter. Thus the guilt was shifted to that household and the mob that had sought to triumph over Alypius, was shamed.

So Alypius went home a wiser and more experienced man— this man who was to be the future steward of Your Word and judge of so many causes in Your Church.

Chapter 10—Alypius and Nebridius Accompany Me to Milan

I found Alypius in Rome, and he became bound to me with the strongest possible ties of friendship. He went with me to Milan so that we would not be separated, and also to obtain some law practice, for which he had qualified, seeking to please his parents more than himself. Alypius had already sat three times as assessor and demonstrated an integrity that seemed strange to many others, though he thought them strange who would prefer gold to integrity.

Alypius' character had also been tested, not only by the bait of covetousness, but by the spur of fear as well. At Rome he was assessor to the secretary of the Italian Treasury. At that time, there was a very powerful senator to whom many were indebted by his favors; many of them feared him as well. As was his usual highhanded way, he demanded to have a favor granted him that was forbidden by the laws. This Alypius resisted. A bribe was promised, but Alypius rejected it with all his heart.

Threats were made, but Alypius trampled them underfoot. This caused all men to marvel at so rare a spirit. Alypius neither coveted the friendship nor feared the enmity of a man at once so powerful and so widely known for his great resources of helping his friends and doing harm to his enemies. Even the official whose counselor Alypius was, although unwilling himself that the favor be granted, would not openly refuse the request. Instead, he passed the responsibility on to Alypius, alleging that it was he that would not permit him to give his assent. The truth was that even if the judge had agreed, Alypius would have simply left the court.

There was one matter, however, which appealed to his love of learning, in which he was very nearly led astray. He discovered that he could have books copied for himself at praetorian rates [public expense]. Nevertheless, his sense of justice prevailed and he changed his mind for the better. He rightly considered that the rule that forbade him was still more profitable than the privilege his office would have allowed him.

These are little things, but "he that is faithful in a little matter is faithful also in a great one."[162] Nor can that possibly be void which Jesus, Your truth said:

> Therefore if you have not been faithful in the unrigh-teous mammon, who will commit to your trust the true riches? And if you have not been faithful in what is another man's, who will give you what is your own?"[163]

Such a man was Alypius, who clung to me at that time and who wavered in his purpose, just as I did, as to what course of life to follow.

Nebridius Accompanies Me To Milan

Nebridius also had come to Milan for no other reason than to join with me in a fervent search for truth and wisdom. He had left his native place near Carthage, leaving behind his fine family estate, his house, and his mother, who would not follow him. Like me, he sighed and he wavered. He was fervent in his quest to find the true life and was an acute analyst of the most puzzling questions.

Three months we went begging, crying out our wants to one another and waiting upon You, that You might give us our meat in due season.[164] And in all the annoyances with which Your mercy endured our worldly pursuits, we sought for the reason why we suffered so—and all was darkness! We turned away groaning and exclaiming, "How long shall these things be?" This we often asked, yet for all our asking we did not relinquish anything, for as yet we had not discovered anything certain that we could grasp in their stead when we gave those others up.

Chapter 11—Frustrated and Aimless

I was especially puzzled when I remembered how much time had passed since my nineteenth year. It was then that I had first fallen in love with wisdom and determined that as soon as I could find her, I would abandon the empty hopes and mad delusions of self-seeking desires.

Now, I was close to thirty and still stuck fast in the same mire. I was still ravenous of the temporal pleasures that flew away and distracted me. I was still proclaiming: "Tomorrow I will discover wisdom. Then, all will become plain and I will see clearly." Or, "Faustus will come and explain everything." Or I would declare:[165]

> O you mighty Academics, is there no certainty that man can grasp for the guidance of his life? No, let us search the more diligently, and let us not despair. See, the things in the Church's books that appeared so absurd to us

before do not appear so now, and may be otherwise and honestly interpreted.

Therefore, I will set my feet upon that step where, as a child, my parents placed me, until the clear truth is discovered. But where and when shall it be sought? Ambrose has no leisure—we have no leisure to read. Where are we to find the books? How or where could I get hold of them? From whom could I borrow them? Let me set a schedule for my days and set apart certain hours for the health of the soul.

A great hope has risen up in us, because the Catholic faith does not teach what we thought it did, and vainly accused it of. Its teachers hold it as an abomination to believe that God is limited by the form of a human body. Do I doubt that I should 'knock' in order for the rest also to be 'opened' unto me? My pupils take up the morning hours; what am I doing with the rest of the day? Why not do this? But, then, when am I to visit my influential friends, whose favors I need? When am I to prepare the lectures that I sell to the class? When would I get some recreation and relax my mind from the strain of work?

Perish everything and let's dismiss these idle musings. Let me devote myself solely to the search for truth. This life is unhappy, and death uncertain. If it comes upon me suddenly, in what state shall I go there and where shall I learn what I have neglected here? Should I not indeed suffer the punishment of my negligence here? However, suppose death cuts off and finishes all care and feeling. This too is a question that calls for inquiry. God forbid that it should be so. It is not without reason, and it is not in vain that the stately authority of the Christian faith has spread over the entire world. God would never have done such great things for us if the life of the soul perished with the death of the body. Therefore, why do I delay in *abandoning my hopes of this world and giving myself wholly to seek after God and the blessed life?*

But wait a moment. This life also is pleasant, and it has a sweetness of its own, not at all negligible. We must not abandon it lightly, for it would be shameful to lapse back into it again. See now, it is important to gain some post of honor. And what more should I desire? I have crowds of influential friends, if nothing else; and, if I push my claims, a governorship may be offered me, and a wife with some money, so that she would not be an added expense. This would be the height of my desire. Many men, who are great and worthy of imitation, have combined the pursuit of wisdom with marriage.

Time was slipping away while I discussed these things, and the winds of opinion veered about and tossed my heart here and there. I delayed my conversion to the Lord; I postponed from day to day the life in You, but I could not postpone the daily death in myself. I was enamored of a happy life, but still feared to seek it in its own dwelling, and so I fled from it while I sought it.

I thought I would be miserable if I were deprived of the embraces of a woman, and I never gave a thought to the medicine that Your mercy has provided for the healing of that infirmity, for I had never tried it. As for fidelity, I imagined that it depended on one's own strength, though I found no such strength in myself. I didn't know that none could be faithful unless You granted it. Certainly You would have given it had I asked with heartfelt desire, casting my care upon You with firm faith.

Chapter 12—Sex and the Question of Marriage

Actually, Alypius is who prevented me from marrying. He said that if I did, it would be impossible for us to live together and have as much undistracted time in our pursuit of wisdom like we had long desired. Alypius was extremely virtuous, which was all the more wonderful, because in his early youth he had fallen into promiscuity, but had not continued in it. Instead, feeling sorrow and disgust at his behavior, he lived from that time to the present holding his passions and desires in check.

I showered him with examples of men that were married but still loved the pursuit of wisdom, men who had pleased God and been loyal and affectionate to their friends. I fell far short of them in greatness of soul. I was gripped with the disease of my insatiable lust and its deadly sweetness, so I dragged my chain along, fearing to be loosed of it. Thus I rejected the words of him who counseled me wisely, as if the hand that would have loosed the chain only hurt my wound. Moreover, the tempter, that serpent of old spoke to Alypius through me. Weaving and lying in his path, my tongue was used to set snares in which his honorable and free feet might be entangled.

Alypius wondered why I, for whom he had such a great esteem, could be stuck so fast in the gluepot of pleasure to maintain that I could not possibly live a celibate life. I answered in defense against his accusing questions, that the hasty and stolen delight of sex that he had once tasted and now hardly remembered, was not to be compared with having it available all the time. Furthermore, if I could have it available all the time in the honorable name of marriage, Alypius should not be astonished at my inability to give it up.

When I talked like this to Alypius, then he also began to desire marriage, not because he was overcome by the lust for such pleasures, but out of curiosity. Alypius thought my life was so happy, that he wanted to know what it was that, without it, my life seemed to me to be no life at all, but a punishment. Alypius who wore no chain of slavery, was amazed at my slavery to sex. His amazement awakened the desire for that experience in him, and from that he would have gone on to experiment with it as well. Had he done so, perhaps he would have fallen into the very slavery that amazed him in me, since he was ready to enter into "a covenant with death,"[166] for "whoever loves danger will perish by it."[167]

The question of matrimonial honor in the ordering of a good married life and the bringing up of children interested us but only slightly. What afflicted me most and what had already enslaved me was the habit of satisfying my insatiable lust. However, Alypius was about to be enslaved through merely a curious wonder.

This is the state we were in until You, O Most High, who never forsakes our lowliness, took pity on our misery and came to our rescue in wonderful and secret ways.

CHAPTER 13—BETROTHED

Active efforts were undertaken to secure a wife for me. I wooed. I was engaged. My mother took the greatest pains in the matter. Her hope was that, when I was once married, I would be washed clean in health-giving baptism for which I was being daily prepared. She joyfully saw this, taking note that her desires and promises were being fulfilled in my faith. Nevertheless, when, at my request and her own impulse, she daily called upon You with strong, heartfelt cries to show her a vision disclosing information about my future marriage, You would not.

My mother did see some fantastic things in the course of her prayers that she said had some reference to me. She told me about them, but not with the same confidence she had when You had shown her anything. She always told me that she could distinguish between Your revelations and the dreams of her own soul by a certain feeling impossible to describe.

Nevertheless, the matter of marriage was pressed forward, and proposals were made for a girl who was two years too young to marry.[168] However, because she pleased me, I agreed to wait for her.

Chapter 14—Plans and Hopes Dashed

Many of my friends after talking about how they detest the turbulent irritations of human life, often considered and were now almost determined to pursue a peaceful life, away from the turmoil of men. We thought this could be done by pooling our resources and putting what we each owned into a common household. We thought that in the sincerity of our friendship nothing should belong more to one than to the other, and that we should have one common cash fund, the whole of which was to belong to everyone equally.

We decided that our group would consist of ten persons, some of whom were very rich, especially Romanianus, my fellow townsman and intimate friend from childhood days. He had been brought up to the court on grave business matters and was the most earnest of us all about the project. His support of the idea carried great weight in convincing the others because his estate was far more ample than theirs. We had also resolved that each year, two of us would serve as managers and provide all that was needed while the rest were left undisturbed. However, when we began to ponder whether our wives would permit this—some were married and others hoped to be—our ingenious plan collapsed and was discarded.

From this we began to sigh and groan again, and our steps took to the broad and beaten ways of the world. Many thoughts were in our hearts except "Your counsel stands fast forever."[169] Therefore, in Your counsel You mocked ours, and prepared Your own plan. It was Your purpose "to give us food in due season, to open Your hand, and to fill our souls with blessing."[170]

Chapter 15—The Mother of My Son Leaves

Meanwhile my sins were being multiplied. My mistress was torn from my side as an impediment to my marriage, and my heart, which clung to her, was torn and wounded till it bled. She returned to Africa, vowing to You never to know another man and leaving with me my natural son by her.

Nevertheless, unhappy as I was, and weaker than a woman, I could not bear a delay of two years before I could marry the bride I sought. Therefore, since I was not a lover of wedlock so much as a slave of lust, I procured another mistress—not a wife, of course. Thus in bondage to a lasting habit, the disease of my soul was nursed and kept in its vigor. It raged and even increased until it would be staunched in the realm of matrimony. Nor indeed was the wound healed that had been caused by cutting away my former mistress. It only ceased burning and throbbing, and began to fester, all the more dangerous because it was less painful.

Chapter 16—The Root of My Misery

Unto You be the praise, Lord. Unto You be the glory, O Fountain of mercies. I became more wretched and You drew nearer. Your right hand was ever ready to pluck me out of the mire and to cleanse me, but I didn't know it. Nor did anything call me back from a still deeper plunge into carnal pleasure except the fear of death and of Your future judgment, which, amid all the wavering of my opinions, never left my mind.

I discussed with my friends, Alypius and Nebridius, the nature of good and evil. I maintained that, in my judgment, Epicurus would have carried off the palm if I had not believed what Epicurus would not believe—that after death there remains a life for the soul, and places of recompense.

I said to my friends, "Suppose we are immortal and live in the enjoyment of perpetual bodily pleasure, without any fear of losing it. Why, then, should we not be happy, or why should we search for anything else?"

I didn't know that the root of my misery was that I was so fallen and blinded I couldn't discern the light of virtue and beauty which must be embraced for its own sake. Nor did I know that the eye of flesh couldn't see these, only the inner vision can. Neither did I consider the reason why I found delight in discussing these perplexing issues with my friends, shameful as they were. For I could not be happy without friends, even according to the notion of happiness I had then, no matter how rich the store of my carnal pleasures might be. Yet I truly loved my friends for their own sakes, and felt that they in turn loved me for my own sake.

O crooked ways! Woe to the audacious soul, which hoped that by forsaking You it, would find some better thing! It tossed and turned, upon back and side and belly—but the bed is hard, and You alone give it rest.[171]

You are near, O God. You deliver us from our wretched wanderings and establish us in Your way. You comfort us and say, "I will carry and will deliver you."[172]

BOOK SEVEN

False Wisdom of Neoplatonism

Augustine converts to Neoplatonism. He examines his growing disbelief of the Manichean conceptions of God and evil, and his growing understanding of God's incorruptibility, though his thought is still bound by materialistic notions of reality. Augustine rejects astrology and turns to the study of Neoplatonism. He embarks on an analysis of the differences between Platonism and Christianity and gives a remarkable account of his appropriation of Plotinian wisdom and his experience of a Plotinian ecstasy. Finally, Augustine begins diligent study of the Bible, especially the writings of the apostle Paul. His pilgrimage is now drawing toward its goal of knowing Jesus Christ and being drawn to Him in hesitant faith.

Chapter 1—Seeking to Understand the Substance of God

Dead now was that evil and shameful youth of mine, and I was passing into full manhood.[173] Nevertheless, as I increased in years, so did my pride. I could not comprehend any substance but what I could see with my own eyes.

I no longer thought of You, O God, by the analogy of a human body. Ever since I inclined my ear to philosophy I had avoided this error, and the truth on this point I rejoiced to find in the faith of our spiritual mother, Your Catholic Church. Yet I could not see how else to understand You. And I, a man (and such a man!) sought to apprehend You, the sovereign and only true God. In my inmost heart, I believed that You are incorruptible, inviolable and unchangeable. Though I knew not how or why, I could still see plainly and without doubt that the corruptible is inferior to the incorruptible, the inviolable obviously superior to its opposite, and the unchangeable better than the changeable.

My heart cried out violently against all phantasms,[174] and with this one clear certainty I endeavored to brush away the swarm of unclean flies that swarmed around the eyes of my mind. But they were scarcely scattered before they gathered again, buzzing against my face, and clouding my vision. I no longer thought of God in the analogy of a human body, yet I was constrained to comprehend You to be some kind of body in space, either infused into the world, or infinitely diffused beyond the world. This was the incorruptible, inviolable, unchangeable substance, which I thought was better than the corruptible, the violable, and the changeable.[175] If something were missing the dimensions of space, it appeared to me to be absolutely nothing. It couldn't even be a void, because if a body is taken out of space, or if space is emptied of all its contents (of earth, water, air, or heaven), it still remains an empty space—a spacious nothing, as it were.

Being so dense-hearted and unclear even to myself, I then held that whatever had neither length nor breadth nor density nor solidity, and did not or could not receive such dimensions, was absolutely nothing. For at that time my mind dealt only with ideas that resembled the forms with which my eyes are still familiar. Nor could I see that the act of thought, by which I formed those ideas, was itself immaterial, and yet it could not have formed them if it were not itself a measurable entity.

I thought about You, O Life of my life, as stretched out through infinite space, interpenetrating the entire mass of the world. I thought about You reaching out beyond in all directions, to immensity without end. That way, the earth could have You, the heavens have You, all things have You, and all of them would be limited in You, while You are placed nowhere at all. The atmosphere above the earth does not block the light of the sun, so the light penetrates it, not by bursting nor dividing, but filling it entirely. Therefore, I imagined that the body of heaven and air and sea, and even of the earth, was entirely open to You; open in all its greatest parts as well as the smallest, ready to receive Your presence by a secret inspiration which, from within or without all, orders all things You have created.

This was my supposition, because I was unable to think of anything else. Nevertheless, it was untrue. Because, in this way, a greater part of the earth would contain a greater part of You, while a smaller part, a smaller fraction of You. All things would be full of You in the sense that there would be more of You in an elephant than in a sparrow, because one is larger than the other and fills a larger space. This would make the portions of Yourself present in the several portions of the world in fragments, great to the great, small to the small. But You aren't such a one. But as yet, You had not enlightened my darkness.

Chapter 2–The Omnipotence of God

It was not sufficient for me, O Lord, to be able to oppose those deceived deceivers and those mute orators—mute because Your Word did not sound forth from them. I saw no reason to confront them with the question that Nebridius used to ask in the old Carthaginian days, shaking all of us who heard it: *What could this imaginary people of darkness, which the Manicheans usually set up as an army opposed to You, have done to You if You had refused to fight?*

Had the reply been that they could have hurt You, and then You would be violable and corruptible. If, on the other hand, the dark could have done You no harm, then there was no cause for any battle at all. There was less cause for a battle in which a part of You, one of Your members, a child of Your own substance, were mixed up with opposing powers, not of Your creation. Especially should that part of Your substance become corrupted, deteriorated and changed by them from happiness into misery, so that it could not be delivered and cleansed without Your help. This offspring of Your substance was theorized to be the human soul, to which Your Word—free, pure, and entire—could bring help when it was being enslaved, contaminated, and corrupted. However, this was true only on the hypothesis that the Word was itself corruptible because it is one and the same substance as the soul.

Therefore, if they admitted that Your nature, whatever You are, is incorruptible, then all these assertions of theirs were false and should be rejected with horror. However, if Your substance is corruptible, then this is self-evidently false and should be abhorred at first utterance. This line of argument, then, was enough against those deceivers who ought to be cast out as vomit from an over-filled stomach. For out of this dilemma they could find no way of escape without dreadful blasphemy of both mind and tongue, when they think and speak such things about You.

Chapter 3—On the Origin of Evil

I was firmly persuaded, and declared that, You our Lord, are the true God. It was You who made not only our souls but our bodies as well; You were free from stain and never changing. Nevertheless, I could not readily and clearly understand what was the cause of evil. Whatever the cause, I realized that the question must be analyzed in such a way that no answer would compel me to believe that the unchangeable God was changeable—lest I should become the very thing that I was seeking (evil). Therefore, I pursued the search with a quiet mind. I was confident that what the Manicheans, whom I strictly avoided, had said could not be true. I now realized that when they asked what was the origin of evil their answer was dictated by a wicked pride, which would rather affirm that Your nature is capable of suffering evil than that their own nature is capable of doing it.

I directed my attention to understand what I was now told, that free will is the cause of our doing evil and that Your just judgment is the cause of our having to suffer the consequences. However, I couldn't see this clearly. So in trying to draw the eye of my mind up out of that pit, I was plunged back into it again, and trying often, I was just as often plunged back down.

One thing lifted me up toward Your light: I had come to know that I had a will as certainly as I knew that I had life. Therefore, when I willed or was unwilling to do something, I was utterly certain that it was none but myself who willed or was unwilling. Immediately, I realized that therein was the cause of my sin. I could see that what I did against my will caused me to suffer rather than succeed. I did not regard such actions as faults, but rather as punishment. However, I must quickly confess that I was not unjustly punished, since I believed You to be most just.

Who was it that put this in me, and implanted the root of bitterness in me despite the fact that I was altogether the handiwork of my most sweet God? If the devil is to blame, who made the devil? If he was a good angel, who by his own wicked will became the devil, how did there happen to be in him that wicked will by which he became a devil? A good Creator made him wholly a good angel!

These constant questions caused me to again be cast down and impotent. Yet I was not plunged into that hell of error where no man confesses to You, and where I thought that You suffered evil, rather than men suffering it.

CHAPTER 4—THE INCORRUPTIBILITY OF GOD

Though I struggled to solve these difficulties, I now assumed as settled truth that the incorruptible must be superior to the corruptible. Furthermore, I acknowledged that You, O God, whatever You are, are incorruptible. For there has never been, nor will be, a soul able to conceive of anything better than You, who are the highest and best good.[176] Since the incorruptible is to be placed above the corruptible, as I now admit, it followed that I could rise in my thoughts to something better than my God, if You were not incorruptible.

When I discovered that the incorruptible was to be preferred over the corruptible, I was able to see where I ought to seek You and where I should look for the source of evil, the corruption which can in no way profane Your substance. For it is obvious that corruption in no way, by no inclination, by no necessity and by no unforeseen chance injures God. Because He is God, and what He wills is good, and He himself is that good. To be corrupted is not good.

You are not compelled to do anything against Your will, since Your will is not greater than Your power. It would have to be greater if You were greater than Yourself, for the will and power of God are God Himself. What can take You by surprise, since You know everything and there is no variety of nature that You don't know?

What more should we say about why that substance which God is cannot be corrupted? If this were so it could not be God?

CHAPTER 5—PERPLEXED BY EVIL

I continued my search for an answer to my question of where evil originated. However, in my searching I sought the origin of evil in an evil way. I missed seeing the evil in my search! I gathered before me in the sight of my spirit all creation, including all that we see of earth, sea, air, stars, trees and animals, and all that we do not see, the firmament of the sky above, the angels and all spiritual things. However, in my imagination, I arranged them in this place or that as if they were bodies too.

I pictured Your creation as one vast mass, composed of various kinds of bodies. Some of these actually were bodies, some of which I imagined spirits were like. I pictured this mass as vast, though not in its full dimensions, for these I could not know. I imagined it as large as I could possibly think, but still finite on every side. But You, O Lord, I viewed as surrounding the mass on every side and penetrating it, still infinite in every direction, as if there were a sea everywhere, and everywhere through measureless space nothing but an infinite sea. This great sea contained within itself some sort of sponge, huge but still finite, so that the sponge would in all its parts be filled from the immeasurable sea.[177]

I conceived Your creation itself to be finite, and filled by You, the infinite. I said, "Behold God, and behold what God has created! God is good and mighty, and incomparably better than all His works."

He who is good has created all things good, look how He encircles and fills them. Where, then, is evil, from where does it come and how has it crept in? What is its root and what is its seed? Has it no being at all? Why, then, do we fear and shun what has no being? Or if we fear it needlessly, then surely that fear is evil by which the heart is unnecessarily stabbed and tortured. Indeed fear is a greater evil since we have nothing real to fear, and yet do fear. Therefore, either that which we fear is evil, or the act of fearing is in itself evil. But, then, from where does it come, since God who is good has made all these things good?

God is the greatest and highest Good, and has created these lesser goods, but both Creator and created are all good. From where, then, comes evil? Or, again, was there some evil matter out of which God made and formed and ordered it, but left something in his creation that He did not convert into good? But why should this be? Was God powerless to change the whole lump so that no evil would remain in it, if He is the Omnipotent? Finally, why would He make anything at all out of such stuff? Why did He not, rather, annihilate it by His same almighty power?

Could evil exist contrary to God's will? And if it were from eternity, why did God permit it to be nonexistent for unmeasured intervals of time in the past, and why, then, was He pleased to make something out of it after so long a time? Or, if God wished now all of a sudden to create something, would not an almighty being have chosen to annihilate this evil matter and live by Himself, the perfect, true, sovereign, and infinite Good? Or, if it were not good that He who was good should not also be the framer and creator of what was good, then why was that evil matter not removed and brought to nothing, so that God might form good matter, out of which He might then create all things? For God would not be omnipotent if He were unable to create something good without being assisted by that matter which had not been created by Him.

Such perplexities revolved in my wretched heart. I was overwhelmed with these gnawing cares lest I die before I discovered the truth. Still the faith of Your Christ, our Lord and Savior, as taught me by the Catholic Church, stuck fast in my heart. As yet it was unformed on many points and diverged from the rule of right doctrine, but my mind did not utterly lose it. Every day, I drank in more and more of it.

Chapter 6—The Foolishness of Astrology

By now I had also repudiated the deceptive foretelling and immoral foolishness of the astrologers. Let Your mercies, out of the depth of my soul, confess this to You also, O my God. Who else is it that calls us back from the death of all errors except the Life which does not know how to die and the Wisdom which gives light to minds that need it, though needing no light itself. You, O God, govern the entire universe, even to the fluttering of the leaves on the trees.

You, and You alone provided strength for my firm stand against Vindicianus, a clever old man, and Nebridius, a remarkably talented young man. The former declared vehemently and the latter frequently, though with some reservation, that no art existed by which we foresee future things. The guesses of men often have the help of chance, and out of many things that they foretold some came to pass unawares to the predictors. They simply landed on the truth by making so many guesses.

You also provided a friend for me who only consulted the astrologers out of curiosity. He knew a good deal about it, which he said he had heard from his father, never realizing how far his ideas would help to overthrow my belief of that art.

My friend's name was Firminus. He had received a liberal education and was a cultivated lawyer. It so happened that he consulted me, as a friend, about some affairs of his, wondering how they would be viewed according to his so-called horoscope. Though I was leaning toward Nebridius' opinion, I didn't hesitate to speculate about the matter or to tell him the thoughts that came into my irresolute mind. However, I did add that I was almost persuaded that astrology was empty and ridiculous.

Firminus then told me that his father had been very interested in astrology, and that he had a friend who was also interested. Their combined study and discussions fanned the flame of their affection for this folly. They even went so far as to observe the moment when their animals gave birth, observing the position of the heavens with regard to them. They did this so they could gather fresh evidence for this so-called art.

Rich Boy – Poor Boy

Firminus' father told him that when Firminius' mother was about to give birth to him, a female slave of a friend of his father's was also pregnant. This could not be hidden from her master, who kept accurate record of birth dates, even of his dogs. So it happened that, under the most careful observations for both his wife and the servant, and with exact calculations of the days, hours, and minutes, both women were delivered at the same moment. This compelled both men to cast the same horoscope, down to the minute, for the son, Firminus, and for the young slave.

As soon as the women began labor, they sent word to the other as to what was happening in their respective houses and had messengers ready to dispatch to one another as soon as they had information of the actual birth. Each, of course, knew instantly the exact time. It turned out, Firminus said, that the messengers from the respective houses met one another at a point equidistant from either house, so that neither could discern any difference either in the position of the stars or any other of the most minute points.

Nevertheless, Firminus was born in a high estate in his parents' house. He ran his course through the prosperous paths of this world, increased in wealth, and was elevated to honors. At the same time, the slave born under the yoke of bondage, continued to serve his masters. Firminus, who knew him, was able to bear witness of this report.

Upon hearing and believing these things related by such a reliable person, all my resistance melted away. First, I endeavored to reclaim Firminus from his superstition. I told him that after inspecting his horoscope, if I could truly foretell, I ought to have seen parents eminent among their neighbors, a noble family in its own city, a good birth, a proper education, and liberal learning. However, if that servant had consulted me with the same horoscope, since he had the same one, I ought to tell him that I saw the lowliness of his origin, the abjectness of his condition, and everything else different and contrary to the former prediction.

Not By Art, But By Chance

If, by casting up the same horoscopes I made contrary analyses, or speak falsely by making identical readings, then surely it followed that whatever was truly foretold by the analysis of the horoscopes was not by art, but by chance. And whatever was said falsely was not from incompetence in the art, but from the error of chance.

An opening was being made in my darkness as I began to consider other implications involved here. Suppose that one of the fools who followed such an occupation, whom I longed to assail and reduce to confusion, argued against me that Firminus had supplied false information, or that his father had informed him falsely.

I then turned my thoughts to those that are born twins and generally come out of the womb with a short interval between them. Whatever importance the astrologers ascribe to it in the nature of things cannot be noted by human observation or expressed in the tables they examine when beginning to pronounce the truth. However, such pronouncements cannot be true. For looking into the same horoscopes, the astrologer must have foretold the same future for both Esau and Jacob,[178] whereas the same future did not turn out for them. The astrologer must therefore speak falsely. If he is to speak truly, then he must read contrary predictions into the same horoscopes. But this would mean that it was not by art that he would speak the truth, but by chance.

For You, O Lord, most righteous ruler of the universe, works by a secret impulse, whether those who inquire or those inquired of know it or not, so that the inquirer may hear, according to the secret merit of his soul, what he ought to hear from the depths of Your righteous judgment. Therefore let no man say to You, "What is this?" or, "Why is that?" Let him not speak so, for he is only a man.

Chapter 7—Impeded by Stuff

By now, O my Helper, You had freed me from those chains. But still I wondered, "Where does evil come from?" You didn't allow me to be carried away from the faith by these fluctuations of thought. I still believed that You exist and that Your substance is unchangeable. I believed that You care for and will judge all men. I believed in Christ, Your Son and our Lord, and the Holy Scriptures, which the authority of Your Catholic Church pressed on me. I also believed that You have planned the way of man's salvation to that life which is to come after this death.

With these convictions safe and immovably settled in my mind, I eagerly inquired, "Where did evil originate?" What torments my travailing heart then endured! What sighs, O my God! Yet even then Your ears were open though I knew it not. When in stillness earnestly I sought, those silent regrets of my soul were loud cries to Your mercy. No man knew, but You knew what I endured. How little of it could I express in words to the ears of my dearest friends! How could the whole tumult of my soul, for which neither time nor speech was sufficient, come to them? Yet the whole of it went into Your ears, all of which I bellowed out in the anguish of my heart.

My desire was before You, and the light of my eyes was not with me, for it was within, and I was without. Nor was that light in any place. I still thought only of things that are contained in a place, and among them could find no place to rest.

Things didn't satisfy me so that I could say, "It is sufficient; it is well." Nor did things allow me to turn back to where it might be well enough with me. For I was higher than things, though lower than You. You are my true joy if I depend upon You, and You made that which You created lower than me subject to me.

This was the true way of salvation for me: To continue in Your image, and by serving You have dominion over the body. However, when I lifted myself proudly against You, it was as if I were "running stubbornly against [You] with [Your] strong, embossed shield."[179] Then, even the lower things were placed above me and pressed down on me so that there was no respite or breathing space. They thrust in on me from every side, in crowds and masses, and when I tried to think, the images of bodies pushed themselves into my way blocking my way back to You. It was as if they would say to me, "Where are you going, unworthy and unclean one?" All these had sprung out of my wound, for You had humbled the haughty as one that is wounded. My swelling pride separated me from You, and my bloated cheeks blinded my eyes.

CHAPTER 8—GOD IS FAITHFUL

Nevertheless, O Lord, You are forever the same. You are not forever angry with us, for You have compassion on our dust and ashes.[180]

It was pleasing in Your sight to correct my deformity, and by inward stings You disturbed me so that I was impatient until You cleared my inward sight. By the secret hand of Your healing, my swelling was lessened and the disordered and darkened eyesight of my mind was daily made whole by the stinging salve of wholesome grief.

CHAPTER 9—FINDING TRUTH IN THE PHILOSOPHERS

You showed me how You "resist the proud, but give grace to the humble."[181] You have mercifully shown men the way of humility in the way that Your Word "was made flesh and dwelt among men."[182] You provided me, through a person filled with monstrous pride, some books of the Platonists translated from Greek into Latin. Though not in the same words, I discovered in reading them that, "in the beginning was the Word, and the Word was with God, and the Word was God. The same was in the beginning with God. All things were made by Him; and without Him was not anything made that was made."[183] That which was made by Him is "life, and the life was the light of men. And the light shined in darkness; and the darkness comprehended it not." [184]

Furthermore, I read that the soul of man, though it "bears witness to the light," yet itself "is not the light; but the Word of God, being God, is that true light that lights every man who comes into the world." And further, that "He was in the world, and the world was made by Him, and the world knew Him not."[185] But in these books I did not find that, "He came unto His own, and His own received Him not. And as many as received Him, to them gave He power to become the sons of God, even to them that believed on His name."[186]

Similarly, I read that God the Word was born "not of flesh nor of blood, nor of the will of man, nor the will of the flesh, but of God."[187] But nowhere did I find that, "the Word was made flesh, and dwelt among us."[188]

I discovered in those books, expressed in many and various ways, that the Son "being in the form of God, did not consider it robbery to be equal with God,"[189] for He was naturally of the same substance. But, in those books I didn't read that He…

...made Himself of no reputation, taking the form of a bondservant, and coming in the likeness of men. And being found in appearance as a man, He humbled Himself and became obedient to the point of death, even the death of the cross. Therefore God also has highly exalted Him and given Him the name which is above every name, that at the name of Jesus every knee should bow, of those in heaven, and of those on earth, and of those under the earth, and that every tongue should confess that Jesus Christ is Lord, to the glory of God the Father.[190]

Facts About the Creator But No Relationship

I read further in them that before all times and beyond all times, Your only Son remained unchangeably coeternal with You. I read that of His fullness all souls receive that they may be blessed, and that by participation in that wisdom which abides in them, they are renewed that they may be wise. But the books didn't say that, "in due time, Christ died for the ungodly" and that You "spared not Your only Son, but delivered Him up for us all."[191] "For You have hidden these things from the wise and prudent, and have revealed them unto babes."[192] Now they "that labor and are heavy laden" might come unto Him and He might refresh them." Because He is "meek and lowly in heart."[193]

"The humble He guides in judgment, and the humble He teaches His way...looking on our affliction and our pain and forgiving all our sins."[194] However, those who strut in the high boots of what they consider to be superior knowledge will not hear Him who says, "Learn of me, for I am meek and lowly in heart, and you shall find rest for your souls."[195] Though they know God, they don't glorify Him as God, nor are they thankful. Therefore, they "became futile in their thoughts, and their foolish hearts were darkened. Professing to be wise, they became fools."[196]

I also read there how they "changed the glory of the incorruptible God into an image made like corruptible man—and birds and four-footed animals and creeping things,"[197] namely, that Egyptian idolatry for which Esau lost his birthright. Therefore, Your first-born people worshiped the head of a four-footed beast instead of You, turning back in their hearts toward Egypt and prostrating Your image (their own soul) before the image of an ox that eats grass.

These things I found there, but I did not feed on them. For it pleased You, O Lord, to take away the reproach of his minority from Jacob, that the elder should serve the younger and You might call the Gentiles. I had sought strenuously after that gold which You did allow Your people to take from Egypt, since wherever it was it was Yours.[198] You said to the Athenians by the mouth of Your apostle that in You "we live and move and have our being,"[199] as one of their own poets had said. And truly these books came from there. But I did not set my mind on the idols of Egypt, which they fashioned of gold "changing the truth of God into a lie and worshiping and serving the creature more than the Creator."[200]

Chapter 10—Augustine Meets Truth

These books admonished me to turn into myself, so I entered my inward soul guided by You. I was able to do this because You were my helper. So, I entered, and with the eye of my soul, such as it was, saw above the same eye of my soul and above my mind the Immutable (Unchangeable) Light. It was not the common light that all flesh can see, nor was it simply a greater one of the same sort, as if the light of day were to grow brighter and brighter and flood all space. It was not like that light, but different, yes, very different from all earthly light. Nor was it above my mind in the same way as oil is above water, or heaven above earth, but it was higher. Because it made me, I was below it, because I was made by it.

He who knows the Truth knows that Light, and he who knows it knows eternity. Love knows it, O Eternal Truth and True Love and Beloved Eternity! You are my God, to whom I sigh both night and day. When I first knew You, You lifted me up so I could see that there was something to be seen, though I was not yet fit to see it. You beat back the weakness of my sight, shining forth upon me Your dazzling beams of light, and I trembled with both love and fear.

I realized that I was far away from You in the land of unlikeness, as if I heard Your voice from on high: "I am the food of strong men; grow and you shall feed on me. You shall not change me, like the food of your flesh into yourself, but you shall be changed into my likeness." I understood then that You chasten man for his iniquity, and make my soul to be eaten away as though by a moth.[201]

I said, "Is Truth, therefore, nothing, because it is not diffused through space—neither finite nor infinite?" You cried to me from afar, "I AM WHO I AM."[202] I heard this as things are heard in the heart, and there was no room for doubt. I should have more readily doubted that I am alive than that Truth exists—the Truth which is "clearly seen, being understood by the things that are made."[203]

Chapter 11—Reality Compared to God

I viewed all the other things that are beneath You, O God, and realized that they are neither wholly real nor wholly unreal. They are real in so far as they come from You, but they are unreal in so far as they are not what You are. For that is truly real which remains unchangeable. It is good, then, for me to hold fast to God, for if I do not remain in Him, neither shall I abide in myself; but He, remaining in Himself, renews all things. And You are the Lord my God, since You stand in no need of my goodness.

CHAPTER 12—THE GOODNESS OF ALL CREATION

It became clear to me that all things are good even if they are corrupted. They could not be corrupted if they were supremely good, but unless they were good they could not be corrupted. If they were supremely good, they would be incorruptible. However, if they were not good at all, there would be nothing in them to be corrupted.

Corruption harms, but unless it could diminish goodness, it could not harm. Therefore, either corruption does not harm, which cannot be, or, as is certain, all that is corrupted is thereby deprived of good. But if they are deprived of all good, they will cease to be. If they exist at all and cannot be at all corrupted, they will become better, because they will remain incorruptible.

What can be more monstrous than to assert that things become better by losing all good? If, then, they are deprived of all good, they will cease to exist. So long as they are, they are good. Therefore, whatsoever is, is good.

Evil, then, the origin of which I had been seeking, has no substance at all, because if it were a substance, it would be good. For either it would be an incorruptible substance and so a supreme good, or a corruptible substance, which could not be corrupted unless it were good. Therefore, I understood, and it was made clear to me, that You made all things good, nor is there any substance at all not made by You. All that You made is not equal, each by itself is good, and the sum of all of them is very good, for our God made all things very good.[204]

CHAPTER 13—PRAISE GOD

To You, there is no such thing as evil in Your entire creation. This is so, because there is nothing from beyond creation that can burst in and destroy the order that You have appointed for it. However, in the parts of creation, some things do not harmonize with others and are considered evil. Yet those same things harmonize with others and are good, and in themselves are good.

All these things, which do not harmonize with each other, still harmonize with the inferior part of creation, which we call the earth (having its own cloudy and windy sky of like nature with itself).

Far be it for me, then, to say, "These things should not be." For if I could see nothing but these, I would indeed desire something better. Still I ought to praise You, if only for these created things.

> *Praise the LORD from the earth, You great sea creatures and all the depths; Fire and hail, snow and clouds; Stormy wind, fulfilling His word; Mountains and all hills; Fruitful trees and all cedars; Beasts and all cattle; Creeping things and flying fowl; Kings of the earth and all peoples; Princes and all judges of the earth; Both young men and maidens; Old men and children.*
> *Let them praise the name of the LORD.*[205]

All Your angels in heaven praise You, O God. They praise You in the heights, "and all Your hosts, sun and moon, all stars and light, the heavens of heavens, and the waters that are above the heavens"[206] praise Your name. Seeing this, I no longer desired a better world, because my thought ranged over all. With better judgment I reflected that the things above were better than those below, yet that all creation together was better than the higher things alone.

CHAPTER 14—BEHOLDING GOD

There is no health in those who find fault with any part of Your creation, just as there was no health in me when I found fault with so many of Your works. Because my soul dared not to be displeased with You, it would not allow that what displeased me came from You. Therefore, my soul wandered into the notion of two substances. There it could find no rest and talked foolishly. Turning from that error, it made a god for itself that extended through infinite space and thought this was You. My soul set up this god in its heart, causing it to again become the temple of its own idol, which is an abomination to You.

However, You soothed my brain, though I was unaware of it, and closed my eyes lest they should see futility. That is how I ceased from preoccupation with self by a little, and my insanity was lulled to sleep. I awoke in You, and beheld You as the Infinite, but not in the way I had thought—and this vision was not derived from the flesh.

CHAPTER 15—GOD HOLDS ALL CREATION IN HIS TRUTH

When I looked around at other things, I saw that it was to You that all owed their being, and that they were all finite in You, they are in You, though not as in a space. You hold all things in the hand of Your truth, because all things are true in so far as they are, and because falsehood is nothing except the existence in thought of what does not exist in fact. I saw that all things harmonize, not only in their places but also in their seasons.

Furthermore, I saw that You are eternal. You did not *begin* to work after unnumbered periods of time, because all ages, both those that are past and those that shall pass, neither go nor come except through Your working and abiding.

CHAPTER 16—THE WILL TURNED AWAY FROM GOD

I saw, and found it not odd, that bread that is distasteful to an unhealthy palate is pleasant to a healthy one; or that light, which is painful to sore eyes, is a delight to sound ones. Your righteousness displeases the wicked, so they find even more fault with the viper and the little worm, which You have created good, fitting in as they do with the inferior parts of creation. The wicked themselves also fit in here, and proportionately more so as they become unlike You. However, they harmonize with the higher creation proportionately as they become like You.

But what is wickedness?

I discovered that it was no substance, but a perversion of the will turned away from You, O God. It is the will turned toward these lower things, casting away its inmost treasure and becoming bloated with external good.[207]

CHAPTER 17—AN ECSTATIC VISION

I marveled that I now loved You, and no imaginary one in Your stead. Nevertheless, I was not stable enough to enjoy my God steadily. Instead I was transported to You by Your beauty, and then torn away from You by my own weight, sinking with grief into these lower things. This weight was carnal habit, but Your memory dwelt with me. I never doubted in the least that there was One for me to cling to, but I was not yet ready to firmly take hold of You.

The body, which is corrupted, presses down the soul, and the earthly dwelling weighs down the mind, which reflects upon many things. My greatest certainty was that Your "invisible *attributes* are clearly seen, being understood by the things that are made, *even* [Your] eternal power and Godhead."[208] I realized that I had found the unchangeable and true eternity of truth above my changeable mind when:

- I marveled at how I could appreciate the beauty of bodies, both celestial and terrestrial.

- Truth supported me in making correct judgments about things changeable and

- I concluded, "This ought to be thus; this ought not"—when I inquired how it was that I could make such judgments (since I did, in fact, make them).

By degrees I was led upward from bodies to the soul, which perceives them by means of the bodily senses. From there to the soul's inward faculty, to which the bodily senses report outward things—a capacity that belongs even to the beasts. Then up to the reasoning power, to whose judgment is referred the experience received from the bodily sense.

When this power of reason within me discovered that it was changeable, it raised itself up to its own intellectual principle, and withdrew its thoughts from experience, abstracting itself from the contradictory throng of imagination in order to seek that light in which it was bathed. Then, without any doubting, it cried out that the unchangeable was better than the changeable. From this it follows that the mind somehow knew the unchangeable, for, unless it had known it in some fashion, it could have had no sure ground for preferring it to the changeable.

With the flash of a trembling glance, my soul arrived at *that which is*,[209] and I saw Your invisibility, understood by means of the things that are made. However, I was unable to sustain my gaze. My weakness rushed back, and I lapsed again into my accustomed ways. I carried along with me nothing more than a loving memory of my vision, and an appetite for what I had smelled, but was still unable to eat.

CHAPTER 18—EMBRACING JESUS

I sought a way to get strong enough to enjoy You, but I did not find it until I embraced that "Mediator between God and man, the man Christ Jesus,"[210] "who is over all, the eternally blessed God."[211] Jesus came calling and said, "I am the way, the truth, and the life."[212] He mingled with our fleshly humanity the heavenly food I was unable to receive. For "the Word was made flesh" so that Your wisdom, by which You created all things, might become milk for our infancy. As yet, I was not humble enough to hold the humble Jesus, nor did I understand what lesson His weakness was meant to teach me.

Your Word, the eternal Truth, that is far exalted above the highest parts of Your creation, lifts His subjects up toward Himself. But in this lower world, He built for Himself a humble habitation of our own clay, so that He might pull people down from themselves and win over those whom He is to bring under subjection. He lowers their pride and heightens their love, so that they might go no farther in self-confidence, but instead become weak, seeing at their feet the Deity made weak. Jesus became weak by sharing our coats of skin so that people might cast their exhausted selves upon Him and be uplifted by His rising.

Chapter 19—The Nature of the Incarnation of Christ

Nevertheless, I thought otherwise. I saw in our Lord Christ only a man of eminent wisdom to whom no other man could be compared, especially because He was miraculously born of a virgin. I saw Jesus as being sent to set the example of despising worldly things for the attainment of immortality, and exhibiting His divine care for us in that way. Because of this, I held that Jesus had <u>earned</u> his great authority as leader.

However, concerning the mystery contained in "the Word was made flesh," I could not even form an idea. From what I had learned in the books about Him—that He ate, drank, slept, walked, rejoiced in spirit, was sad, and talked with his disciples—I realized that His flesh alone was not bound unto Your Word, but also that there was a bond with the human soul and body. Everyone knows this who knows the unchangeableness of Your Word, and this I knew by now, as far as I was able, and I had no doubts at all about it. These are all properties of the soul and mind, and are subject to change:

- To move the limbs by an act of will, at another time not to move.

- To feel some emotion at one time, but at another time not to feel it.

- To speak intelligibly through verbal signs at one time, at another, not.

If these things were falsely written about Jesus, everything else would risk being false as well. There would remain in those books, then, no saving faith for the human race.

Therefore, because the books were written truthfully, I acknowledged a perfect man to be in Christ. Not the body of a man only, nor, in the body, an animal soul without a rational one as well, but a true man. This man I held to be superior to all others, not only because He was a form of the Truth, but also because of the supreme excellence and perfection of His human nature, due to His participation in wisdom.

Alypius, on the other hand, supposed the Catholics to believe that God was clothed with flesh and that besides God and the flesh there was no soul in Christ. He didn't think that Jesus had a human mind.[213] Because Alypius believed that the actions recorded about Jesus could not have been performed except by a living rational creature, he moved the more slowly toward Christian faith.[214] When he later learned that this was the error of the Apollinarian heretics, he rejoiced in the Catholic faith and accepted it.

I must confess that it was even later before I learned that, "The Word was made flesh," in the Catholic truth could be distinguished from the falsehood of Plotinus. Refuting heretics makes the tenets of Your Church and sound doctrine stand out boldly. "For there must also be factions (heresies) among you, that those who are approved may be recognized among you."[215]

Chapter 20—Augustine's Desire to Seem Wise

Having read the books of the Platonists, and having been taught by them to search for the non-physical Truth, I saw how Your invisible things are understood through the things that are made. Even when I was thrown back, I still sensed what it was that the dullness of my soul would not allow me to contemplate. I was assured that You were, and were infinite, though not diffused in finite space or infinity. That You truly are, who are ever the same, varying neither in part nor motion. And that all things are from You, as is proven by this statement alone: they exist.

Of all this I was convinced, yet was too weak to enjoy You. I chattered away as if I were an expert, but had I not sought Your Way in Christ our Savior, my knowledge would have turned out not to be instruction but destruction.

Full, now of what was in fact my punishment, I had begun to desire to seem wise. I did not mourn my ignorance, but rather was puffed up with knowledge. Where was that love that builds upon the foundation of humility, which is Jesus Christ?[216] When would these books of philosophy teach me this? I now believe that it was Your pleasure that I studied these books before studying Your Scriptures. That way it was impressed on my memory how they affected me. Afterward, when Your Scriptures subdued me, and when my wounds were touched by Your healing fingers, I could discern and distinguish the difference between presumption and confession. I could see the difference between those who saw where they were to go even if they did not see the way, and the Way, which leads not only to the observing, but also the inhabiting of the blessed country.

Had I first been molded in Your Holy Scriptures, and if You had grown sweet to me through my familiar use of them, and if I had afterward fallen on those volumes, they might have pushed me off the solid ground of godliness. Or, if I had stood firm in that wholesome disposition which I had acquired there, I might have thought that wisdom could be attained by the study of those [Platonist] books alone.

CHAPTER 21—AUGUSTINE DISCOVERS PAUL

With great eagerness, I fastened upon the venerable writings of Your Spirit and principally upon the apostle Paul. I had thought that he sometimes contradicted himself and that the text of his teaching did not agree with the testimonies of the Law and the Prophets, but now all these doubts vanished away. I saw that those pure words had but one face, and I learned to rejoice with trembling. So I began.

I soon discovered that whatever truth I had read [in the Platonists] was here combined with the exaltation of Your grace. Therefore, he who sees must not glory as if he had not received, not only the things that he sees, but also the very power of sight, for what does he have that he has not received as a gift? By this he is not only exhorted to see, but is also to be cleansed, that he may grasp You, who are ever the same. Likewise, he who cannot see You afar off may yet enter upon the road that leads to reaching, seeing, and possessing You. For although a man may "delight in the law of God according to the inward man," what shall he do with that other "law in his members, warring against the law of [his] mind, and bringing [him] into captivity to the law of sin which is in [his] members"?[217]

You are righteous, O Lord, but we have sinned and committed iniquities, and have done wickedly. Your hand has grown heavy upon us, and we are justly delivered over to that ancient sinner, the lord of death. For he persuaded our wills to become like his will, by which he strayed away from Your truth. What shall a "wretched man" do? "Who shall deliver him from this body of death,"[218] except Your grace through Jesus Christ our Lord? This Jesus, whom You have begotten, coeternal with Yourself, and created in the beginning of Your ways,[219] in whom the prince of this world found nothing worthy of death, yet he killed Him. And so the handwriting that was all against us was blotted out.

The books of the Platonists tell nothing of this. Their pages do not contain the expression of this kind of godliness:

- the tears of confession
- Your sacrifice
- a troubled spirit
- a broken and a contrite heart
- the salvation of Your people
- the espoused City
- the earnest of the Holy Spirit
- the cup of our redemption

No man in these books sings: "Shall not my soul be subject unto God, for from him comes my salvation? He is my God and my salvation, my defender; I shall no more be moved."[220] In them, no one hears Jesus calling, "Come unto me all you who labor." They refuse to learn of Him because he is "meek and lowly of heart," for "You have hidden those things from the wise and prudent, and have revealed them unto babes."

It's one thing to see the land of peace from a wooded mountaintop and fail to find the way there, to attempt impassable ways in vain, opposed and waylaid by fugitives and deserters under their captain, the "lion" and "dragon."[221] But it's quite another to stay on the highway that leads there, guarded by the hosts of the heavenly Emperor, on which there are no deserters from the heavenly army to rob the passers-by, for they shun it as a torment.[222]

These thoughts sank wondrously into my heart, when I read Paul, the "least of Your apostles"[223] and trembling, considered all Your works.

BOOK EIGHT

Embraced by Christ

Augustine is converted to Christ. He is greatly moved by the conversion of the famous orator and philosopher, Marius Victorinus, as told by Simplicianus. Augustine desires to emulate him, but he's still bound by his lack of sexual restraint and preoccupation with worldly affairs. A court official, Ponticianus, tells him and Alypius the conversion stories of Anthony and two agents of the imperial "secret service." These stories send Augustine into a violent turmoil, in which his divided will struggles against himself. He is nearly successful in deciding to be sexually restrained, but is still held back. A child's song, overheard by chance, finally sends him to the Bible, in which a text from Paul resolves his crisis and conversion becomes a fact. Alypius joins Augustine, and Monica rejoices when she hears the news.

Chapter 1—Coming to Jesus

O my God, let me remember with gratitude and confess to You Your mercies toward me. Let my bones be bathed in Your love, and let them declare: "LORD, who is like You?[224] You have loosed my bonds, I will offer to You the sacrifice of thanksgiving."[225] How You broke them I will declare, and all who worship You will say when they hear these things: "Blessed be the LORD in heaven and earth, great and wonderful is His name."[226]

Your words had stuck fast in my heart, and I was fenced in by You on every side. I was now certain of Your eternal life, although I had seen it "through a glass darkly."[227] I was relieved of all doubt that there is an incorruptible substance and that it's the source of every other substance. Furthermore, I didn't crave greater certainty about You any longer, but rather greater steadfastness in You.

However, as for my temporal life, everything was uncertain and my heart had to be purged of the old leaven. "The Way," Jesus, the Savior, pleased me well, but I was still reluctant to pass through the narrow gate.

Questions and Answers

You put into my mind to visit Simplicianus, a faithful servant of Yours. It seemed good to me as well, because Your grace shined in him. I had been told that from his youth up he had lived in entire devotion to You. He was already an old man, and because of his great age, which he lived in zealous discipleship to Jesus, he appeared likely to have gained much wisdom, which he had. Setting before him all my questions, I desired him to tell me from his experience what would be the best way for someone who felt as I did to walk in Your way.

I saw the Church full, but one man was going this way and another that. Still, I could not be satisfied with the life I was living in the world. My passions had ceased to excite me with hopes of honor and wealth as of old, and it was a tremendous burden to continue in such servitude. Compared with Your sweetness and the beauty of Your house, which I loved, those things delighted me no longer. But I remained tightly bound by the love of women. True, the apostle didn't forbid me to marry, though he exhorted me to something better. He wished earnestly that all men were as he was.

However, I was weak and chose the easier way, and for this single reason, my whole life was one of inner turbulence and listless indecision. I was compelled by many influences to agree to marriage, though unwilling, which bound me hand and foot. I had heard from the mouth of Truth that "there are eunuchs who have made themselves eunuchs for the Kingdom of Heaven's sake."[228] Then He said, "He that is able to receive it, let him receive it."

Men who don't have the knowledge of God, or have been unable from the good things that are seen to find Him who is good, live futile lives. But I was no longer fettered in that futility; I had overcome it. From the united testimony of Your entire creation, I had found You, our Creator, and Your Word—God with You, and together with You and the Holy Spirit, one God—by whom You have created all things.

Still another sort of wicked men exists, who "when they knew God, they glorified him not as God, neither were thankful."[229] I had also fallen into this, but Your right hand held me up and carried me away, and You placed me where I could recover. For You have said to men, "Behold the fear of the Lord, that is wisdom,"[230] and, "Do not be wise in your own eyes,"[231] because "professing to be wise, they become fools."[232]

Nevertheless, I had now found the goodly pearl. I should have sold all that I had and bought it—yet I hesitated.

Chapter 2—The Roman Victorinus is Converted

Therefore, I went to Simplicianus, the spiritual father of Ambrose (then a bishop), whom Ambrose truly loved as a father. I told him the extent of my wandering, but when I mentioned that I had read certain books of the Platonists which Victorinus had translated into Latin, Simplicianus congratulated me that I had not fallen upon the writings of other philosophers. (Victorinus was formerly a professor of law at Rome, and I had been told that he died a Christian.) These other books were full of lies and deceit, "according to the basic principles of the world,"[233] whereas in the Platonists, the pathway led to belief in God and His Word at every turn.

To encourage me to emulate the humility of Christ, which is hidden from the wise and revealed to babes, Simplicianus told me about Victorinus, whom he had known intimately at Rome. I must repeat what he said to me about Victorinus, because the story contains glorious proof of Your grace, which ought to be confessed to You.

That old man, Victorinus, was highly trained and skilled in all the liberal arts. He had read, criticized, and explained many of the writings of the philosophers and was the teacher of many noble senators. As a mark of his distinguished service in office, he had both merited and obtained a statue in the Roman Forum, which men of this world esteem a great honor. This man who, up to an advanced age, had been a worshiper of idols, participated in the blasphemous rites that nearly all the nobility of Rome were wedded to.

> Victorinus had inspired the people with the love of Osiris and,
> "The dog Anubis, and a medley crew
> Of monster gods who 'gainst Neptune stand in arms
> 'Gainst Venus and Minerva, steel-clad Mars,"[234]

Rome had once conquered, and now worshiped, all of this. Victorinus had with thundering eloquence defended all of this for many years. However, despite all, he did not blush to become a child of Your Christ, a babe at Your baptismal font, bowing his neck to the yoke of humility and submitting his forehead to the humiliation of the cross.

O Lord, Lord, "who bowed the heavens and descended, who touched the mountains and they smoked,"[235] by what means did You find Your way into the heart of Victorinus? He read the Holy Scriptures, as Simplicianus said, and diligently searched for and studied all the Christian writings.

Victorinus privately told Simplicianus, "You must know that I am a Christian." To which Simplicianus replied, "I will not believe it, nor will I count you among the Christians, until I see you in the Church of Christ." Victorinus then asked, with a gleam in his eye, "Is it the walls that determine whether one is a Christian?" This was how he often affirmed his Christianity. Simplicianus would give the same answer, and just as often the joke about the walls was repeated.

Victorinus was afraid of offending his friends—proud demon worshipers. He feared that a storm of hostility would descend upon him from the heights of Babylonian dignity, as from the tops of the cedars of Lebanon, which the Lord had not yet broken down.

However, Victorinus steadily gained strength from studying and asking questions about the faith. He began to fear that Christ would deny him before the holy angels if he were afraid to confess Jesus before men. Victorinus felt guilty because he was ashamed of the sacraments and the humility of Your Word, though he was not ashamed of the sacrilegious rites of those proud demons, whose pride he had imitated and whose rites he had shared. From this he became bold-faced against pride and shamefaced toward the truth.

Victorinus Confesses Christ

Suddenly and unexpectedly, Victorinus said to Simplicianus (as he told me himself), "Let's go to the church; I wish to become a Christian." Simplicianus went with him, scarcely able to contain himself for joy. Victorinus was admitted to the first sacraments of instruction, and not long afterward submitted his name to receive the baptism of regeneration. All of Rome marveled at this and the Church rejoiced. The proud saw and were enraged, but they just gnashed their teeth and melted away! Victorinus was Your servant, O Lord, and as such he paid no attention to their pride and insane lying.

At Rome, those who were about to enter into Your grace, would memorize a creedal statement and declare it from a platform in full view of the Church. When the hour arrived for Victorinus to make his public profession of faith, the Church officials offered to allow him to make his more privately, as was the custom for those who were afraid because of bashfulness. However, Victorinus chose to profess his salvation in the presence of the holy congregation. Salvation was not in the law that he taught and openly professed, so why wouldn't he name Your Word before the sheep of Your flock? He had not been bashful in uttering his own words before the mad multitude!

Therefore, when Victorinus ascended the platform to make his profession, as the people recognized him, they whispered his name to each other in great joy. Who was there among them that did not know him? A low murmur ran through all those rejoicing: "Victorinus! Victorinus!" At the sight of him, there was a sudden burst of exaltation, then, just as suddenly the people were quiet so they could hear him. He pronounced the true faith with an excellent boldness, and all desired to take him to their very heart, which they did by their love and joy. The Church lovingly received him with outstretched arms.

CHAPTER 3—VICTORY COMES WITH STRUGGLE

O God, You are good! But why do some rejoice more at the salvation of a soul that has been delivered from greater danger than over one who has never lost hope, or never been in such imminent danger? O most merciful Father, You "rejoice more over one that repents than over ninety-nine just persons that need no repentance."[236]

We love to hear how the lost sheep is brought home again on the shepherd's shoulders while the angels rejoice.[237] We're delighted when the piece of money is restored to its place in the treasury and the neighbors rejoice with the woman who found it.[238] The joy of the solemn festival of Your house moves us to tears when the story is read about the younger son who "was dead and is alive again, was lost and is found." It's You who rejoices both in us and in Your angels, who are holy through holy love. You are ever the same because You know unchangeably all things which remain neither the same nor forever.

What, then, happens in the soul when it's more delighted at finding or having restored to it the things it loves than if it had always possessed them? Indeed, many other things bear witness that this is so—all things are full of witnesses, crying out, "So it is."

A commander triumphs in victory, yet he could not have conquered had he not fought—the greater the danger in battle, the more joyful the triumph. Also, a storm tosses the voyagers, threatens shipwreck, and everyone turns pale in the presence of death. Then the sky and sea grow calm and they rejoice as much as they had feared. And a loved one is sick and his pulse indicates danger. All who desire his safety are themselves sick at heart, but then he recovers, though still unable to walk with his former strength. However, there is more joy now than there was before when he walked sound and strong.

Pleasure Comes Through Difficulty

By difficulties people obtain the very pleasures of human life—not only those which rush upon us unexpectedly and involuntarily, but also those which are voluntary and planned. There is no pleasure in eating and drinking unless the pains of hunger and thirst have gone before. Drunkards eat salty meats in order to create painful thirst so that when they drink, their thirst is quenched causing pleasure. It's also customary that a woman engaged to be married, not be immediately given in marriage so that her husband-to-be will not esteem her any less than he longed for her as his betrothed.

This can be seen in lowest of dishonorable pleasure, but is also apparent in pleasures that are permitted and lawful as is the sincerity of honest friendship, and the immense pleasure of he who was dead and lives again and he who had been lost and was found.

Greater joy is everywhere preceded by greater pain. What does this mean, O Lord my God, when You are an everlasting joy to Yourself, and heavenly creatures about You are ever rejoicing in You? What does it mean that this portion of creation ebbs and flows, alternately in want and abundance? Is this their mode of being? You assigned to all things their proper place and their proper season, to all the kinds of good things and to all Your just works, but is this what You have allotted from the highest heaven to the lowest earth, from the beginning of the world to the end, from the angels to the worm, or from the first movement to the last?

O my God. How high You are in the highest and how deep in the deepest! You never depart from us, and yet only with difficulty do we return to You.

Chapter 4—Thwarting the Devil

Go on, O Lord, and act. Stir us up and call us back, inflame us and draw us to You, stir us up and grow sweet to us…let us now love You, let us run to You. Many men return to You out of a deeper pit of darkness than that of Victorinus. These men draw near to You and are illuminated by that light which gives those who receive it power from You to become Your sons. However, if they are less well known, even those who know them rejoice less for them. When many rejoice together, the joy of each one is more full because they warm one another; they catch fire from each other.

Moreover, those who are well known influence many toward salvation and take the lead with many following them. Therefore, even those who went before them rejoice greatly, because they do not rejoice over them alone. Nevertheless, it must never be that in Your tabernacle the rich are welcomed before the poor, or those born to nobility esteemed above the others.

"God has chosen the foolish things of the world to put to shame the wise, and God has chosen the weak things of the world to put to shame the things which are mighty."[239] You sounded forth these words by the tongue of "the least of the apostles."

When Paul, the proconsul, had his pride overcome by the onslaught of the apostle, he took up the easy yoke of Christ and became an officer of the great King. He also desired to be called Paul instead of his former name, Saul, as a testimony to such a great victory.[240] The enemy is more overcome in one upon whom he has a greater hold, but the proud he controls more readily through their concern about their status. Through them, he controls more by means of their influence.

Therefore, the more the world prized the heart of Victorinus (which the devil had held in an impregnable stronghold) and the tongue of Victorinus (that sharp, strong weapon with which the devil had slain so many), all the more joyfully should Your sons rejoice because our King has bound the strong man. They saw his vessels taken from him and cleansed, and made fit for Your honor and "profitable to the Lord for every good work."[241]

Chapter 5—Overcoming My Stubborn Will

When Simplicianus told me the story of Victorinus, I was eager to imitate him. In fact, this was Simplicianus' purpose in telling me the story. He also told me that in the reign of the Emperor Julian, a law was passed forbidding Christians to teach literature and law. Victorinus, in ready obedience to the law, chose to abandon his "school of words" rather than Your Word, by which You make the tongues of the illiterate eloquent.

Victorinus seemed not so much brave as happy to me, because he had found a reason for giving his time wholly to You. This was what I longed to do, but I was still bound by the iron chain of my own will. The enemy held fast my will, making it a chain with which he bound me tight. Out of my perverse will came lust, and the service of lust ended in habit, and habit, not resisted, became necessity. By these links, which is why I called it "a chain," hard bondage held me in slavery. My new will, which had begun to spring up in me freely to worship You and to enjoy You, O my God, the only certain Joy, was not yet able to overcome my former willfulness, made strong by long indulgence. Therefore, my two wills—the old and the new, the carnal and the spiritual—raged in conflict within me. They tore my soul apart by their dispute.

I came to understand from my own experience what I had read, how "the flesh lusts against the Spirit, and the Spirit against the flesh."[242] I truly lusted both ways, yet more in what I approved of in myself than that which I disapproved of in myself. I was not really involved in that which I disapproved of, because here I was more of an unwilling sufferer than a willing actor. Nevertheless, it was through me that habit had become an armed enemy against me. I had willingly come to be what I unwillingly found myself to be.

Who can, with any justice, speak against it when just punishment follows the sinner? I no longer had my usual excuse that I hesitated to forsake the world and serve You because my perception of the truth was uncertain. Now it was certain. Nevertheless, I was still bound to the earth. I refused to be Your soldier, and was as afraid of being free from all entanglements as I should have feared being entangled.

Convicted but Not Convinced

I was sweetly burdened with the baggage of the world, as one in slumber. My thoughts of You were like the efforts of those who desire to wake up, but who are still overpowered with drowsiness and fall back into deep sleep. Nobody wishes to sleep forever, yet a person will usually defer shaking off his drowsiness when there is a heavy lethargy in his limbs. He is glad to continue sleeping, even when his reason disapproves and the hour for rising has come.

I was assured that it was much better for me to surrender to Your love than to continue yielding to my own lust. Your love satisfied and overwhelmed me, while my lust pleased and fettered me. I had no answer when You called me saying, "Awake, you who sleep, arise from the dead, and Christ will give you light."[243]

On all sides, You showed me that Your words are true. Convicted by the truth, I had no reply but the drawling and drowsy words: "Presently, presently. Leave me alone this little while." But "presently, presently," had no present, and my "leave me alone this little while" went on for a long time.

To no avail, I "delighted in Your law in the inner man" while "another law in my members warred against the law of my mind and brought me into captivity to the law of sin which is in my members." The law of sin is the tyranny of habit, and by it, the mind is drawn and held, even against its will. Yet the mind deserves to be held so because it so willingly falls into the habit. "O wretched man that I am! Who shall deliver me from this body of this death?"[244] Your grace alone through Jesus Christ our Lord, O God, is all that can deliver me.

CHAPTER 6—PONTICIANUS VISITS AUGUSTINE

Now I will tell and confess unto Your name, O Lord, my helper and my redeemer, how You delivered me from the chain of sexual desire that so tightly bound me, and from the slavery of worldly business.[245]

With increasing anxiety I went about my usual duties, and daily cried out to You. I groaned under the burden of my business, but attended Your church as frequently as I could. Alypius was with me, and after a third term as assessor was at last released from his legal post. Now he was seeking private clients to whom he could sell his legal advice as I sold the power of speaking (as if it could be supplied by teaching).

For the sake of our friendship, Nebridius had agreed to teach under Verecundus, a citizen of Milan, professor of grammar, and a very intimate friend. Verecundus fervently desired, and by right of friendship demanded from us, the faithful aid he greatly needed. Nebridius was not drawn to teaching by any desire of gain, because he could've made much more out of his learning had he been so inclined. However, he was a sweet and kindly friend and so was unwilling to slight our request out of respect for our friendship. Therefore, he acted very discreetly, taking care not to become known to those persons who had great reputations in the world. This way, he avoided all the distractions of mind, and reserved as many hours as possible to pursue or read or listen to discussions about wisdom.

One day, when Nebridius was away, Ponticianus, a fellow countryman of ours from Africa that held high office in the emperor's court, came to visit Alypius and me at our house. What he wanted with us I do not know, but we sat down to visit. While there, he noticed a book on a game table before us. When he opened it, he saw that it was the apostle Paul, for he imagined that it was one of my wearisome legal texts. At this, he looked up at me with a smile and expressed his delight and wonder that he had so unexpectedly found this book and only this one, lying before my eyes.

Ponticianus, it turns out, was a Christian and a faithful one at that. Daily he prostrated himself in the church before You, our God, in fervent prayer. When I told him that I had given much attention to these writings, a conversation followed in which he spoke of Anthony, the Egyptian monk, whose name was held in high esteem among Your servants, although up to that time unfamiliar to me. When Ponticianus learned this, he lingered on the topic, giving us an account of this eminent man, and marveling at our ignorance. We in turn were amazed to hear of Your wonderful works so fully manifested in recent times occurring in the true faith and the Catholic Church. We all were in awe— we, that these things were so great, and he, that we had never heard of them.

From this, Ponticianus conversation turned to the multitudes then in monasteries and their manners, which are so fragrant to You. He talked of the teeming solitude of the wilderness, of which we knew nothing at all. There was even a monastery at Milan, outside the city's walls, full of good brothers under the fostering care of Ambrose—and we were ignorant of it.

God's Secret Agents

Ponticianus continued talking with us, and we listened intently and in silence. He told us how, on a certain afternoon, at Trier,[246] when the emperor was occupied watching the gladiatorial games, Ponticianus and three friends went out for a walk in the gardens close to the city walls. As they walked two-by-two, one strolled away with him, while the other two went on by themselves. As they rambled, the first two came upon a certain cottage where some of Your servants lived—some of the "poor in spirit" ("of such is the Kingdom of Heaven")—here they found the book in which was written the life of Anthony!

One of the men began to read the book and was captivated by it. While reading, he meditated on embracing just such a life, giving up his worldly employment to seek You alone. These two belonged to the group of officials called "secret service agents."[247] Suddenly, being overwhelmed with a holy love and a sober shame, as if in anger with himself, he fixed his eyes on his friend and said:

> *Tell me, I beg you, what goal are we seeking in all these toils of ours? What is it that we desire? What is our motive in public service? Can our hopes in the court rise higher than to be 'friends of the emperor'?*[248] *How frail, how filled with peril is that pride! Through what dangers must we climb to a greater danger? And when will we succeed? But if I chose to become a friend of God, I can become one now.*

As the man spoke, he was caught in the birth pangs of new life. He turned his eyes again to the page and continued reading. The man was inwardly changed, as You saw, and the world dropped away from his mind, which soon became plain to the others. As he read, his heart became like a stormy sea, and more than once he groaned. Finally he saw the better course, and resolved to pursue it.

Having become Your servant, the man told his friend: "I have broken loose from those hopes we had, and I am determined to serve God. I enter into that service from this hour in this place. If you are reluctant to imitate me, do not oppose me." The other replied that he would continue bound in his friendship, to share in so great a service for so great a prize. So both became Yours, and began to "build a tower", counting the cost, namely, forsaking all that they had and following You.[249]

Shortly after, Ponticianus and his companion, who had walked with him in the other part of the garden, came in search of the two. When they found them, they reminded them to return, as the day was waning. However, the first two, making known to Ponticianus their resolution and purpose, and how a resolve had sprung up and become confirmed in them, asked them not to be offended if they refused to join them.

Ponticianus and his friend, although not detoured from their former course, (as he told us) wept themselves and congratulated their friends on their godliness, commending themselves to their prayers. With hearts inclining again toward earthly things, Ponticianus and the other man returned to the palace. However, the other two, set their affections on heavenly things and remained in the cottage. Both of these men had fiancées who likewise dedicated their virginity to You when they heard of this.

Chapter 7 – Warring Against the Flesh

Such was the story Ponticianus told. While he was speaking, You, O Lord, turned me toward myself. You forced me to come out of hiding from self-scrutiny and set me face-to-face with myself so I could see how ugly I was, and how crooked, sordid, and stained with sin. As I looked, I loathed myself, but where to hide I didn't know. If I sought to turn my gaze away from self, Ponticianus would continue his narrative, and You would oppose me to myself. You thrust me before my own eyes that I might discover my iniquity and hate it. I had known it, but acted as though I didn't. Instead, I winked at it and forgot it.

How I loved those who had given themselves entirely to You to be saved, and abhorred myself when compared with them. Many years, perhaps twelve, had passed since my nineteenth, when, upon the reading of Cicero's Hortensius, I was roused to obtain wisdom. Yet here I was, still postponing the abandonment of this world's happiness to devote myself to the search. Not for just the finding alone, but for the bare search for it as well. I ought to have preferred wisdom above the treasures and kingdoms of this world—more than all bodily pleasures, though they were to be had for the taking.

I was a despicable youth, extremely sinful from the very outset. I asked for purity from You, praying, "Lord, help me to be pure, but not yet." I was afraid that if You heard me too soon, I would be cured too soon of my disease of lust. I just wanted to have it satisfied rather than its fire extinguished. So I wandered the perverse path of godless superstition. I wasn't really sure where it would lead but preferred it to the Truth, which I didn't seek in reverence, but opposed in malice.

I thought I had delayed rejecting worldly hopes and following You because there was nothing certain to direct my course. However, the day had arrived in which I was revealed to myself. My conscience chided me:

> *Where are you, O my tongue? You said that you were unwilling to cast off the baggage of pride for uncertain truth. But now it is certain, and still that burden oppresses you. At the same time those who have not worn themselves out with searching for it as you have, nor spent ten years and more in thinking about it, have had their shoulders unburdened and have received wings to fly away.*

I was confused, and plagued with horrible shame. Nevertheless, Ponticianus continued to speak. When he finished his story and completed the business he came for, he went his way.

With what scourges of rebuke did I not whip my soul to make it follow me, as I was struggling to go after You? Yet it drew back. My soul refused and would not make an effort. All its arguments were exhausted and refuted, but it resisted in sullen unrest, fearing the cutting off of that habit by which it was being wasted to death, as if that were death itself.

CHAPTER 8—MY BATTLE OF THE WILLS

As this heated quarrel with my soul was raging inside my heart, I became agitated in both mind and countenance. I seized Alypius and exclaimed:

> *What is the matter with us? What is this? What did you hear? The uninstructed start up and take heaven, and we—with all our learning but so little heart—see where we wallow in flesh and blood! Because others have gone before us, are we ashamed to follow, and unashamed not to follow?*

I scarcely knew what I said, and in my excitement quickly turned away. All the while Alypius looked at me in silent astonishment. I didn't sound like myself, instead, my face, eyes, color, and tone of voice expressed my meaning more clearly than words.

We had a small garden by our house that was ours to use. The landlord didn't live there, so the entire house was available to us. The storm in my soul hurried me out into this garden, where no one would interrupt the fiery struggle raging inside of me. That is, until it reached the end that You knew would come—though I didn't know.

I was frantic for health, and dying for life. I knew what an evil thing I was, but didn't know what a good thing I was shortly to become.

I fled into the garden, with Alypius following my every step. I had no secrets that he didn't share, and how could he leave me in such distress? We sat down, as far from the house as possible. I was greatly disturbed in my spirit. I was enraged with myself because I had not entered Your will and covenant, O my God, though all my bones cried out for me to enter.

The entry into God's will is not by ships or chariots or feet. In fact, it's not as far as we had gone from the house to where we were seated. To go along that road and to reach the goal requires nothing but your will to go. However, it must be a strong and single will, not staggering and swaying about this way and that. It can't be a changeable, twisting, fluctuating will that wrestles with itself, one part falling as another rises.

The fever of my indecision caused my body to writhe and tremble. It was similar to what men do when they want to act but can't, either because they have no arms or legs, or because their limbs are bound by weakness or disease, or incapacitated in some other way. Therefore, if I tore my hair, struck my forehead, or entwined my fingers and clasped my knee, I did so because I willed it. However, I might have willed it and still not have done it, if the nerves had not obeyed my will. I did many things, in which the will and power to do were not the same.

Nevertheless, I didn't do the one thing that seemed infinitely more desirable to me. Before long I would have power to will, because shortly when I willed, I would will with a single will. For in the power of willing is the power of doing, but as yet I could not do it. Therefore, my body more readily obeyed the slightest wish of the soul in moving its limbs at the order of my mind than my soul obeyed itself to accomplish in the will alone its great resolve.

CHAPTER 9—UNDERSTANDING HUMAN WILL

How can there be such a strange anomaly? And why is it? Let Your mercy shine on me, O God, that I may seek and find an answer, amid the dark maze of human punishment and the darkest remorse of the sons of Adam.

What is the source of such an anomaly? And why should it be? The mind commands the body, and the body obeys, but the mind commands itself and is resisted. The mind commands the hand to be moved and there is such readiness that the command is scarcely distinguished from the obedience in act. Yet the mind is mind, and the hand is body. The mind commands the mind to will, and yet though it is itself it does not obey itself.

What is this strange anomaly and why should it be? I repeat: The will commands itself to will, and can't give the command unless it so wills. Yet what is commanded isn't done. But in actuality, the will does not will entirely. Therefore, the will does not command entirely. As far as it wills, it commands. And as far as it does not will, the thing commanded is not done.

The will commands that there be an act of will—not another, but itself. But it does not command entirely. Therefore, what is commanded does not happen; for if the will were whole and entire, it would not even command it to be, because it would already be. It is, therefore, no strange anomaly partly to will and partly to be unwilling. This is actually an infirmity of mind, which can't rise up while pressed down by habit, even though it is supported by the truth. Therefore, two wills are in place. One will isn't whole, and what is present in one is lacking in the other.

CHAPTER 10—TWO WILLS

Let this perish from Your presence, O God, as foolish talkers and deceivers of the soul perish. When we observe that there are two wills in the act of deliberation, we must go on to affirm that there are two kinds of minds in us: one good, the other evil. They are themselves evil when they hold these evil opinions. They will become good only when they hold the truth and consent to the truth that Your apostle declared: "For you were once darkness, but now *you are* light in the Lord."[250] They desired to be light, though not "in the Lord," but in themselves. These minds conceived the nature of the soul to be the same as what God is, and so have become a thicker darkness than they were before. For in their dread arrogance they have gone farther away from You, "the true Light, that lights every man that comes into the world." Mark what you say and blush for shame; draw near to Him and be enlightened, and your face will not be ashamed.[251]

While I was deliberating whether to serve the Lord my God now, as I had long purposed to do, it was I who willed and it was also I who was unwilling. Either case, it was me. I neither willed with my entire will nor was I entirely unwilling. Therefore, I was at war with myself and torn apart by myself. This strife was against my will, though it didn't reveal the presence of another mind, but the punishment of my own. Thus it was no more I who did it, but the sin that dwelt in me[252]—the punishment of a sin freely committed by Adam, and I was a son of Adam.

For if there were as many opposing natures as there are opposing wills, there would not be two but many more. If a man tries to decide whether he should go to Church or to the theater, the Manicheans at once cry out, "See, here are two natures—one good, drawing this way, another bad, drawing back that way. How else can this indecision between conflicting wills be explained?"

However, I reply that both impulses are bad—that which draws to them and that which draws back to the theater. They don't believe that the will drawing them can be anything but good. Suppose, then, that one of us tries to decide, and through the conflict of his two wills should waver whether to go to the theater or to our Church. Wouldn't they also waver about the answer here? For either they must confess, which they are unwilling to do, that the will that leads to our Church is as good as that which carries their own adherents and those captivated by their mysteries. Or they must imagine that there are two evil natures and two evil minds in one man, both at war with each other. Then it will not be true what they say, that there is one good and another bad. Otherwise, they must be converted to the truth, and no longer deny that when anyone deliberates there is one soul fluctuating between conflicting wills.

Two Wills, One Substance

Let these foolish talkers no longer maintain that when they perceive two wills to be contending with each other in the same man the contest is between two opposing minds, of two opposing substances, from two opposing principles—the one good and the other bad. Thus, O true God, You reprove and refute and convict them. Both wills may be bad. For example:

- When a man tries to decide whether he should kill another by poison or by the sword.

- Whether a man should take possession of this field or that one belonging to someone else, when he cannot get both.

- Whether a man should squander his money to buy pleasure or hold onto his money through the motive of covetousness.

- Whether a man should go to the circus or to the theater if both are open on the same day.

- Whether a man should rob another man's house.

- Whether a man should commit adultery if the opportunity presents itself.

All these things occur in the same space of time and all may be equally longed for, although impossible to do at one time. Therefore, the mind is pulled in many different directions by many antagonistic wills, in view of the vast range of human desires. Even the Manicheans don't affirm that there are so many different substances.

The same principle applies in the action of good wills. I asked these foolish deceivers, "Is it a good thing to delight in reading the apostle, or to delight in a sober psalm, or to discuss the gospel?" To each of these, they will answer, "It is good." But what do we do if all delights us equally and all at the same time? Don't different wills distract the mind when a man is trying to decide what he should choose? Yet they are all good, but at odds with each other until one is chosen.

When the choice is made, the now united will may go forward on a single track instead of remaining divided in many ways as it was before. Likewise, when eternity attracts us from above, and the pleasure of earthly delight pulls us down from below, the soul does not will either the one or the other with all its force, but still it's the same soul that does not will this or that with a united will. Therefore, it's torn with confusion, because for truth's sake it prefers this, but for custom's sake does not lay the other aside.

CHAPTER 11—PURITY BECKONS

This is why I was sick and tormented, accusing myself more bitterly than ever, rolling and writhing in my chain till it should be utterly broken. By now I was held but slightly, but still was held. You, O Lord, pressed upon me in my inmost heart with severe mercy, redoubling the lashes of fear and shame. You didn't do this to prevent me from falling and breaking that slender remaining tie, but to help me recover strength and so You could chain me even more securely.

I kept saying to myself, "See, let it be done now; let it be done now." And as I said this I all but came to a firm decision. I all but did, yet not quite. However, I didn't fall back to my old condition either, but stood aside for a moment to catch my breath. When I tried again, I lacked only a very little of reaching the resolve, and then somewhat less, and then all but touched and grasped it. However, I still didn't quite reach or touch or grasp the goal, because I hesitated to die to death and to live to life. The worst way, to which I was chained by habit, was stronger in me than the better way, which I had not tried. Up to the very moment in which I was to become another man, the nearer it approached, the greater the horror struck me. Nevertheless, it didn't strike back, nor turn me aside, but held me in suspense.

In fact, it was my old mistresses that still enthralled me. Thoughts of them tugged at my fleshly garments and softly whispered: "Are you going to part with us? From that moment will we never be with you any more? From that moment will not this and that be forbidden to you forever?" What were these thoughts suggesting in those words "this or that"? What is it they suggested, O my God? Let Your mercy guard the soul of Your servant from the wickedness and shame these thoughts suggested!

Self Against Self

I scarcely heard the thoughts, for they were not openly showing themselves and opposing me face to face, but muttering, as it were, behind my back. They furtively plucked at me as I was leaving, trying to make me look back at them. Still they delayed me, so that I hesitated to break loose and shake myself free of them and leap over to the place to which I was being called. Unruly habits kept calling to me: "Do you really think you can live without sex?"

Though the habits continued to call, the call was very faint. The modest dignity of sexual purity appeared to me in the direction I had set my face toward, but where I still trembled to go. The allure was cheerful but not wanton, modestly beckoning me to come and doubt nothing. She extended her holy hands to receive and embrace me, full of a multitude of good examples…countless young men and women, multitudes of youth and older, grave widows and ancient virgins. Purity herself was in the midst, not barren, but a fruitful mother of children, her joys, fathered by You, O Lord, her husband.

Purity smiled on me with a challenging smile as if to say:

> Can you not do what these young men and women do? Or can any of them do it of themselves, and not rather in the Lord their God? The Lord their God gave me to them. Why do you try to stand in your own strength and fall? Cast yourself on Him; fear not. He will not

flinch and you will not fall. Cast yourself on Him without fear, for He will receive and heal you.

I blushed violently, because I still heard the muttering of those memories and hung suspended. Again Purity seemed to speak:

> *Stop your ears against those unclean members of yours, that they may be disciplined. They tell you of delights, but not according to the law of the Lord Your God.*

The struggle raging in my heart was nothing but the contest of self against self. Through it all, Alypius remained close beside me, waiting in silence for the outcome of my extraordinary agitation.

CHAPTER 12—AUGUSTINE AND ALYPIUS BECOME CHRISTIANS

When deep reflection had drawn up out of the secret depths of my soul and had heaped all my misery up before the sight of my heart, a mighty storm arose, accompanied by a mighty rain of tears. So that I might fully give way to my tears and cries of repentance, I slipped away from Alypius. It seemed to me that solitude was more appropriate for the business of weeping. I went far enough away so that even his presence was no restraint upon me. This was how I felt at the time, and he realized it. I probably said something before I moved and he noticed that my voice was choked with weeping. So he stayed where we had been sitting, wondering what was happening.

I flung myself down under a fig tree—how I don't know—and let my tears run their course. The streams of my eyes gushed out an acceptable sacrifice to You, O God. In words to this effect, I cried: "O Lord—how long? How long, O Lord? Will You be angry forever? Oh, do not remember former iniquities against us."[253] For

I felt that I was still captivated by them. I sent up these sorrowful cries: "How long, how long? For tomorrow and tomorrow? Why not now? Why not this very hour make an end to my uncleanness?"

Pick it up, read it!

While I was saying these things and weeping bitter tears of remorse, I heard the voice of a child coming from the neighboring house. They were chanting over and over again, "Pick it up, read it. Pick it up, read it." Immediately I stopped weeping and began to wonder whether it was usual for children in some kind of game to sing such a song, but I couldn't remember ever having heard anything like it. Therefore, damming the torrent of my tears, I rose to my feet. I could only think that this was a divine command to open the Bible and read the first passage I saw. For I had heard[254] how Anthony, who had accidentally entered the church while the gospel was being read, received the admonition of Scripture as if what was read had been addressed to him: "Go, sell what you have and give it to the poor, and you shall have treasure in heaven; and come, follow me."[255] He was converted to You by these words.

I hurried back to the bench where Alypius was sitting, because I had put down the apostle's book when I had left there. Taking it, I opened it and in silence read the paragraph on which my eyes first fell: "Let us walk properly, as in the day, not in revelry and drunkenness, not in lewdness and lust, not in strife and envy."[256] I wanted to read no further, nor did I need to. For instantly, as the sentence ended, there was infused in my heart something like the light of full certainty and all the gloom of doubt vanished away.[257]

I marked the page and closed the book and began to calmly tell Alypius everything. He in turn told me what had been happening in him, of which I knew nothing, and then asked to see what I had read. I showed him, and he read even further than I had. I didn't know what followed, but it was this, "Receive one who is weak in the faith."[258] Alypius told me that he applied this to himself, and with these words of warning he was strengthened. By exercising his resolve for good, he joined me in full commitment without hesitation. Alypius was a man of good character, and in that respect, was always far different from and better than I was.

Then we went in to my mother, and to her great joy told her what happened. When we explained how our full conversion had occurred, she leapt for joy in triumph and blessed You, God, who are "able to do exceedingly abundantly above all that we ask or think."[259] She saw that You had granted her far more than she had ever asked in her pitiful and solemn prayers. You so converted me to You that I sought neither a wife nor any other of this world's hopes, but instead set my feet on that rule of faith which so many years before You had shown her in a dream about me. You turned her grief into gladness greater than anything she had hoped, and dearer and purer than the desire she had of having grandchildren.

BOOK NINE

Augustine's Mother Dies

This Book marks the end of Augustine's autobiography. He tells about resigning from his professorship and of his days at Cassiciacum where he prepared for baptism. He is baptized along with Adeodatus and Alypius. Soon thereafter, they return to Africa. Augustine remembers the joy he shared with his mother in Ostia and then tells of her death and burial, and his grief. This book closes with a moving prayer for the souls of Monica, Patricius, and all his fellow citizens of the heavenly Jerusalem.

CHAPTER 1—SWEETNESS BEYOND COMPARE

"O LORD, truly I *am* Your servant; I *am* Your servant, the son of Your maidservant; You have loosed my bonds. I will offer to You the sacrifice of thanksgiving."[260] Let my heart and my tongue praise You, and let all my bones say, "Lord, who is like unto You?" Let my soul say so, and You answer and say unto my soul, "I am your salvation."

Who am I, and what is my nature? What evil does not reside in my deeds and me—if not in my deeds, my words—if not in my words, my will? But You, O Lord, are good and merciful. Your right hand reached into the depths of my death and emptied the abyss of corruption from the bottom of my heart. The result is that I did not will to do what I willed, and began to will to do Your will.

Where was my free will during all those years? From what deep, secret retreat was it called forth in a single moment? What happened to enable me to give my neck to Your "easy yoke" and my shoulders to Your "light burden?" Christ Jesus, You are "my Strength and my Redeemer."

How sweet it suddenly was to be without the "sweetness" of sexual play! It was now a joy to put away what I used to fear I would lose. You cast them away from me, O true and highest Sweetness, and in their place entered in Yourself. This was by far sweeter than all pleasures, though not to flesh and blood. It was brighter than all light, but more secret than all mysteries. And it was more exalted than all honor, though not to them that are exalted in their own eyes.

Now my soul was free from the gnawing cares of seeking and getting, of wallowing in the mire and scratching the itch of lust. I chattered on like a child to You, O Lord my God. You are my light, my riches, and my salvation.

Chapter 2—Leaving Public Office

It seemed right to me, in Your sight, not to snatch my tongue's service abruptly out of the speech market, but to withdraw quietly. That way, the young men who were unconcerned about Your law or peace, but were concerned with frivolous suits and legal maneuverings, might no longer purchase weapons for their frenzy from my mouth. Fortunately, there were only a few days before the "vintage vacation"[261] and I was determined to endure them. Since You now owned me, I planned to close shop and no longer offer myself for sale.

You knew my plan, and except for a few of my friends, it was unknown to other men. We agreed not make my departure public. Though in our climb from the "valley of tears" and our singing of "the song of degrees," You gave us sharp arrows and hot burning coals to stop any deceitful tongue that opposed us under the guise of good counsel.

God, You pierced our hearts with Your love, and we carried Your words, as it were, thrust through our vital organs. Examples of Your servants that You changed from black to shining white and from death to life, crowded into our thoughts, burning and consuming our sluggish tempers, thus preventing us from toppling back into the abyss. The fire purged us, so that every breath of our detractors' deceitful tongues fanned the flame, but did not blow it out.

Closing My Practice

My vow to You and my purpose in leaving public office had supporters, who would praise it for the sake of Your name, which You have sanctified throughout the earth. Nevertheless, it could appear to be a self-promoting move if I left before the vacation time that was now so near. If I had left such a public office ahead of time and in view of the general public, those who noticed would have talked about me a great deal, as if I were trying to appear a great person. What purpose would be served if people argued about my conversion so that my good would be spoken of as evil?

Furthermore, that same summer my lungs had grown weak from too much literary labor. Breathing was difficult, and the pain in my chest revealed that my lungs were affected. Too loud or prolonged speaking quickly fatigued me. This infirmity had at first been a trial for me, because I would have been compelled of necessity to lay down my burden of teaching, or, if I was cured and became strong again, I would at least have to take a leave of absence for a time. However, the full desire to be still that I might know that You are the Lord[262] arose and was confirmed in me. You know, my God, that I then began to rejoice that I had this reason to leave. I knew that it would help temper the disappointment of those who, for their sons' freedom, wished me to have no freedom of my own.

Full of joy, then, I endured until my time ran out—perhaps twenty days. Nevertheless, it was stressful to go through with it, because the greediness that helped support the drudgery was gone. I would have been overwhelmed if it had not been replaced by patience. Some of Your servants, my brethren, may say that I sinned in this, since having fully and from my heart enlisted in

Your service, I permitted myself to sit a single hour in the chair of falsehood. I will not dispute it, but haven't You, O most merciful Lord, pardoned and forgiven this sin in the holy waters of baptism as well, along with all the other sins, horrible and deadly as they were?

CHAPTER 3—NEBRIDIUS CONVERTS TO CHRISTIANITY

Verecundus was very disturbed by this new happiness of mine, since he was still firmly held by his chains and saw that he would soon lose my companionship. He was not yet a Christian, though his wife was. Indeed, he was more firmly chained by her than by anything else, and held back from that journey on which we had set out. Furthermore, he declared that he didn't wish to be a Christian on any terms except those that were impossible. However, he courteously invited us to use his country home as long as we needed to stay there. O Lord, You will recompense him for this "in the resurrection of the just,"[263] seeing that You have already given him "the lot of the righteous."[264]

While we were traveling in Rome, Verecundus was overtaken with sickness. While the sickness was running its course, he became a Christian and departed this life as one of the faithful. Thus You had mercy on him, and not on him only, but on us as well. Had we remembered the great kindness of our friend and had been unable to count him in Your flock, we would be tortured with intolerable grief. Thanks be unto You, our God; we are Yours. Your exhortation, consolation, and faithful promises assure us that You will repay Verecundus for that country home at Cassiciacum where we found rest in You from the fever of the world. You'll do this with the perpetual freshness of Your paradise in which You have forgiven him his earthly sins, in that fruitful mountain of Yours flowing with milk.

One Grieves, Another Rejoices

Verecundus was full of grief, but Nebridius was filled with joy. Nebridius was not yet a Christian, and had fallen into the pit of deadly error—he believed that the flesh of Your Son, the Truth, was an illusion.[265] Yet he had risen up out of that pit and now held the same belief that we did. Though not yet initiated in any of the sacraments of Your Church, Nebridius was an earnest inquirer after truth.

Not long after our conversion and regeneration by Your baptism, Nebridius also became a faithful member of the Catholic Church. He served You in purity and abstinence among his own people in Africa, and brought his entire household to Christ.

You released Nebridius from the flesh, so he now lives in Abraham's bosom, whatever is signified by that term "bosom." Nevertheless, my sweet friend, Nebridius, Your son by adoption, O Lord, now lives there and is not a freedman any longer. There he resides, for what other place could there be for such a soul? He lives in that abode about which he used to ask me so many questions— poor ignorant one that I was. He no longer inclines his ear to my mouth, but his spiritual mouth he places to Your fountain. There he drinks of wisdom as often as he desires and is happy without end. I don't believe, though, that he is so inebriated by that heavenly drink that he would forget me since You, O Lord, who are the drink, are mindful of me.

Thus we comforted the unhappy Verecundus, our friend. We reconciled him to our conversion and exhorted him to a faith fit for his condition since he was married. We waited for Nebridius to follow since he was so close, which he was just about to do when our notice to leave public office expired. The days had seemed long and many because of my eagerness for leisure and liberty in which I might sing to You from my inner self: "My heart has said to You, I have sought Your face; Your face, O Lord, will I seek."[266]

Chapter 4—Augustine Laments the Error of the Manicheans

Finally the day came on which I was actually to be relieved from my professorship of law—I had already been released in intention. It was done. You delivered my tongue as You had already delivered my heart. I blessed You with great joy for doing so, and retired with my friends to the villa.[267] My books testify to what I accomplished there in writing, which was now hopefully devoted to Your service, though in this pause it was as if I were still panting from my exertions in the school of pride.[268] These were books in which I engaged in dialogue with my friends, and also those written in private before You alone. Also included are my letters to Nebridius, who was still absent.[269]

When would there be enough time to describe all the wonderful blessings which You bestowed on us during that time—especially since I am hurrying on to still greater mercies? I remember these things. It's pleasant to confess to You, O Lord, the inward goads by which You subdued me, how You brought me low, leveling the mountains and hills of my thoughts, straightening my crookedness, and smoothing my rough ways.

I also remember how You subdued Alypius, my heart's brother, to the name of Your only Son, our Lord and Savior Jesus Christ. He at first refused to have Jesus' name inserted in our writings. At first, he preferred the smell of the cedars of the schools,[270] which the Lord has now broken down, rather than of the wholesome herbs of the Church, which is hostile to serpents.[271]

Subdued by the Psalms

O my God, how I cried out to You when I read the psalms of David. Those hymns of faith and joyful songs of devotion leave no room for swelling pride! I was still a novice in Your true love, a student keeping holiday at the villa, with Alypius, a student like myself. My mother was also with us—in woman's garb, but with a man's faith. She exuded the peacefulness of age and the fullness of motherly love and Christian piety.

O the cries I sent up to You in those Psalms, and how I was drawn toward You by them! I burned to sing them throughout the entire world against the pride of the human race. Yet they are sung throughout the entire world, and none can hide from Your heat.

With strong and bitter regret I was indignant at the Manicheans! Yet I also pitied them, for they were ignorant of those medicines,[272] the sacraments, and raved insanely against the cure that would have made them sane! I wished they could have been somewhere close by, and could have seen my face and heard my words when, in that time of leisure, I pored over the Fourth Psalm. I wish they could have seen how that psalm affected me.

"Hear me when I call, O God of my righteousness! You have relieved me in my distress; Have mercy on me, and hear my prayer."[273] I wish the Manicheans could have heard what I said in comment on those words, without my knowing that they heard, lest they think that I was speaking it just on their account. I wouldn't have said quite the same things, in quite the same way, had I known that I was heard and seen by them. If I had so spoken, the words wouldn't have meant the same thing to them as they did to me when I spoke by myself, for myself, out of the private affections of my soul before You.

By turns I trembled with fear and warmed with hope and rejoiced in Your mercy, O Father. All these feelings were expressed in my eyes and voice when Your Spirit said, "O sons of men, how long will you be slow of heart, how long will you love vanity, and seek after falsehood?" I had loved vanity and sought after falsehood.

You, O Lord, had already magnified Your Holy One, raising him from the dead and setting him at Your right hand, so that He would send from on high His promised "Paraclete, the Spirit of Truth." Already He had sent Him, and I knew it not. He had sent him because He was now magnified, rising from the dead and ascending into heaven. Until then "the Holy Spirit was not yet given, because Jesus was not yet glorified."[274]

The prophet cried: "How long, O you sons of men, *Will you turn* my glory to shame? *How long* will you love worthlessness *and* seek falsehood? But know that the LORD has set apart for Himself him who is godly."[275] He cries, "How long?" He cries, "But know that…" And I, so long loving worthlessness and seeking after falsehood, heard and trembled. These words were spoken to such a one as I had been. The lies that I once accepted as truth were nothing but worthlessness and falsehood.

Out of remorse, I loudly and earnestly spoke many things that I wish the Manicheans had heard. They still "loved worthlessness and sought falsehood." Perhaps they would have been troubled, and would have vomited up their error. You would have heard them when they cried to You, for by a real death in the flesh Jesus died for us and now makes intercession for us with You.

I read on further, "Be angry, and do not sin."[276] I was deeply touched, O my God, because I had learned to be angry with myself for past things, so that in the future I wouldn't sin. Yes, to be angry with good reason, for it was not another nature out of the species of darkness that had sinned for me as they who are not angry with themselves affirm. They store up for themselves dire wrath against the day of wrath and the revelation of Your righteous judgment.

Out of Darkness and into the Light

Furthermore, the good things I saw were not outside of me, though invisible to the eyes of flesh in the light of the earthly sun. They that have their joys from without sink easily into emptiness and are spilled out on those things that are visible and temporal, and in their starving thoughts they lick their very shadows. If only they would grow weary with their hunger and would say, "Who will show us any good?" We would answer, and they would hear, "O Lord, the light of Your countenance shines bright upon us." We are not that Light that enlightens every man, but we are enlightened by You, so that we who were formerly in darkness may now be light in You.

If only these lost ones could have beheld the inner Light Eternal. Now that I had tasted it, I gnashed my teeth because I could not show it to them unless they brought me their heart in their roving eyes and said, "Who will show us any good?" However, even in the inner chamber of my soul where I was angry with myself and inwardly pricked, You had begun to grow sweet to me and to "put gladness in my heart." There I had offered my sacrifice, slaying my old man, and hoping in You with the new resolve of a new life with my trust placed in You.

As I read the cry of the psalmist, I cried aloud and felt its inward meaning. I didn't wish to increase in worldly goods that are wasted by time. I now possessed, in Your eternal simplicity, other corn and wine and oil.

With a loud cry from my heart, I read the following verse: "Oh, in peace! Oh, in the Selfsame!"[277] See how he says it: "I will both lie down in peace, and sleep."[278] Who will withstand us when the truth of this saying is made manifest: "Death is swallowed up in victory?"[279] Surely You, who does not change, are the Selfsame, and in You is rest and oblivion to all distress. There is none other beside You, nor are we to toil for those things that are not You. Only You, O Lord, make me to dwell in hope.

These things I read and was enflamed. However, I still didn't know what to do with those deaf and dead Manicheans to whom I myself had belonged. I had been a bitter and blind opponent against the Scriptures, though they are honeyed with the honey of heaven and luminous with Your light. Therefore, I was grieved at these enemies of the Scriptures.

A Toothache Healed

When shall I call to mind all that happened during those holidays? I have not forgotten, nor will I be silent about the severity of Your scourging, and the amazing quickness of Your mercy. During that time You tortured me with a toothache. When it had become so painful that I was unable to speak, it came into my heart to urge all my friends who were present to pray for me to You, the God of all health. I wrote my prayer request on a tablet and gave it to them to read. Then, as we bowed our knees in prayer, the pain disappeared! But what pain? How did it go? I confess that I was terrified, O Lord my God, because from my earliest years I had never experienced such pain.

Your purposes were profoundly impressed upon me, and rejoicing in faith, I praised Your name. Nevertheless, that faith allowed me no rest in respect of my past sins, which were not yet forgiven through Your baptism.

CHAPTER 5—AMBROSE NOTIFIED OF AUGUSTINE'S CONVERSION

Now that the vacation was over, I gave notice to the citizens of Milan that they should provide their scholars with another word-merchant. I gave as my reasons my determination to serve You and also my insufficiency for the task—my difficulty in breathing and the subsequent pain in my chest.

I wrote letters to notify Your bishop, the holy man Ambrose, of my former errors and my present resolution. I also asked his advice as to which of Your books it was best for me to read so that I would be ready and fit to receive so great a grace. He recommended Isaiah the prophet, and I believe it was because Isaiah foreshows the gospels more clearly than others, as well as the calling of the Gentiles. However, I couldn't understand the first part, so I imagined the rest to be like it. Therefore, I set it aside with the intention of taking it up again later when better practiced in the words of our Lord.

CHAPTER 6—ADEODATUS, AUGUSTINE'S SON

When the time arrived for me to submit my name, we left the country and returned to Milan. Alypius also resolved to be born again in You at the same time. He was already clothed with humility suitable for Your sacraments, and bravely tamed his body so that he could walk the frozen Italian soil with his bare feet.

Adeodatus, my son after the flesh, the offspring of my sin, accompanied us. You made of him a noble lad. Though barely fifteen years old, his intelligence excelled that of many learned men. I confess to You Your gifts, O Lord my God, creator of all, who have power to reform our deformities. There was nothing of me in that boy but the sin. It was You who inspired us to foster him in Your discipline, and none other. Your gifts I confess to You.

I wrote a book entitled, *De Magistro*,[280] a dialogue between Adeodatus and me. You know that everything attributed to my communicant are his, though he was then only sixteen. Many other gifts even more wonderful I found in him. His talent was a source of awe to me. Who but You could be the worker of such marvels?

You quickly removed Adeodatus' life from the earth, but I recall him to mind with a sense of security. I fear nothing for his childhood or youth, or for his entire life. We accepted him as our companion to be trained along with us in Your discipline as if he were the same age in grace as we were. So we were baptized and the anxiety about our past life left us.

During those days, I couldn't get enough of the wondrous sweetness of meditating on the depth of Your counsels concerning the salvation of the human race. I wept freely in Your hymns and Scripture songs, and was deeply moved by the voices of Your sweet-speaking Church! Their voices flowed into my ears and Your truth was poured into my heart. Often, the tide of my devotion overflowed, and my tears ran down. I was happy in all these things.

CHAPTER 7—PERSECUTION, MARTYRS AND MIRACLES

The church of Milan had only recently begun having everyone sing together. We eagerly did so with earnestness of voice and heart. It had only been about a year since Justina, the mother of the boy-emperor Valentinian, had persecuted Your servant Ambrose on behalf of her heresy—she had been seduced by the Arians. Many devoted people kept guard in the church, prepared to die with their bishop, Your servant. Among them was my mother, Your handmaid. She assumed a leading role during those anxious days and lived there in prayer. Though we were not entirely melted by the heat of Your Spirit, we nevertheless were excited by the alarmed and disturbed city.

This was when the Eastern Church custom began of singing hymns and psalms. This was so the people wouldn't be worn out with the tedium of lamentation. This custom, retained from then until now, has been imitated by nearly all Your congregations throughout the rest of the world.[281]

By a vision, You made known to Your renowned bishop the spot where lay the bodies of Gervasius and Protasius, the martyrs. You had preserved these men uncorrupted in Your secret storehouse for many years, so that You could produce them at the proper time to check a woman's fury—not just any woman, but a queen! When they were discovered and their remains brought with due honor to the basilica of Ambrose, many who were troubled by unclean spirits—the devils manifesting—were healed as they were carried along the road.

There was also a well-known man of the city, blind many years, who, when he had asked and learned the reason for the people's joy, rushed out and begged his guide to take him there. When he arrived, he begged to be permitted to touch his handkerchief to the coffin of Your saints—their death was precious in Your sight. When he had done this, and put it to his eyes, they were immediately opened. The fame of all this spread abroad, and from this Your glory shone more brightly. Also from this, the mind of that angry woman, the queen, though not embracing a full faith, was restrained from the fury of persecution.

Thanks to You, O my God. Where have You led my memory, that I should confess such things as these to You? I had forgotten them and passed them over, though they were great. However, at that time, when the sweet smell of Your ointment was so fragrant, I didn't run after You.[282] Therefore, I wept more bitterly as I listened to Your hymns, having so long hungered for You. Now I could breathe as much as the space allowed in this straw house.[283]

CHAPTER 8—MONICA'S DEVOTION

You, O Lord, make men of one mind to dwell in a single house. You also brought Evodius to join our company. He was a young man of our city, who, while serving as a secret service agent, was converted to You and baptized, whereupon he had left his secular service in preparation for Yours. We were together, and resolved to serve together in our devout purpose.

We looked for a place where we would be most useful in our service to You, and had planned on going back to Africa together. When we had gone as far as Ostia on the Tiber, my mother died.

I must hurry, or many things will be left out. Nevertheless, O my God, receive my confession and thanksgiving for the unnumbered things about which I am silent.

I will not omit anything I recall concerning my mother. She was Your handmaid who birthed me in her flesh, so that I could be born into this world's light. She also birthed me in her heart, so that I would be born to life eternal. I will not speak of _her_ gifts, but of _Your_ gift in her, because she neither made herself nor trained herself. You created her, and neither her father nor her mother knew what kind of person she would be.

Following the discipline of Christ, mother was trained in Your fear in the house of one of Your faithful servants, a sound member of Your Church. Yet my mother did not attribute this good training of hers as much to the diligence of her own mother as to that of a certain elderly maidservant who had nursed her father. This elderly servant carried mother's father around on her back, as women carry babies. She was highly respected by the heads of that Christian household because of her long service, extreme age and excellent character.

The care of her master's daughters was also committed to this precious elderly saint, and she performed her task with diligence. She was quite good at restraining them with a holy severity when necessary and instructing them with a sober wisdom. No matter how thirsty the children were, this servant woman wouldn't allow the children to drink even water except at mealtime. This way, she took precautions against an evil custom and added the wholesome advice:

> You drink water now because you don't control the wine. However, when you are married and mistresses of the pantry and cellar, you may not care for water, but the habit of drinking would be fixed.

Her method of instruction, and her authority, restrained the longing of their tender age. She regulated even the thirst of the girls so they no longer wanted what they ought not to have.

My mother told me that she once had a love for wine. During mother's childhood, when her parents sent her to draw wine from the cask, she would hold a cup under the tap to fill the bottles. Before she poured the wine into the bottle, she would wet her lips with a little of it—more than this her taste refused. She didn't do this out of any craving for drink, but out of the overflowing joy of that time in her life. She was young, and her youthful spirit bubbled over in innocent curiosity that is usually beaten down by the seriousness of old folks. Therefore, adding daily a little to that little, she slipped into the habit of eagerly drinking her little cup nearly full of wine, for "he who despises small things will fail little by little."[284]

Where was that wise older woman and her strict prohibition? Could anything prevail against our secret diseases if Your medicine, O Lord, did not watch over us? Though father, mother and nurturers are absent, You are present. You who have created us and called us, also work some good for our salvation through those in authority over us.

A Slave's Taunt

What did You do at that time, O my God? How did You heal my mother? How did You make her whole? Did You bring forth words from another woman's soul in the form of a hard and bitter insult? Didn't these words cut like a surgeon's knife, and with one thrust drain the infection of puss? The slave girl who often accompanied mother to the cellar began quarreling with her little mistress, as she sometimes did when the two were alone, throwing back in mother's teeth this vice of hers. This accusation, along with the insult of being called a drunkard, stung my mother. It was then that she saw her own vile behavior and immediately condemned and renounced it.

As the flattery of friends corrupts, so often the taunts of enemies instruct. Yet You repay them, not for the good You work through their means, but for the malice they intended. That angry slave girl wanted to infuriate her young mistress, not to cure her. That's why she spoke up while they were alone. Perhaps it was because their quarrel just happened at that time and place, or perhaps she was afraid of punishment for having told of it.

But You, O Lord, ruler of heaven and earth, change to Your purpose the deepest floods, and You control the turbulent tide of the ages. You healed one soul by the unsoundness of another. That way, nobody upon hearing of such a thing, could attribute it to his own power if another person whom he wishes to reform is reformed through a word of his.

Chapter 9—A Tribute to Monica

Mother was raised modestly and soberly, and was made subject to her parents by You, more than by her parents to You. When she was old enough to be married, she was given to a husband whom she served as her lord. Immediately, she began showing You to her husband by her behavior, in that You made her fair and reverently friendly, and admirable to her husband. She endured with patience his infidelity and never allowed any conflict with her husband on this subject. Mother prevailed upon You, and for Your mercy upon him until he would become faithful to her by believing in You.

Moreover, even though earnest in friendship, my father was also violent in anger. Mother had learned that an angry husband should not be resisted, either in deed or in word. Then, when she saw an opportune time after he had calmed down and peace was restored, mother would give him a reason for her conduct, if he had been excited unreasonably.

Many wives whose husbands were gentler than mothers bore the marks of beatings on their disfigured faces. Privately, they would blame the behavior of their husbands, but she would blame their tongues. Mother would admonish them seriously, though in a joking manner. She said that from the moment the wedding vows are read wives must consider them as instruments by which they are made servants. Then, always mindful of their condition, wives must not rise up in opposition to their husbands.

These women knew what a furious, bad-tempered husband mother endured. Therefore, they marveled that it had never been rumored, nor was there any mark to show, that Patricius had ever beaten his wife, or that there had been any domestic strife between them, even for a day. When these women asked her confidentially the reason for this, she taught them the rule I mentioned above. Those who observed it confirmed the wisdom of it and rejoiced...those who didn't were bullied and miserable.

Even mother's mother-in-law was conquered by her submission. She was at first prejudiced against mother by the lies of malicious servants, but mother conquered by submission, persevering through it with patience and meekness. Finally, the mother-in-law told her son about the lies of the meddling servants that had caused a rift between herself and her daughter-in-law, begging him to punish them for it. True to his mother's wish, and in the interest of family discipline to insure future harmony, he had those servants beaten who were identified as troublemakers. She promised a similar reward to anyone else, that in thinking to please her, they would say anything evil of her daughter-in-law. After this no one dared to do so, and they lived together with a wonderful sweetness of mutual good will.

O my God, my Mercy. Another great gift You gave to my mother, was that when possible she acted as a peacemaker between differing and discordant people. When mother heard bitter things on either side of a controversy—the kind of bloated and undigested discord which often belches forth bitter words, or when crude malice is breathed out by sharp tongues to a present friend against an absent enemy—she would say nothing about the one to the other except words of reconciliation. This may seem trivial, but I know countless persons who, because of the horrible infection of sin, repeat angry words spoken in passion against each other to an enemy, and then add words that were never said at all. It's not enough to simply avoid making the matter worse by keeping our mouth shut; we must also seek to smother harsh words with kind ones. Such a one was my mother. You were her most intimate instructor, because You taught her in the school of her heart.

Finally, toward the end of his earthly life, mother won her husband over to You. From then on she had no cause to complain of unfaithfulness in him because he became one of the faithful.

Mother was the servant of Your servants, and all who knew her greatly praised, honored, and loved You in her. They, through the witness of the fruits of a holy life, recognized You were present in her heart. Mother had "been the wife of one man."[285] She honored her parents, and guided her own home in piety. Mother was known for good works. She brought up her children, travailing in labor with them as often as she saw them swerving from You.

Mother served us as if she had been the daughter of us all. All of us, who lived together before mother's death in You, saw how she devoted as much care as if she were the mother of us all.

CHAPTER 10—SHARING CHRISTIAN ECSTASY WITH MOTHER

As the day approached when mother was to depart this life—a day which You knew, but which we didn't—she and I stood alone, looking out a window from which the garden could be seen. Here in this place, removed from the crowd, we were resting for the voyage after the stress of a long journey.

We talked quietly, "forgetting those things which are behind and reaching forward to those things which are ahead."[286] We were in the present time, and in the presence of Truth discussing the nature of the eternal life of the saints. For "eye has not seen, nor ear heard, nor have entered into the heart of man the things which God has prepared for those who love Him."[287]

We opened our hearts wide, thirsting for those heavenly streams of Your fountain: "For with You is the fountain of life."[288] We wanted to be sprinkled with its waters and be filled to our capacity so that we could weigh the truth of such a profound mystery.

Our conversation brought us to a point of heightened physical sense, and we were immersed in an intense illumination of physical light. We were surrounded by the sweetness of the eternal life to come, though nothing is worthy of its comparison. We were lifted heavenward with a more ardent love toward the One and Only, and gradually passed through all the levels of bodily objects. We even passed through the heavens where the sun, moon and stars shine on the earth. By an inner musing, we soared higher still, speaking of and marveling at Your works.

Seeking an Encounter with Wisdom

We came at last to our own minds and then went beyond them so we could climb as high as that region of unfailing plenty. This is where You fed Israel with the food of truth and where life is that Wisdom by whom all things are made, both which have been and which are to be. Wisdom is not made, but is as wisdom has been and forever will be. "To have been" and "to be hereafter" do not apply to wisdom, but only "to be." Wisdom is eternal and "to have been" and "to be hereafter" are not.

While we were talking and straining after wisdom, we barely touched her with all the efforts of our hearts. With a sigh, we left the first fruits of the Spirit bound to that ecstasy, and returned to the sound of our own voice, where the spoken word has both beginning and end.[289] What is like unto Your Word, O Lord, who remains in Himself without becoming old, and "renews all things?"[290]

What we said was something like this:

> If to anyone the turmoil of the flesh were silenced; the
> illusions of earth, water and air were silenced and the
> poles were silent as well; the very soul grew silent to itself,
> and went beyond itself by not thinking of itself; if fancies
> and imaginary revelations were silenced; if every tongue
> and every sign and every transient thing—for if anyone
> could hear them they would say, 'We did not create
> ourselves, but were created by Him who abides
> forever'—having uttered this should be silent; having
> stirred our ears to hear Him who created them, and if
> then He alone spoke, not through them but by Himself,
> that we might hear His word, not in fleshly tongue or
> angelic voice, nor sound of thunder, nor the obscurity of
> a parable, but might hear Him for whose sake we love
> these things, if we could hear Him without these, as we
> now strain ourselves to do, we then with rapid thought
> might touch on that Eternal Wisdom which abides over
> all.
>
> If this could be sustained, and other visions of a far
> different kind be taken away, and this one should so
> enrapture, absorb and envelop its beholder in these
> inward joys, that his life might be eternally like that one
> moment of knowledge which we now sighed after,
> wouldn't this be the reality of the saying, 'Enter into the
> joy of Your Lord'?[291]
>
> When shall such a thing be? Will it not be 'when we
> all shall rise again,' and shall it not be that 'all things will
> be changed'?[292]

Such a thought I expressed, and if not in this manner and in
these words, still, O Lord, You know that on that day, mother and
I were talking so.

This world, with all its joys, seemed cheap to us even as we spoke. Then my mother said:

> Son, I no longer have any pleasure in anything in this life. Now that my hopes in this world are satisfied, I don't know what more I want here or even why I'm here. There was one thing for which I wished to tarry in this life, and that was to see you become a Catholic Christian before I died. My God has answered this more than abundantly. Now I see you as His servant, rejecting all earthly happiness. What more am I to do here?

CHAPTER 11—MOTHER'S DEATH

I don't remember what I said in reply to mother's statement. However, it was scarcely five days later, certainly not much more, that she was gravely ill with a fever. While she was sick, she fainted one day and was for a short time unconscious. We hurried to her aid, and when she regained her senses, mother looked at my brother[293] and me and asked, "Where was I?" Then looking intently at us, mute in our grief, she said, "Here in this place you will bury your mother."

I was silent, holding back my tears. My brother said something about wishing mother the happier choice of dying in her own country and not abroad. When she heard this, she looked at him intently and with an anxious countenance, because he savored such earthly concerns. Then, gazing at me mother said, "See how he speaks." Soon after, she said to us both: "Lay this body anywhere, and do not let the care of it be a trouble to you at all. Only this I ask: that you will remember me at the Lord's altar, wherever you are." After she had expressed her wish as clearly as she could, she became silent, and in heavy pain her sickness increased.

However, as I thought about Your gifts, O invisible God, which You plant in the heart of Your faithful ones and from which such marvelous fruits spring up, I rejoiced and gave thanks to You. I remembered how she had always been so concerned about her burial place, by the body of her husband, which she had provided and prepared for herself. Mother and father had lived peaceably together, so her desire had always been that the two of them, so united on earth, should lie in the same grave—so little is the human mind capable of grasping things divine. This futile thought had left mother's heart because of the bounty of Your goodness.

I joyfully marveled at what mother had told me when she asked, "What is there here for me to do any more?" She appeared at that time not to desire to die in her own country. Later I heard that during our stay in Ostia, she had told some of my friends about her contempt of this life and the blessing of death. They were amazed at the courage God had given her, a woman, and asked her if she dreaded having her body buried so far from her home town. She replied: "Nothing is far from God. I don't fear that He wouldn't know the place from where He will resurrect me at the end of time."

So it was, that on the ninth day of her sickness, in the fifty-sixth year of her life and the thirty-third of mine,[294] mother's religious and devout soul was released from the body.

Chapter 12—Grieving for Monica

I closed mother's eyes, and suddenly a great sadness overcame my heart. Tears flooded from my eyes, but at the strong urging of my mind the fountain was staunched. Nevertheless, sorrow rippled through me in great convulsions.

When mother breathed her last, her grandson, Adeodatus began wailing. We quieted him, like I was quieting my own childlike feelings. Mine were seeking escape in tears through the youthful voice of my heart, but were held back and silenced. We didn't consider it fitting to celebrate mother's death with tearful wails and grieving. This is how those who die unhappy or are altogether dead are mourned. However, mother neither died unhappy nor did she altogether die, for of this the witness of her good life assures us. Her "sincere faith"[295] and other manifest evidence convinced us of her eternal life.

What, then, hurt me so grievously in my heart? Was it because the sweet and dear habit of living together with mother was suddenly broken? I was full of joy because of her testimony in her last illness. She praised my dutiful attention and called me kind. She recalled with great affection that she had never heard any harsh or reproachful sound from my mouth against her. However, O my God who made us, how can the honor I paid her compare with her service to me? I was left destitute of great comfort in her, and my soul was stricken. My life was torn apart because it had been made one out of hers and mine together.[296]

When Adeodatus stopped weeping, Evodius picked up the Psalms and began to sing. The entire household joined in singing, "I will sing of mercy and justice to You, O LORD."[297] When others heard what we were doing, many of the brethren and religious women came together. While those whose duty it was to prepare for the funeral went about their task, I visited in another part of the house with those who thought I should not be left alone.

By this balm of truth, I softened my anguish known only to You. Those visiting with me were unaware of it and listened intently, thinking I was free of any sorrow. But in Your ears, where none of them heard, I reproached myself for the mildness of my feelings, and restrained the flow of my grief, which bowed a little to my will. The convulsion of grief returned, and I knew what I repressed in my heart, even though it did not make me burst forth into tears or even change my countenance. I was greatly annoyed that these human feelings had such power over me, which in the due order and destiny of our natural condition must necessarily happen. So with a new sorrow, I sorrowed for my sorrow and was wasted with twofold sadness.

Grieving for Mother

Therefore, when the body was carried out, we went and returned without tears. I didn't weep during either of the prayers that we poured forth to You, when the sacrifice of our redemption was offered up to You for her. This was done with the body placed by the side of the grave as is the custom there, and before it's lowered into it. However, I was grievously sad in secret throughout the day. With a troubled mind, I entreated You, as I could, to heal my sorrow…but You did not. I now believe that, by this one lesson, You were fixing in my memory the power of the bonds of habit, even on a mind which no longer feeds upon deception.

It occurred to me then, that it would be good to go and bathe. I had heard that the Greek word for bath, balneum, took its name from the word balaneion, because it washes anxiety from the mind. This also I confess to Your mercy, "O Father of the fatherless."[298] I bathed and felt the same as I had before because the bitterness of my grief was not sweated from my heart.

I slept, but when I awoke, I found that my grief was still very deep. As I lay there on my bed, those true verses of Ambrose came to my mind:

O God, Creator of us all,
Guiding the orbs celestial,
Clothing the day with lovely light,
Appointing gracious sleep by night:
Your grace our wearied limbs restore
To strengthened labor, as before,
And ease the grief of tired minds
From that deep torment which it finds.[299]

Little by little, my former memories of Your handmaid, my mother, returned. My recollection of her devout life toward You, her holy tenderness and attentiveness toward us, which had suddenly been taken away, provided comfort for me to weep in Your sight. So I wept for her and for me, about her and about me. Thus I released the tears that before I had repressed. I allowed them to flow at will and spread them out as a pillow beneath my heart. My heart rested on those tears, for Your ears were near me, not the ears of a man who would have made callous comments about my weeping.

Now, I confess to You in writing, O Lord! Read it, all who will and comment how you will. My mother, who was for a while dead to my eyes and who had for many years wept for me that I might live in Your eyes, was very dear to me. Therefore, if I've sinned in weeping for my mother for part of an hour, don't laugh at me. Instead, be generous in love and weep with me. Weep for my sins against You, the Father of all the brethren or Your Christ.

Chapter 13—A Prayer for the Souls of all Believers

Now that my heart is healed of that wound—so far as it can be charged against me as a carnal affection—I pour out to You, O God, on behalf of Your handmaid, tears of a very different sort. These tears flow from a spirit broken by the thought of the danger of every soul that dies in Adam. Mother had been "made alive" in Christ[300] even before she was freed from the flesh, and had lived to praise Your name both by her faith and by her life. However, I wouldn't dare to say that from the time You regenerated her by baptism, no word came out of her mouth against Your precepts.

Your Son, the Truth, has declared that, "whoever says, 'You fool!' shall be in danger of hell fire."[301] There would be doom even for the life of a praiseworthy man if You judged it with Your mercy set aside. But You don't stringently inquire after our sins, so we hope with confidence to find some place in Your presence. When someone recounts his actual merits to You, what is he doing but recounting to You Your own gifts? Oh, if only men would know themselves as men, then "he that glories" would "glory in the LORD"![302]

Therefore, O my Praise and my Life, O God of my heart, forgetting for a moment mother's good deeds for which I give joyful thanks to You, I now beseech You for her sins. Listen to me through that Medicine of Your wounds, who was hung on the tree and who now sits at Your right hand "making intercession for us."[303] I know that she acted in mercy, and from the heart forgave her debtors their debts.[304] I ask You also to forgive her debts, whatever she contracted during so many years since the water of salvation. Forgive her, O Lord; forgive her, I pray, "enter not into judgment" with her.[305] Let Your mercy be exalted above Your justice, for Your words are true and You have promised mercy to the merciful, that the merciful shall obtain mercy.[306] This is Your gift: to have mercy on whom You will and to have compassion on whom You have compassion.[307]

I believe You have already done what I ask. Nevertheless, "accept, I pray, the freewill offerings of my mouth, O LORD."[308] For when the day of mother's death was close, she took no thought to have her body sumptuously wrapped or embalmed with spices.

Nor did she covet a handsome monument, or even care to be buried in her own country for that matter. About these things she gave no instructions at all, but only wished to have her name remembered at Your altar. That was where she had served without missing a single day, and where she knew that the holy sacrifice was dispensed which blots out our sin. That is also where the enemy is vanquished who, when he summed up her offenses and searched for something to bring against her, could find nothing in her in Him.

Secure in Christ

Who will restore to God the innocent blood? Who will repay the price with which He bought us, so as to take us from Him? To the sacrament of our redemption Your handmaid bound her soul by the bond of faith. Let none separate her from Your protection. Let not the "lion" and "dragon" bar her way by force or fraud. For she will not reply that she owes nothing, lest she be convicted and duped by that cunning deceiver. Rather, she will answer that Jesus forgives her sins. No one is able to repay the price that He, who owed us nothing, paid for us all.

Therefore, let mother rest in peace with her husband. She was married to no other man than he, and she obeyed him patiently, bringing fruit to You that she might also win him for You. O Lord my God, inspire Your servants, my brothers. Inspire Your sons, my masters, who with voice and heart and writings I serve, that as many of them that read these confessions might also at Your altar remember Monica, Your handmaid, together with Patricius, once her husband. These two You used to bring me into this life in a manner I know not.

May those who read these confessions remember my parents with pious affection in this transitory life, and remember my brothers under You, our Father, in our Catholic mother. May they remember my fellow citizens in the eternal Jerusalem, for which Your people sigh in their pilgrimage from birth until their return. Thus will be fulfilled what my mother desired of me, more richly in the prayers of so many gained for her through these confessions of mine than by my prayers alone.

BOOK TEN

Probing the Depths of Self

Now Augustine moves from autobiography to self-analysis. He turns from memories of the past to the mysteries of memory itself. Doing so, Augustine examines his motive for writing "Confessions," and seeks to chart the path by which men come to God. However, this brings him into an intricate analysis of memory and its relation to the self and its powers. Then, Augustine explores the meaning and mode of true prayer. In his conclusion, he embarks on a detailed analysis of the appetite and the various temptations that the flesh and the soul have inherited. Finally he comes to see how necessary and right it was for Jesus, the Mediator between God and man, to have been the God-Man.

CHAPTER 1—I WANT TO KNOW GOD

Let me know You, O my Knower; let me know You even as I am known.[309] O Strength of my soul, enter it and prepare it for You so that You may have and hold it, without "spot or blemish."[310] This is my hope, therefore I have spoken, and in this hope I rejoice whenever I rejoice in harmony with You.

As for the other things of this life, they deserve less of our supplication. The more we are prayerful about them, the less men care for them—though for some we should be prayerful all the more. "You desire truth"[311] and "he who does the truth comes to the light."[312] This is what I wish to do through confession in my heart before You, and in my writings before many witnesses.

CHAPTER 2—MY REASON FOR CONFESSING

What is there in me that could be hidden from You, Lord, to whose eyes the abyss of my conscience are exposed, even if I were unwilling to confess it to You? In doing so I would only hide You from myself, not myself from You. My groaning is witness to the fact that I am dissatisfied with myself, but You shine forth and satisfy.

You are beloved and desired, so that I blush for myself, renounce myself and choose You, for I can neither please You nor myself except in You. To You, then, O Lord, I am completely exposed, whatever I am, and I have already said with what gain I may confess to You. I do not confess with words and sounds of the flesh but with the words of the soul and with the sound of my thoughts, which Your ear hears. When I'm wicked, to confess to You means nothing less than to be dissatisfied with myself. However, when I am truly devout, it means not attributing my virtue to myself.

You, O Lord, bless the righteous, but first You justify him while he is yet ungodly. Therefore, my confession, O my God, is made unto You silently in Your sight—yet not silently. As far as sound is concerned, it is silent. But in strong affection it cries aloud. I do not give voice to something that sounds right to men, which You have not heard from me before, nor do You hear anything from me which You did not first say to me.

CHAPTER 3—WHY THESE CONFESSIONS?

What is it to me that men hear my confessions as if it were they who were going to cure all my infirmities? People are curious to know the lives of others, but slow to correct their own. Why are they anxious to hear from me what I am, when they are unwilling to hear from You what they are? And how can they tell when they hear what I say about myself whether I speak the truth, since no man knows what's in a man "except the spirit of the man which is in him"?[313]

However, if men were to hear from You something concerning themselves, they would not be able to say, "The Lord is lying." For what does it mean to hear from You about themselves but to know themselves? Furthermore, who is he that knows himself and says, "This is false," unless he himself is lying? "Love believes all things"[314]—at least among those who are bound together in love by its bonds—therefore, I confess to You, O Lord. I do this so that men may also hear. I can't prove to them that I confess the truth, yet those whose ears love opens will believe me.

But will You, O my inner Physician, make clear to me what profit I am to gain in doing this? You have "forgiven and covered"[315] my sins so that You could make me blessed in You. This was done by transforming my soul by faith and Your sacrament. Therefore, when the confessions of my past sins are read and heard, may hearts be stirred so they will stop dozing along in despair, saying, "I cannot." Instead, awake these hearts in the love of Your mercy and the sweetness of Your grace. Let these hearts see that he that is weak is strong, provided he is made conscious of his own weakness.

Those who are good will be pleased to hear about the past errors of one who is now free of them. These folk will be delighted, not because of the errors, but because the errors once were and are so no longer.

O Lord my God, my conscience makes daily confession to You far more confident in the hope of Your mercy than in my own innocence. Therefore, what profit is there in confessing to men in Your presence through this book, both what I am now, as well as what I have been? For I have seen and spoken of my harvest of things past. But what am I *now*, at this very moment of making my confessions? Many different people desire to know, both those who know me and those who don't. Some have heard about me or from me, but they aren't close to my heart. They have the desire to hear me confess what I am within, where they can neither see nor hear. They desire as those willing to believe—but will they understand? For the love by which they are good tells them that I am not lying in my confessions, and the love in them believes me.

Chapter 4—My Desire for these Confessions

What do people hope to gain in this? Will they wish me happiness when they learn how near I have approached You by Your gifts? Will they pray for me when they learn how much I'm still held back by my own weight? To such as these I will declare myself. For it is no small gain, O Lord my God, that many people should give thanks to You on my account and that many should entreat You for my sake. Let the brotherly soul love in me what You teach him should be loved, and let him grieve in me what You teach him should be grieved.

Let it be the soul of a brother that rejoices or is sorrowful with me, and not a stranger. Let it not be one of those "foreigners, Whose mouth speaks vain words, And whose right hand *is* a right hand of falsehood."[316] But let my brother do it who, when he approves of me, rejoices for me, but when he disapproves of me is sorry for me. Whether my brother approves or disapproves, I know that he loves me.

To such I will declare myself. Let them be refreshed by my good deeds and sigh over my evil ones. My good deeds are Your acts and Your gifts; my evil ones are my own faults and Your judgment. Let them breathe expansively at the one and sigh over the other. Let hymns and tears ascend in Your sight out of their brotherly hearts, which are Your censers.[317] O Lord, who takes delight in the incense of Your holy temple, have mercy upon me according to Your great mercy, for Your name's sake. Do not, on any account whatever, abandon what You have begun in me. Go on, rather, to complete what is yet imperfect in me.[318]

The Fruit of My Confessions

This, then, is the fruit of my confessions—not what I was, but what I am. I don't desire to confess this before You alone, in secret praise with trembling and a secret sorrow with hope. I want to confess in the hearing of the believing sons of men as well. These are the companions of my joy and sharers of my mortality. These are my fellow citizens and fellow pilgrims, those who have gone before and those who are to follow after, and the comrades of my present way as well. These are Your servants, my brothers, whom You desire to be Your sons. They are my masters, whom You have commanded me to serve if I desire to live with and in You.

However, Your Word would mean little if it were only words with no preceding action. Therefore, I confess both in act and word. I do this under Your wings, in a danger too great to risk if it were not that under Your wings my soul is subject to You.

My weakness is known to You. I am insufficient, but my Father lives forever, and my Defender is sufficient for me. He is the Selfsame who begat me and watches over me. You are the Selfsame who are all my good. You are the Omnipotent, who are with me, even before I am with You. To those, therefore, whom You commanded me to serve, I will declare, not what I was, but what I now am and what I will continue to be. However, I don't judge myself. Therefore, let me be heard.

CHAPTER 5—GETTING TO KNOW GOD

You, O Lord, are who judges me. No man "knows the things of a man, except the spirit of the man which is in him."[319] However, there is something of a man that "the spirit of the man which is in him" does not know itself. But You, O Lord, made him and knows him completely. Though in Your sight I despise myself and count myself nothing but dust and ashes, even I know something about You that I don't know about myself, for "now we see through a glass darkly," not yet "face to face."[320]

Therefore, as long as I journey away from You, I am more present with myself than with You. I know that You can't suffer violence, but I don't know what temptations I can resist and those I can't. But there is hope, because You are faithful and will not allow me to be tempted beyond my ability to resist. Instead, with the temptation You will also make a way of escape so that I will be able to bear it.

I would therefore, confess what I know about myself, and will confess what I don't know about myself as well. What I do know of myself, I know from Your enlightening of me. What I don't know of myself, I will continue to not know until the time when my "darkness is as the noonday"[321] in Your sight.

CHAPTER 6—ALL CREATION REVEALS GOD

I am fully certain that I love You, O Lord. You have smitten my heart with Your Word, and I have loved You. The heavens, the earth, and all that is in them—on every side—tell me to love You, and they never cease to tell this to all men, "so that they are without excuse."[322] Wherefore, still more deeply You will have mercy on whom You will have mercy, and compassion on whom You will have compassion.[323] For otherwise, both heaven and earth would broadcast Your praises to deaf ears.

What is it that I love in loving You? Not physical beauty, nor the splendor of time. It's not the radiance of the light, which is so pleasant to our eyes, or the sweet melodies of various kinds of music. Nor is it the fragrant smell of flowers and ointments and spices, it's not manna and honey or the limbs embraced in physical love. It's not these that I love when I love You, my God.

Nevertheless, it's true that I love a certain kind of light and sound, fragrance and food, and embrace in loving my God. For You are the light and sound and fragrance and food and embracement of my inner man. You are the light that shines into my soul which no physical place can contain, where time does not snatch away the lovely sound, where no breeze disperses the sweet fragrance, where no eating diminishes the food, and where there is an embrace that can't be torn asunder. This is what I love when I love my God.

What is this God? I asked the earth, and it answered, "I am not He." Everything in the earth made the same confession. I asked the sea and the deeps and the creeping things, and they replied, "We are not your God; seek above us." I asked the fleeting winds, and the entire air with its inhabitants answered, "Anaximenes[324] was deceived; I am not God." I asked the heavens, the sun, moon, and stars; and they answered, "Neither are we the God whom you seek."

God Speaks Through Beauty and Order

I replied to all these things that surround me: "You have told me about my God, that you are not He. Tell me something about Him." With a loud voice they all cried out, "He made us." My question had come from observing them, and their reply came from their beauty of order.

I then turned my thoughts inward to myself and said, "Who are you?" And I answered, "A man." There is in me both a body and a soul—the one without, the other within. In which of these should I have sought my God? I had already sought with my body from earth to heaven as far as I was able to see with my eyes. However, the inner part is the better part. As both ruler and judge, the messengers of my senses reported the answers of heaven and earth and everything therein that said, "We are not God, but He made us."

My inner man knew these things through the ministry of the outer man. The inner man, my soul, knew all this through the senses of my body.[325] I asked the entire frame of earth about my God, and it answered, "I am not He, but He made me."

Isn't this beauty of form visible to all whose senses are unimpaired? Why, then, does it not say the same things to all? Animals, both small and great, see but are unable to question its meaning. Their senses are not endowed with the reason that would enable them to judge the evidence their senses report.

Ask the Creator, Not the Creation

However, man can frame the question so that "His invisible *attributes* are clearly seen, being understood by the things that are made."[326] But men love these created things too much. They are brought into subjection to them, and as subjects, are unable to judge.

Created things don't reply to their questioners unless they can make rational judgments. Creatures will not alter their beauty of form if one man simply sees what another both sees and questions. Therefore, the world seems to be one way to this man and another to that. The world appears the same way to both, but is mute to this one and speaks to that one.

Actually, creation speaks to all, but the only ones who understand it compare the voice received from without with the truth within. Truth says to me, "Neither heaven nor earth nor anybody is your God." Their very nature tells this to the one beholding them. "They are a mass, less in part than the whole." Now, O my soul, you are my better part, and to you I speak; since you animate the entire mass of your body, giving it life, whereas no body furnishes life to a body. But your God is the life of your life.

Chapter 7—The Power of Life

So what is it that I love when I love my God? Who is He that is beyond the topmost point of my soul? Yet by this very soul I will mount up to Him. I will soar beyond that power of mine by which I am united to the body, and by which its entire structure is filled with life. Yet it's not by that vital power that I find my God. Otherwise, "the horse and the mule, which have no understanding,"327 might also find Him. They have the same vital power by which their bodies live.

Besides the power by which I animate my body, there is another by which I endow my flesh with sense. This is a power that the Lord provided for me that commands that the eye is not to hear and the ear is not to see. Rather, I am to see by the eye and to hear by the ear. This power also gives to each of the other senses its own proper place and function. Through this diversity, I, the single mind, act.

However, I will soar beyond this power of mine, because horses and mules have it too. They also perceive through their bodily senses.

Chapter 8—The Mystery of Memory

I will soar beyond this power of my nature, still rising by degrees toward Him who made me. I will enter the fields and spacious halls of memory, where are stored as treasures the countless images that have been brought into them from all manner of things by the senses. There, in the memory, is stored what we think about, either by enlarging or reducing our perceptions, or by altering one way or another that which the senses have made contact with. Memory also holds everything else that has been entrusted to it and stored up in it that oblivion has not yet swallowed up and buried.

When I go into this storehouse, I ask for what I want be brought forth. Some things appear immediately, but others require a longer search. When found, they are dragged out, as it were, from some hidden recess. Other things rush out in crowds, while on the other hand, something else sought and inquired for, leaps into view as if to say, "Is it not we, perhaps?" These I brush away with the hand of my heart from the face of my memory, until finally the thing I want makes its appearance out of its secret cell.

Some things suggest themselves without effort and in continuous order, just as they are called for. These things that come first give place to those that follow, and in so doing are treasured up again to be available when I want them. All of this happens when I repeat a thing from memory.

All these things, each one of which came into memory in its own particular way, are stored up separately and under the general categories of understanding. For example, light, colors, and the shape of things enter through the eyes. Sounds enter through the ears, odors enter through the nose, and flavors through the mouth. The nerves of the body permit entry to the sensations of what is hard or soft, hot or cold, smooth or rough, heavy or light, and whether external or internal to the body. Thus the vast cavern of memory, with its countless mysterious recesses receives all these things and stores them for recall when required.

What is Stored in Memory

Each experience enters by its own door and is stored in the memory. Yet the things themselves do not enter—only the images of the things perceived are there for thought to remember. Who knows how these images are formed, even if it's evident which of the senses brought which perception in and stored it? Even when I'm in darkness and silence I can bring forth colors in my memory if I wish. I can discern between black and white and the other shades as I wish, and at the same time, sounds don't break in to disturb what is drawn in by my eyes. This is key, because the sounds are also stored there, yet as it were, apart.

I can summon sounds too, if I please, and they are immediately present in memory. Although my tongue is at rest and my throat is silent, I can sing. However, those images of color, which are as truly present as before, do not interpose themselves or interrupt while another treasure that had flowed in through the ears is being thought about. Similarly, all the other things that were brought in by all the other senses, I can recall at my pleasure. I can distinguish the scent of lilies from that of violets while actually smelling nothing, and I prefer honey to beer, a smooth thing to a rough, even though I am neither tasting nor handling them, but only remembering them.

All this is done within myself, in that huge hall of my memory. For in it, heaven, earth, and sea are present to me, and whatever I can ponder about them, except what I have forgotten. There I also meet myself and remember myself[328]—what, when, or where I did a thing, and how I felt when I did it. There also, is everything that I remember, either having experienced it myself or been told about it by others. Out of the same storehouse, with these past impressions, I can construct first this, now that. I can see an image of things that I either have experienced or have believed on the basis of experience, and from these I can further construct future actions, events, and hopes. I can meditate on all these things as if they were present as well.

"I will do this or that," I say to myself in that vast recess of my mind. With its full store of so many and such great images, I declare "and this or that will follow upon it." "O that this or that could happen!" "God prevent this or that." I speak to myself in this way. When I speak, the images of what I am speaking about are present out of the same store of memory. If the images were absent I could say nothing at all about them.

The Power of Memory

Great is this power of memory, exceedingly great, O my God. It's a large and boundless inner hall! Who has plumbed the depths of it? Yet it's a power of my mind, and it belongs to my nature. However, I don't myself apprehend all that I am. Thus the mind is far too narrow to contain itself. But where can that part of it be which it does not contain? Is it outside and not in itself? How can it be that the mind cannot grasp itself?

A great marvel rises in me, and astonishment seizes me. Men go forth to marvel at the heights of mountains and the huge waves of the sea. The broad flow of the rivers, the vastness of the ocean, and the orbits of the stars mesmerize them, yet they neglect to marvel at themselves. Nor do they wonder how it is that, when I spoke of all these things, I was not looking at them with my eyes. Yet I couldn't have spoken about them had it not been that I was actually seeing in my memory those mountains and waves and rivers and stars that I've seen. In my memory, I saw that ocean which I believe in, and with the same vast spaces between them as when I saw them outside me.

However, when I saw these things outside me, I did not take them into me by seeing them—the things themselves are not inside me, only their images are. Yet I knew through which physical sense each experience had made an impression on me.

CHAPTER 9—MEMORY'S UNLIMITED CAPACITY

This is not all that the unlimited capacity of my memory stores up. All that I have learned of the liberal sciences, and have not forgotten, has been removed to an inner place, which is not a place. Of these things it is not the images that are retained, but the things themselves. For what literature and logic are, and what I know about how many different kinds of questions there are, these are stored in my memory as they are. I have not taken in the image and left the thing outside.

It's not as though a noise had sounded and passed away like a voice heard by the ear. It leaves a trace by which it can be called into memory again as if it were still sounding in my mind, though it no longer sounded outside. Nor is it the same as an odor that, even after it has passed and vanished into the wind, affects the sense of smell. This then conveys into the memory the *image* of the smell, which is what we recall and re-create. Likewise, food once in the belly now has no taste and yet does have a kind of taste in the memory, or like anything that is felt by the body through the sense of touch. These still remain as an image in the memory after the external object is removed. For these things themselves are not put into the memory. Only the images of these things are gathered with a marvelous quickness and stored, as it were, in the most wonderful filing system, and are then produced in a marvelous way by the act of remembering.

CHAPTER 10—MEMORY OF LITERATURE AND SCHOLASTICS

There are three kinds of questions: Whether a thing is? What it is? Of what kind it is? Do I, then, retain the image of the sounds these words of which literature and scholastics are composed? I know that the sounds pass through the air with a noise and now no longer exist. But the things themselves, which were signified by those sounds I never could reach by any sense of the body nor see them at all except in my mind. Therefore, what I have stored in my memory was not their signs, but the things signified.

How these sounds entered me, let them tell who can. For I examine all the gates of my flesh, but can't find the door by which any of them entered. For the eyes say, "If they were colored, we reported that." The ears say, "If they gave any sound, we gave notice of that." The nostrils say, "If they smell, they passed in by us." The sense of taste says, "If they have no flavor, don't ask me about them." The sense of touch says, "If it had no bodily mass, I did not touch it, and if I never touched it, I gave no report about it."

Where, then, and how did these things enter into my memory? I don't know. When I first learned them, it was not that I believed them on the credit of another man's mind, but I recognized them in my own. I saw them as true, took them into my mind and laid them up, so to say, where I could get at them again whenever I wanted. There they were, then, even before I learned them, but they were not in my memory. Where were they, then? How does it come about that when they were spoken of, I could acknowledge them and say, "So it is; it's true"? Were they already in my memory, though far back and hidden in the more secret recesses, so that unless the teaching of another drew them out, I would never have been able to think of them at all?

Chapter 11—Learning Builds by Careful Observation

Thus we discover that learning those things whose images we do not take in by our senses, but which we intuitively know without images and as they actually are, is nothing else except the gathering together of those same things which the memory already contains. These things are held in an indiscriminate and confused manner. Learning assembles them by careful observation because they are at hand in the memory. Though they formerly lay hidden, scattered, or neglected, they now come easily to present themselves to the mind which is familiar with them.

How many things of this sort has my memory stored up? How many have already been discovered and laid up for ready reference? These are the things we may be said to have learned and now know. However, if I cease to recall them even for short intervals of time, they are again so submerged that they must be drawn out again as if new from the same place. It's as if they slide back into the further reaches of the memory, for there is nowhere else for them to have gone, and must be collected again so that they can become known. In other words, they must be gathered up from their dispersion.

Chapter 12—Memory of Time and Space

The memory also contains the principles and the unnumbered laws of numbers and dimensions. None of these have been impressed on the memory by a physical sense, because they have neither color, sound, taste, nor sense of touch. I have heard the sound of the words by which these things are signified when they are discussed, but the sounds are one thing, the things another. The sounds are one thing in Greek and another in Latin, but the things themselves are neither Greek nor Latin nor any other language.

I've seen the lines of the craftsmen, the finest of which are like a spider's web, but mathematical lines are different. They are not the images of such things as the eye of my body has shown me. The man who knows them does so without any thought of physical objects, but knows them within himself. I have perceived with all the senses of my body the numbers we use in counting, but the numbers by which we count are far different from these. They are not the images of these, they simply are. Let the man who doesn't see these things mock me for saying them, and I'll pity him while he laughs at me.

Chapter 13—The Power of Memory to Recall

All these things I hold in my memory, and I remember how I learned them. I also remember many things that I have heard falsely argued against them. Even if they are false, it's not false that I have remembered them. I also remember that I have distinguished between the truth and false objections, and now I see that it's one thing to distinguish these things and another to remember that I distinguished them when I have thought about them.

I remember two things: I've often understood these things. I store in my memory what I distinguish and comprehend of them. That way, I may later remember them just as I now understand them. I remember that I remembered, so that if afterward I call to mind that I was once able to remember these things it will be through the power of memory that I recall it.

Chapter 14—The Mind is Separate from the Body

The memory also retains the feelings of the mind, not in the manner in which the mind itself experienced them, but differently according to a power peculiar to memory. Without being joyous now, I can remember that I once was joyous. Likewise, without being sad, I can recall my past sadness. I can remember past fears without fear, and former desires without desire. Again, the contrary happens. Sometimes when I am joyous I remember my past sadness, and when sad, remember past joy.

This is not to be marveled at as far as the body is concerned; for the mind is one thing and the body another.[329] Therefore, if when I'm happy I recall some past bodily pain, it's not so strange—but even as this memory is experienced, it's identical with the mind. For example, when we tell someone to remember something we say, "See that you bear this in mind." When we forget a thing, we say, "It didn't enter my mind" or "It slipped my mind." Thus we call memory itself "mind."

Since this is so, how can it be that when I am joyful I can still remember past sorrow? Thus the mind has joy, and the memory has sorrow—the mind is joyful from the joy that is in it, yet the memory is not sad from the sadness that is in it. Is it possible that the memory does not belong to the mind? Who will say so? The memory is doubtless the "belly of the mind." Joy and sadness are like sweet and bitter foods that when committed to the memory is "passed into the belly" where they can be stored but no longer tasted. It's ridiculous to use this as an analogy, but they are not dissimilar.

Four Basic Emotions

From memory I produce the statement that there are four basic emotions of the mind: desire, joy, fear, and sadness. Whatever analysis I'm able to make of these, by dividing each into its particular species and defining it, I still find what to say in my memory. It's from my memory that I draw it out. However, I'm not moved by any of these emotions when I call them to mind by remembering them. Moreover, before I recalled them and thought about them, they were there in the memory, which is how they could be brought forth in remembrance.

Perhaps, just as food is brought up out of the belly of a cow chewing its cud, so also these things are drawn up out of the memory by recall. But why, then, doesn't the man who is thinking about the emotions, and is thus recalling them, feel in the midst of his reflection the sweetness of joy or the bitterness of sadness? Is the comparison unlike in this because it is not complete at every point?

Who would willingly speak on these subjects, if as often as we used the term sadness or fear, we would be compelled to be sad or fearful? However, we couldn't speak of them if we didn't find them in our memories. Not merely as the sounds of the words, because their images are impressed on it by the physical senses, but also the idea of the things themselves. We didn't receive this by any gate of the flesh, but the mind recognizes it through the experience of its own passions. This, then, the mind has entrusted to the memory, or else the memory itself has retained it without it being entrusted to the memory.

CHAPTER 15—IMAGES IN THE MEMORY

Whether all this is by means of images or not, who can rightly say? If I name a stone or name the sun, those things aren't present to my senses themselves. However, their images are present in my memory. I name some pain of the body, yet it's not present when there is no pain, but if there were not some image of it in my memory, I couldn't even speak of it, nor would I be able to distinguish it from pleasure.

I name bodily health when I am sound in body, and the thing itself is indeed present in me. At the same time, unless there were some image of it in my memory, I could not possibly call to mind what the sound of this name signified. Nor would sick people know what was meant when health was named, unless the same image were preserved by the power of memory, even though health was absent from their body.

I can name the numbers we use in counting, and it's not their images but the numbers themselves that are in my memory. I name the image of the sun, and this too is in my memory. I don't recall the image of that image, but that image itself, for the image itself is present when I remember it. I name memory and I know what I name. But where do I know it except in the memory itself? Is it also present to itself by its image and not by itself?

Chapter 16—Remembering to Forget, Forgetting to Remember

When I mention forgetfulness, and understand what I mean by it, how could I understand it if I didn't remember it? If I don't refer to the sound of the name, but to the thing which the name signifies, how could I know what that sound signified if I had forgotten what the name means? Therefore, when I remember memory, then memory is present to itself by itself, but when I remember forgetfulness then both memory and forgetfulness are present together—the memory by which I remember the forgetfulness, which I remember.

What is forgetfulness except the deprivation of memory? How, then, is that present to my memory which, when it controls my mind, I cannot remember? If what we remember we store up in our memory...and if we could never know the thing signified by the word when we heard it, unless we remembered forgetfulness...then forgetfulness is contained in the memory. It's present so that we don't forget it, but since it's present, we do forget.

From this, we can infer that when we remember forgetfulness, it's not present to the memory through itself, but through its image. If forgetfulness were present through itself, it wouldn't lead us to remember, but only to forget.

Who will work this out someday? Who can understand how it is?

Truly, O Lord, I toil with this and labor in myself. I've become a troublesome field that requires hard labor and heavy sweat. For we are not now searching out the tracts of heaven, or measuring the distances of the stars or inquiring about the weight of the earth.

Remembering Forgetfulness

It is I myself—I, the mind—who remember. This isn't much to marvel at, if what I myself am isn't far from me. What is nearer to me than myself? I'm unable to comprehend the force of my own memory, though I couldn't even call my own name without it. But what shall I say, when it's clear to me that I remember forget-fulness? Should I affirm that what I remember is not in my memory? Or should I say that forgetfulness is in my memory so that I shouldn't forget?

Both of these views are absurd. Is there a third view? How can I say that the image of forgetfulness is retained by my memory, and not forgetfulness itself when I remember it? How can I say this? In order for the image of anything to be imprinted on the memory the thing itself must necessarily have been present first. If not present, how then could the image have been imprinted?

I remember this or that event from Carthage, and I remember all the other places where I've been. I remember the faces of men whom I've seen and things reported by the other senses. I remember both health and sickness of my body. However, when either was not present, my memory received images from them so that they remained present so I could see them and reflect upon them in my mind, if I choose to remember them in their absence.

If, therefore, forgetfulness is retained in the memory through its image and not through itself, then this means that forgetfulness itself was once present, so that its image was imprinted. But when it was present, how did it write its image on the memory, since forgetfulness, by its presence, blots out even what it finds already written there? Nevertheless, in some way or another, even though it's incomprehensible and inexplicable, I'm still quite certain that I also remember forgetfulness, by which I remember that something is blotted out.

Chapter 17—The Multiplicity of Memory

Great is the power of memory. It's a true marvel, O my God, a profound and infinite multiplicity! This is the mind, and this I myself am. What, then, am I, O my God? Of what nature am I? Am I a life that is various and manifold, exceedingly vast? The countless halls and caves, the innumerable fields, dens and caverns of my memory are full without measure of numberless things. These things are present either through images, as all bodies are, or in the things themselves, like our thoughts. These things are present by some notion or observation, like our emotions are, which the memory retains even though the mind no longer feels them, so long as whatever is in the memory is also in the mind. Nevertheless, through all these I run to and fro. I penetrate into them on this side and that as far as I can, yet there is nowhere any end.

So great is the power of memory, so great the power of life in man whose life is mortal! What, then, shall I do, O You my true life, my God? I will pass even beyond this power of mine that is called memory. I must pass beyond it so that I may come to You, O lovely Light. What are You saying to me? I soar by my mind toward You, who remains above me.

I will pass beyond this power of mine, called memory, in my desire to reach You where You can't be reached, and in wishing to cling to You where it is possible to cling to You. Even beasts and birds possess memory, or else they could never find their lairs and nests again. Neither could they display many other things they know and do by habit. Indeed, the beasts and birds couldn't even form their habits except by their memories.

Therefore, I will pass even beyond memory that I may reach Him who has differentiated me from the four-footed beasts and the fowls of the air by making me a wiser creature. Thus I will pass beyond memory. But where will I find You, the true Good and the steadfast Sweetness? But where will I find You? If I find You without memory, then I'll have no memory of You. So, how could I find You at all, if I don't remember You?

CHAPTER 18—LOST FROM SIGHT THOUGH NOT FROM MEMORY

The woman who lost her small coin[330] and searched for it with a light would never have found it unless she had remembered it. For when it was found, how could she have known whether it was the same coin if she hadn't remembered it?

I remember losing and finding many things and have learned this from the experience:

When I was searching for anything that was lost and was asked: "Is this it? Is that it?" I answered, "No," until finally what I was seeking was shown to me. But if I had not remembered it, whatever it was, even though it was shown to me, I still wouldn't have found it because I wouldn't have recognized it.

This is how it always is when we search for and find anything that's lost. Still, if anything is accidentally lost from sight—not from memory, as a visible body might be—its image is retained within, and the thing is searched for until it is restored to sight. Then, when the thing is found, it is recognized by the image of it within. We don't say that we've found what we've lost unless we recognize it, and we can't recognize it unless we remember it. Nevertheless, all the while the thing lost to sight was retained in the memory.

Chapter 19—Forgetting Doesn't Mean Forgotten

What happens when the memory itself loses something, like when we forget anything and try to recall it? Where do we search for it but in the memory itself? There, if one thing is offered for another, we refuse it until we find what we are looking for, and when we do find it, we recognize that this is it. However, we couldn't do this unless we recognized it, nor could we have recognized it unless we remembered it. Yet we had forgotten it!

Perhaps it had not entirely slipped out of our memory, but a part was retained by which the other lost part was sought. This because the memory realized it wasn't operating as smoothly as usual and was being hindered by the crippling of its habitual function. Therefore, it demanded the restoration of what was lacking.

For example, if we see or think of some man we know, and, having forgotten his name, try to recall it, if some other thing presents itself, we cannot tie it into the effort to remember, because it was not habitually thought of in association with him. It's consequently rejected, until something comes into the mind on which our knowledge can rightly rest as the familiar and sought-for object.

Where does this name come back from, except from the memory itself? For even when we recognize it by another person reminding us of it, still it is from the memory that this comes. We don't receive it as something new, but when we recall it, we admit that what was said is correct. However, if the name had been entirely blotted out of the mind, we wouldn't be able to recollect it even when reminded of it. We've not entirely forgotten anything if we can remember that we've forgotten it, because a lost notion, one that we've entirely forgotten, we can't even search for.

Chapter 20—The Memory and Happiness

How, then, do I seek You, O Lord? For when I seek You, my God, I seek a happy life. I seek You so that my soul may live[331] because my body lives by my soul, and my soul lives by You. How, then, do I seek a happy life till I can rightly say: "It is enough. This is it." since happiness is not mine? Do I seek it by remembering as though I had forgotten it but knew that I had forgotten it? Do I seek it by longing to learn of it as though it were something unknown, which either I had never known or had so completely forgotten so as not to remember that I had forgotten it?

Isn't the happy life what everyone desires, and is there anyone who doesn't desire it at all? However, where would they have gotten the knowledge of it, that they should so desire it? Where have they seen it that they should so love it? It's somehow true that we have it, but how I do not know.

There is a sense in which, when anyone has his desire, he is happy. Likewise, there are some who are happy in hope. These are happy in an inferior degree to those that are actually happy, but they are better off than those who are happy neither in actuality nor in hope. However, even these, had they not known happiness in some degree, would not then desire to be happy, yet it's certain that they do so desire.

How these folk come to know happiness, I cannot tell, but they have it by some kind of knowledge unknown to me. I doubt that it's in the memory. If it is, then we've been happy once, either each of us individually, or all of us in that man who first sinned and in whom also we all died and from whom we are all born in misery. How this is, I'm not asking now, but I do ask whether the happy life is in the memory.

If we didn't know happiness, then we shouldn't love it. When we hear it mentioned, we acknowledge that we desire it, because we're not delighted with the mention of it only. When a Greek hears the word "happiness" spoken in Latin, he doesn't feel delight because he doesn't know what has been said. But we are as delighted as he would be if he'd heard it in Greek. This is because happiness itself, which Greeks, Latins and men of all the other tongues long so earnestly to obtain, is neither Greek nor Latin. Happiness is known to all. Therefore, if all could with one voice be asked whether they wished to be happy, no doubt they would all answer that they would. This would not be possible unless the thing itself, which we name "happiness," were held in the memory.

Chapter 21—Recalling Happiness

Is this the same kind of memory as one who having seen Carthage remembers it? No. The happy life isn't visible to the eye because it's not a physical object. Is it the sort of memory we have for numbers? No. The man who has these in his understanding does not keep striving to attain more. We know something about the happy life and therefore we love it, but still we wish to go on striving for it that we may be happy.

Is the memory of happiness, then, something like the memory of eloquence? No. Although when some hear the term eloquence, they call it to mind even if they are not themselves eloquent. Furthermore, there are many people who would like to be eloquent, from which it follows that they must know something about eloquence. These people have noticed through their senses that others are eloquent and have been delighted by it, so they long to be this way themselves. However, they wouldn't be delighted if not for some interior knowledge, and they wouldn't desire to be delighted unless they had once been delighted. Nevertheless, as for a happy life, there is no physical perception by which we experience it in others.

Does one remember happiness as one remembers joy? It may be so. I remember my joy even when I'm sad, just as I remember a happy life when I'm miserable. I have never, through physical perception, seen, heard, smelled, tasted, or touched my joy, but I've experienced it in my mind when I rejoiced. That's because the knowledge of joy clung to my memory so that I can recall it to mind, sometimes with disdain and other times with longing depending on the different things I remember that I rejoiced in. I have been bathed with a certain joy even by unclean things, which I now detest and denounce as I call them to mind. At other times, I longingly call to mind good and honest things that are no longer near at hand, causing me to be saddened when I recall my former joy. Where and when did I ever experience my happy life so that I can call it to mind, love it, and long for it?

It's not I alone, or even a few others who wish to be happy, but absolutely everybody. Unless we knew happiness by a knowledge that is certain, we should not wish for it with a will that is so certain. Take this example:

> If two men were asked whether they wished to serve as soldiers, one of them might reply that he would, and the other that he would not. However, if they were asked whether they wished to be happy, both of them would unhesitatingly say that they would. Yet the first one would wish to serve as a soldier while the other would not wish to serve. Both men are wishing from no other motive than to be happy.
>
> Is it, perhaps, that one finds his joy in this and another in that? Thus they agree in their wish for happiness just as they would also agree, if asked, in wishing for joy. Is this joy, then, what they would call a happy life? Although one could choose his joy in this way and the other in that, all have one goal they strive to attain, namely, to have joy.

This joy, then, is something that no one can say he has not experienced. Therefore, it's found in the memory and is recognized whenever the phrase "a happy life" is heard.

Chapter 22–God is the Source of True Happiness

Forbid it, O Lord, put it far from the heart of Your servant, who confesses to You. Far be it from me to think I am happy because of any and all the joy I have. For there is a joy not granted to the wicked but only to those who worship You in thankfulness, and this joy You are Yourself. The happy life is this: To rejoice to You, in You, and for You. This it is and there is no other. Those who think there is another, follow after other joys, and not the true one. Their will is not moved except by some image or shadow of joy.

Chapter 23—The Quest for Happiness Leads to Truth

Is it uncertain that all men wish to be happy? Many are those who don't wish to find their joy in You, which is alone the happy life. Do they not desire the happy life? Do all desire the happy life, but because "the flesh lusts against the spirit and the spirit against the flesh…so that…you do not do what you wish,"[332] you just do what you are able to and be content? This because you don't want to do what you can't do urgently enough to make you able to do it.

Ask men whether they would rather rejoice in truth or in falsehood, and they'll not hesitate to answer, "In truth" rather than say that they wish to be happy. A happy life is joy in the truth. Yet this is joy in You, who are the Truth. O God my Light, You are "the health of my countenance and my God."[333] Everyone wishes for this happy life, which is joy in the truth.

I've had experience with many who wished to deceive, but not one who wished to be deceived. Where, then, did they ever know about this happy life, except where they knew also what the truth is? Men love truth since they are unwilling to be deceived. Therefore, when they love the happy life, which is nothing else but joy in the truth, then they also love the truth. Yet they wouldn't love it if there were not some knowledge of it in the memory.

Men Hate the Truth

Why, then, don't men rejoice in the truth? Why are they unhappy? Because they are so fully preoccupied with other things which do more to make them miserable than those which would make them happy—which they remember so little about. Yet there is a little light in men. Let them walk in it, lest the darkness overtake them.

Why, then, does truth generate hatred, and why does Your servant who preaches the truth come to be an enemy to those who also love the happy life? The happy life is nothing other than joy in the truth, unless truth is loved in such a way that those who love something besides truth and desire what they love to be the truth. Since they're unwilling to be deceived, they are also unwilling to be convinced that they've been deceived.

Therefore, men hate the truth for the sake of whatever it is that they love in place of the truth. They love truth when she shines on them and hate her when she rebukes them. Since they are unwilling to be deceived, but do wish to deceive, they love truth when she reveals herself and hate her when she reveals them. On this account, she will so repay them that those who are unwilling to be exposed by her will indeed be exposed against their will, yet truth will not disclose herself to them.

The human mind is so blind and sick, so base and ill mannered, that it desires to lie hidden, but does not wish that anything should be hidden from it. However, the opposite is what happens—the mind itself is not hidden from the truth, but the truth is hidden from it. Yet even so, for all its wretchedness, it still prefers to rejoice in truth rather than in known falsehoods. It will, then, be happy only when without other distractions it comes to rejoice in that single Truth through which all things else are true.

Chapter 24—Find Truth—Discover God

Behold how great a territory I have explored in my memory seeking You, O Lord! Yet in it all I've still not found You. Nor have I found anything about You, except what I had already retained in my memory from the time I learned of You. For where I found Truth, there I found my God, who is the Truth. From the time I learned this I've not forgotten it. Therefore, since the time I learned of You, You've dwelt in my memory. There is where I find You whenever I call You to remembrance, and delight in You. These are my holy delights, which You have bestowed on me in Your mercy, mindful of my poverty.

Chapter 25—The Abode of God

Where in my memory do You abide, O Lord? Where do You dwell there? What sort of lodging have You made for Yourself there? What kind of sanctuary have You built for Yourself? You have done this honor to my memory to take up Your abode in it, but I must investigate further that part in which You abide.

When I called You to mind, I soared beyond those parts of memory which the beasts also possess, because I didn't find You among the images of physical things. From there I went on to those parts where I had stored the remembered affections of my mind, and I didn't find You there either. Then I entered the inmost seat of my mind, which is in my memory, since the mind remembers itself also, and You weren't there.

You aren't a bodily image, nor the emotion of a living creature (such as we feel when we rejoice or are grief-stricken, when we desire, or fear, or remember, or forget, or anything of that kind), so neither are You the mind itself. You are the Lord God of the mind and of all these things that are changeable, but You are unchangeable over all. Yet You have elected to dwell in my memory from the time I learned of You.

Why do I now inquire about the part of my memory You dwell in, as if indeed there were separate parts? Assuredly, You dwell in it, since I have remembered You from the time I learned of You, and I find You in my memory when I call You to mind.

Chapter 26—The Omnipresence of God

Where, then, did I find You so as to be able to learn of You? You weren't in my memory before I learned of You. So where did I find You so I could learn of You—except in Yourself beyond me.[334]

Place there is none—we go "backward" and "forward" and there is no place. Everywhere and at once, O Truth, You guide all who consult You, and simultaneously answer all even though they consult You on different things. You answer clearly, though all do not hear in clarity. All take counsel of You on whatever point they wish, though they do not always hear what they wish. Your best servant is he who doesn't look to hear from You what he himself wills, but who wills rather to will what he hears from You.

Chapter 27—God's Pursuit of Me

Belatedly I loved You, O Beauty so ancient and so new. See, You were within and I was without, and I sought You out there. Unlovely, I rushed heedlessly among the lovely things You have made. You were with me, but I was not with You. These things kept me far from You, even though they were not at all unless they were in You. You called and cried aloud, and forced open my deafness. You gleamed and shone, and chased away my blindness. You breathed fragrant odors and I drew in my breath, and now I pant for You. I tasted, and now I hunger and thirst. You touched me, and I burned for Your peace.

CHAPTER 28—JOYS OF SORROW CONTEND WITH SORROWS OF JOY

When I come to be united to You with all my being, there will be no more pain and toil for me. My life will be a real life, wholly filled by You. However, since he whom You fill is the one You lift up, I'm still a burden to myself because I'm not yet filled by You. Joys of sorrow contend with sorrows of joy, and I don't know on which side the victory lies.

Woe is me! Lord, have pity on me. My evil sorrows contend with my good joys, and on which side the victory lies I do not know. Woe is me! Lord, have pity on me. Woe is me! Behold, I do not hide my wounds. You are the Physician, I am the sick man— You are merciful, I need mercy.

Isn't the life of man on earth an ordeal? Who is he that wishes for trials and tribulations? You command them to be endured, not loved. For no man loves what he endures, though he may love to endure. Yet even if he rejoices to endure, he would prefer that there were nothing for him to endure.

I desire prosperity in adversity, and in prosperity I fear adversity. What middle ground is there between these two, where human life is not an ordeal? There is woe in the prosperity of this world, woe in the fear of misfortune, and woe in the distortion of joy. There is woe in the adversities of this world—a second woe, and a third, from the desire of prosperity—because adversity itself is a hard thing to bear and makes a wreck of endurance. Is not the life of man upon the earth an ordeal, and that without end?

Chapter 29—God Commands Self-Restraint

My entire hope is in Your exceeding great mercy and that alone. Give what You command and command what You will. You command self-restraint from us, and when I knew that one couldn't be successful unless God gave it to him, even this was a point of wisdom to know whose gift it was.[335]

Through self-restraint we are bound up and brought back together in the One, whereas before we were scattered abroad among the many. One who loves along with You anything else that he does not love for Your sake loves You too little. You, O God, are Love that burns forever and is never quenched. Kindle a fire in me! You command self-restraint. Give what You command, and command what You will!

Chapter 30—Resisting Lust in Dreams

Obviously You commanded that I restrain myself from "the lust of the flesh, the lust of the eyes, and the pride of life."[336] You commanded me to abstain from sex outside of marriage, and as for marriage itself, You have counseled something better than what You allow. Since You gave it, it was done—even before I became a minister of Your sacrament. Nevertheless, in my memory there still exist the images of what my habits had fixed there. These things rush into my thoughts with no power when I am awake. However, when in sleep they rush in, it's not only to give pleasure but also to obtain my consent in doing what very closely resembles the deed itself. These dreams are so vivid, that my mind and my flesh respond as if I'm actually engaged in sexual embrace. My memory seems to persuade me in my dreams what isn't true in reality.

Am I not myself when I dream, O Lord my God? Is there a great difference between myself awake and myself in the moment when I pass from waking to sleeping, or return from sleeping to waking?

Where, then, is the power of reason that resists such suggestions when I am awake? Then, even if the things themselves are forced upon me, I remain unmoved. Does reason cease when the eyes close? Is it put to sleep with the bodily senses? If that is true, then how is it that even in slumber we often resist, and with our conscious purpose in mind, continue to remain pure in them, not yielding agreement to such enticements? There is at least this much difference: When in dreams we succumb to forbidden passion, upon awaking, we return to peace of conscience. By this difference between sleeping and waking we discover that it wasn't we who did it, even though we still feel sorry that in some way it was done in us.

Isn't Your hand, O Almighty God, able to heal all the diseases of my soul. Isn't Your abundant grace able to quench even the sexual passions of my sleep? Increase Your gifts in me, O Lord, so that my soul may follow me to You, wrenched free from the sticky glue of lust, no longer in rebellion against itself, even in dreams. O that my soul would neither commit nor consent to these sexual fantasies that come through sensual images and result in the pollution of my flesh.

The Almighty is "able to do…more than we can ask or think."[337] God can sustain us so that no influence, not even one so slight that a nod might restrain it, would afford gratification to the feelings of a modest person even when sleeping. This could come to pass not only in this life, but even at my present age.

Nevertheless, what I am still in this way of wickedness I've confessed unto my good Lord, rejoicing with trembling in what You have given me and grieving in myself for that in which I'm still imperfect. I'm trusting that You will perfect Your mercies in me, to the fullness of that peace which both my inner and outward being will have with You when death is swallowed up in victory.[338]

CHAPTER 31–OVERCOMING EVILS OF THE DAY

Gluttony

Another "evil of the day"[339] exists to which I wish I were sufficient. Eating and drinking restore the daily losses of the body until that day when You destroy both food and stomach. Then, You will destroy this emptiness with an amazing fullness and will clothe this corruptible with an eternal incorruption. However, the necessity of habit is sweet to me and against this sweetness must I fight, lest I be taken prisoner by it. Therefore, I carry on a daily war by fasting, constantly "bringing my body into subjection,"[340] after which my hunger is satiated by pleasure.

Hunger and thirst are actual pains. They consume and destroy like fever does, unless the medicine of food is at hand to relieve us. Since this medicine at hand comes from the comfort we receive in Your gifts (by means of which land and water and air serve our infirmity), even our calamity is called pleasure.

You have taught me that I should learn to take food as medicine. However, during that time when I pass from the pangs of an empty stomach to the contentment of fullness, the snare of my appetite awaits calling to me. While health is the reason for our eating and drinking, a perilous delight joins itself to them as a handmaid. In fact, she tries to take precedence so that I may want to do for her sake what I say I want to do for health's sake. Neither have the same limit. What is sufficient for health is not enough for pleasure. Moreover, it's often a matter of doubt whether it's the needful care of the body that still cries for food or whether it's the sensual snare of desire still wanting to be served.

My unhappy soul rejoices in this uncertainty, and uses it to prepare an excuse as a defense. My soul is glad that it's unclear as to what is sufficient to maintain health, so that under the pretense of health it may conceal its agenda for pleasure. I endeavor daily to resist these temptations by summoning Your right hand to my help and casting my concern onto You. So far, I've not reached a firm conclusion in this matter.

Carousing

I hear the voice of God commanding: "take heed to yourselves, lest your hearts be weighed down with carousing, drunkenness, and cares of this life."[341] Drunkenness is far from me, and You'll have mercy that it doesn't come near me. However, "carousing" sometimes creeps upon Your servant. Have mercy, O God, that it may be put far from me, for no man can practice self-restraint unless You give it.[342] Many things that we pray for You give us, and whatever good we receive before we prayed for it, we received from You, so that afterward we would know that it came from You.

I've never been a drunkard, but I've known drunkards who were turned into sober men by You. It was also Your doing that those who never were drunkards have not become drunkards. Likewise, it was Your doing that those who have been would not always remain so. Furthermore, it was from You that both would know from whom all this came.

I heard another voice of Yours declare: "Do not follow your base desires [lusts], but restrain your appetites."[343] By Your favor I've also heard this saying in which I have taken much delight: "for neither if we eat are we the better; nor if we do not eat are we the worse."[344] This is to say that neither one, nor the other will make me thrive or be miserable.

Contentment

I heard still another voice: "for I have learned in whatever state I am, to be content. I know how to be abased and I know how to abound...I can do all things through Christ who strengthens me."[345] You can see here a soldier of the heavenly army, not the sort of dust we are. However, remember O Lord, "that we are dust"[346] and that You created man out of the dust,[347] and that he "was lost, and is found."[348] Of course, the apostle Paul couldn't do all this by his own power. He was of the same dust as we are. Paul, whom I love so much, spoke of these things through the breath of Your inspiration: "I can," he said, "do all things through Christ who strengthens me." O God, strengthen me so that I too may be able.

God, give what You command, and command what You will. Paul confessed that he received the gift of grace and that, when he gloried, it was in the Lord. I have heard yet another voice praying that he might receive. "Let neither gluttony nor lust over come me."[349] From this it appears, O my holy God, that You give mercy and grace when Your commands are obeyed.

You have taught me, good Father, that "to the pure all things are pure",[350] but "it is evil for the man who eats in offense."[351] You said that, "every creature of Yours is good, and nothing is to be refused if it is received with thanksgiving",[352] and that "food does not commend us to God."[353] Therefore, "let no one judge you in food or in drink."[354] "Let not him who eats despise him who does not eat, and let not him who does not eat judge him who eats."[355] These things I have learned, thanks and praises be unto You, O my

God and Master. You, who have knocked at my ears and enlightened my heart, deliver me from all temptation!

Uncontrolled Appetites

It's not the uncleanness of meat that I fear, but the uncleanness of an uncontrolled appetite. I know that permission was granted to Noah to eat every kind of flesh that was good for food. I also know that Elijah was fed with flesh. Furthermore, I know that John ate locusts and was not polluted—he who was blessed with a wonderful abstinence. Esau was deceived by his hunger for lentils and David blamed himself for desiring water. Jesus, our King, was tempted not by flesh but by bread. Thus, the people in the wilderness truly deserved their reproof, not because they desired meat, but because in their desire for food they murmured against the Lord.

Set in the midst of these temptations, I strive daily against my appetite for food and drink. It's not the kind of appetite I'm able to deal with by cutting it off once for all and not touching it, as I was able to do with illicit sex. Therefore, the restraint of the throat must be held in between slackness and tightness.

Who, O Lord, is the man who is not in some degree carried away beyond the bounds of necessity? Whoever he is, he is great— let him magnify Your name. However, I'm not such a man, "for I am a sinful man."[356] Yet I too magnify Your name, for He who has "overcome the world"[357] intercedes with You for my sins, numbering me among the weak members of His body. Your eyes saw my days and in Your book are all written down.[358]

Chapter 32—Life is an Ordeal

I'm not tempted much by the pleasant smells. When they're absent, I don't seek them; when they're present, I don't refuse them, and I'm always prepared to go without them. Nevertheless, it's quite possible that I am deceived. For there is a deplorable darkness in which my capabilities are concealed, so that when my mind questions itself concerning its own powers, it doesn't immediately believe itself, because what is already in it is largely concealed unless experience brings it to light.

Therefore, no man ought to feel secure in this life. The whole of life is called an ordeal. It's ordered so that the man who could be made better from having been worse may not also from having been better become worse. Our sole hope, our sole confidence, our only assured promise, is Your mercy.

Chapter 33—Holiness in Music and Song

The delights of the ear drew and held me much more powerfully, but You unbound me and liberated me. I find solace in the melodies that Your words inspire, especially when sung with a sweet and trained voice. However, it's not so that I can cling to them, but to be able to free myself as I wish. It's because of the words that are their life that they gain entry into me and strive for a place of proper honor in my heart, and I can hardly assign them a fitting one. I often give them more respect than is fitting, when I see that my mind is more devoutly and earnestly set aflame by the holy words when they are sung than when they are not. I recognize that all the diverse affections of our spirits have their appropriate measures in the voice and song, to which they are stimulated by a secret unknown correlation. However, the pleasures of my flesh, to which the mind ought never to be surrendered nor weakened, often beguile me while physical sense ignores reason. Having once gained entry to help reason, my soul strives to run on ahead and be the leader. Thus in these things I sin unknowingly, but I come to know it afterward.

On the other hand, when I earnestly avoid this kind of deception, I err out of too great a seriousness. Sometimes I go to the point of wishing that all the melodies of the pleasant songs to which David's Psalter is adapted should be banished both from my ears and from those of the Church itself. It seemed to me that a safer way was one attributed to Athanasius, bishop of Alexandria. He required the readers of the psalm to use such a slight inflection of the voice that it was more like speaking than singing.

However, when I call to mind the tears I shed at the songs of Your Church at the outset of my recovered faith, and how even now I am moved, not by the singing alone but by what is sung, I acknowledge the great value of this custom. So I vacillate between dangerous pleasure and healthful exercise. I'm inclined to approve of the use of singing in the church, so that by the delights of the ear the weaker minds may be stimulated to a devotional mood. Yet when it happens that I am more moved by the singing than by what is sung, I confess to have sinned wickedly, and then I would rather not have heard the singing.

See now what a condition I am in! Weep with me, and weep for me, those of you who can control your inward feelings so that good results always come forth. As for you who don't act this way at all, such things don't concern you. But You, O Lord, my God, give ear. Look and see, and have mercy upon me. Heal me, O God, in whose sight I have become an enigma to myself. This itself is my weakness.

CHAPTER 34—THE TEMPTATIONS OF SIGHT

There remain the delights of these fleshly eyes of mine, about which I must make my confession before others of Your temple. Therefore, I'll finish the list of the temptations of carnal appetite that still assail me, groaning and desiring as I am to be clothed with my house from heaven.[359]

The eyes delight in countless forms and bright and pleasing colors. Let these not take possession of my soul! Rather let God possess it, He made all these things very good indeed. He is still my good, and not these. The pleasures of sight affect me all the time I'm awake. There is no rest from them as there is from the voices of melody, which I can occasionally find in silence. For daylight, that queen of the colors, floods all that I look upon everywhere I go during the day. It flits about me in countless forms and soothes me even when I'm busy about other things and not noticing it. It presents itself so forcibly that if it's suddenly withdrawn, it's looked for with longing, and if it's long absent the mind is saddened.

O Light, which Tobit saw with his eyes closed in blindness when teaching his son the way of life. He went before his son himself in the steps of love, never going astray.[360] Or that Light that Isaac saw when his fleshly "eyes were dim, so that he could not see"[361] because of old age, and it was permitted him unknowingly to bless his sons, but in the blessing of them to know them. Or the Light that Jacob saw when blind in old age yet with an enlightened heart he prophesied of the nation yet to come, pre-signified when laid his hands mysteriously crossed upon his grandsons by Joseph— not as their father, who saw them from without, but as though he were within them—and distinguished them correctly.[362] This is the true Light. It is one, and all are one who see and love it.

Resist the Seductions of the Eyes

However, that physical light of which I was speaking, seasons the life of the world for her blind lovers with a tempting and fatal sweetness. Those who know how to praise You for it, "O God, Creator of Us All," take it up in Your hymn[363] and are not overcome by it in their sleep. Such a man I desire to be. I resist the seductions of my eyes, lest my feet be entangled as I go forward in Your way, and I raise my invisible eyes to You so that You would be pleased to "pluck my feet out of the net."[364] You continually pluck them out, for they are easily ensnared. You cease not to pluck them out, but I constantly remain tightly held in the snares set all around me. However, You who "keep Israel shall neither slumber nor sleep."[365]

What numberless things there are: products of the various arts, manufactures in our clothes, shoes, vessels, and all such things, pictures and statues. All of these are far beyond the necessary and moderate use of them or their significance for the life of holiness. Men have added these for the delight of the eye, copying the outward forms of the things they make, but inwardly forsaking Him by whom they were made and destroying what they themselves have been made to be!

And I, O my God and my Joy, I also raise a hymn to You for all these things, and offer a sacrifice of praise to my Sanctifier. Those beautiful forms that pass through the medium of the human soul into the artist's hands come from that beauty that is above our minds, which my soul sighs for day and night.

The craftsmen and devotees of these outward beauties discover the norm by which they judge them from that higher beauty, but not the measure of their use. Even if they don't see it, it's there guarding them from wandering astray and keeping their strength for You, so as not dissipate it in delights that pass into boredom.

For myself, though I can see and understand that I'm still entangled in my own course with such beauty, but You will rescue me, O Lord, "for Your loving-kindness is before my eyes."[366] I'm captivated in my weakness but You in Your mercy rescue me. Sometimes this happens without my knowing it because I had only lightly fallen, at other times the rescue is painful because I was stuck fast.

Chapter 35—Dangerous Distractions

Besides this there is yet another form of temptation even more complex in its peril. In addition to the fleshly appetite, which strives for the gratification of the senses and pleasures, there is also a certain vain and curious longing in the soul rooted in the same bodily senses. It's cloaked under the name of knowledge and learning, not having pleasure in the flesh, but striving for new experiences through the flesh. This longing, since its origin is our appetite for learning and since sight is the chief of our senses in the acquisition of knowledge, is called "the lust of the eyes."[367]

Seeing is a function of the eyes, but we also use this word for the other senses as well when we exercise them in the search for knowledge. We don't say, "Listen how it glows," "Smell how it glistens," "Taste how it shines," or "Feel how it flashes," since all of these are said to be *seen*. Nor do we simply say, "See how it shines," which only the eyes can perceive, but we also say, "See how it sounds, see how it smells, see how it tastes, see how hard it is." Therefore, the entire round of sensory experience is called "the lust of the eyes." The function of seeing, in which the eyes have the principal role, is applied by analogy to the other senses when they are seeking after any kind of knowledge.

From this, then, one can more clearly distinguish whether it's pleasure or curiosity that is being pursued by the senses. Pleasure pursues objects that are beautiful, melodious, fragrant, savory, and soft. But curiosity, seeking new experiences, will even seek out the contrary of these, not with the purpose of experiencing the discomfort that often accompanies them, but out of a passion for experimenting and knowledge.

The Malady of Curiosity

What pleasure is there in seeing a lacerated corpse, which makes you shudder? Yet if there is one lying close by we flock to it as if to be made sad and pale. People fear lest they should see such a thing even in sleep, just as they would if, when awake, someone compelled them to go and see it or if some rumor of its beauty had attracted them.

This is also the case with the other senses, though it would be tedious to pursue a complete analysis of it. This malady of curiosity is the reason for all those strange sights exhibited in the theater. It's also the reason why we proceed to search out the secret powers of nature that have nothing to do with our destiny, and that don't profit us to know about. Men desire to know about them only for the sake of knowing.

With this same motive of perverted curiosity for knowledge we consult the magical arts. Even in religion itself, this drive prompts us to try God by eagerly seeking signs and wonders, though not desired for any saving end, but only to try Him.

This wilderness is so vast and crammed with snares and dangers. O God, how many of them I have lopped off and cast from my heart as You have enabled me. But when would I dare to say, since so many things of this sort still buzz around my daily life, that no such motive prompts my seeing or creates a vain curiosity in me?

The theaters no longer attract me, nor do I care to inquire about the courses of the stars, and my soul has never sought answers from the departed spirits. All sacrilegious oaths I abhor. However, O Lord my God, to whom I owe all humble and single-hearted service, with what subtle suggestion the enemy still influences me to require some sign from You! But by our King, Jesus, and by Jerusalem, our pure and chaste homeland, I beseech You that if any desires such as are now far from me, so may they always be farther and farther. When I entreat You for the salvation of any man, the end I aim at is something more than the asking. Let it be that as You do what You will, You will also give me the grace to willingly follow Your lead.

Trivial Pursuits

How many of the most minute and trivial things still tempt my curiosity daily, and who can keep count on how often I succumb? How often, when people are telling idle tales, we begin by tolerating them lest we should give offense to the sensitive, and then gradually we come to listen willingly! I don't go to the circus nowadays to see a dog chase a rabbit, but if by chance I pass such a race in the fields, it quite easily distracts me, taking me from even serious thoughts, drawing me after it. I don't turn aside with my horse, but the inclination of my mind follows the chase. By showing me my weakness, You speedily warn me to rise above such a sight and back to You by a deliberate act of thought, or else to despise the whole thing and pass it by. Otherwise, I would become absorbed in the sight, vain creature that I am.

How is it that when I'm sitting at home a lizard catching flies, or a spider entangling them as they fly into her webs, often captures my attention? Is the feeling of curiosity not the same just because these are such tiny creatures? From them I proceed to praise You, the wonderful Creator and Disposer of all things, but it's not this that first attracts my attention. It's one thing to get up quickly and another thing not to fall, and of both my life is full. My only hope is in Your abundant mercy.

When our hearts, that were made to be the repository of such things, are overrun by a throng of flourishing distractions, then our prayers are often interrupted and disturbed by them. Even while we are in Your presence and direct the voice of our hearts to Your ears, such a great business as this is broken off by the inroads of countless idle thoughts.

Chapter 36—Honor God's Gifts

Shall we, then, consider this futile curiosity among the things that are to be but lightly esteemed? Shall anything restore us to hope except Your complete mercy since You have begun to change us? You know to what extent You have already changed me. First of all, You healed me of the lust for vindicating myself, so that You might then forgive all my remaining iniquities and heal all my diseases. Then, You could "redeem my life from destruction and crown me with loving-kindness and tender mercies, and satisfy my mouth with good things."[368] It was You who restrained my pride with Your fear, and bowed my neck to Your "yoke."[369] Now I bear the yoke and it is "light" to me, because You promised to make it so. So in truth it was, though I knew it not when I feared to take it up.

However, O Lord, You alone reign without pride, because You alone are the true Lord—You have no Lord. Has this third kind of temptation left me, or can it leave me during this life? I'm speaking of the desire to be feared and loved of men, with no other view than that I may find in it a joy that is no joy. It's a wretched life and an improper showiness. This is a special reason why we don't love You or devotedly fear You. Therefore "You resist the proud but give grace to the humble."[370] You thunder down on the ambitious designs of the world, and "the foundations of the hills" tremble.[371]

God Resists the Proud

Nevertheless, certain offices in human society require the officeholder to be loved and feared of men. Through this the adversary of our true blessedness presses hard upon us, scattering everywhere his snares of "well done, well done." Then, while we eagerly pick them up, we are caught unawares and isolated from Your truth, fixed on the deceits of men. This way we come to take pleasure in being loved and feared, not for Your sake but in Your stead. By such means as this, the adversary makes men like himself so that he may have them as his own—not in the harmony of love, but in the fellowship of punishment. The enemy is the one who aspired to exalt his throne in the north,[372] that in the darkness and the cold men would have to serve him, mimicking You in perverse and distorted ways.

O Lord, we are Your little flock. Possess us, stretch Your wings above us and let us take refuge under them. You be our glory. Let us be loved for Your sake and let Your word be feared in us. Those who desire to be commended by the men whom You condemn will not be defended by men when You judge, nor will they be delivered when You condemn them. When a man is praised for some gift that You have given him, and he is more gratified at the praise for himself than because he possesses the gift for which he is praised, such a one is praised while You condemn him. In such a case the one who praised is truly better than the one who was praised. For the gift of God in man was pleasing to the one, while the other was better pleased with the gift of man than with the gift of God.

CHAPTER 37—BEWARE THE PRIDE OF PRAISE

These temptations daily try us, O Lord. We are tried unceasingly. Our daily "furnace" is the human tongue.[373] Also in this respect You command us to show restraint. Give what You command and command what You will.

You know the groans of my heart in this matter and the rivers of my eyes. I'm unable to know for certain how clean I am of this plague. Therefore, I stand in great fear of my "secret faults,"[374] which Your eyes perceive, though mine do not. In respect of the pleasures of my flesh and of idle curiosity, I see how far I have been able to hold my mind in check when I abstain from them either by voluntary act of the will or because they simply are not at hand. Then I can inquire of myself how much more or less frustrating it is for me not to have them. This is also true about riches, which are sought after so that they may minister to one or all of these three "lusts." The mind is able to see clearly if, when it has riches, it despises them so that they may be cast aside and it may prove itself.

However, if we desire to test our power of doing without praise, must we then live wickedly or lead a life so atrocious and abandoned that everyone who knows us will detest us? What greater insanity than this can be either said or conceived? Yet if praise, both by custom and right, is the companion of a good life and of good works, we should as little forgo its companionship as the good life itself. But unless a thing is absent I don't know whether I should be contented or troubled at having to do without it.

What is it, then, that I am confessing to You, O Lord, concerning this sort of temptation? That I am delighted with praise, but more with the truth itself than with praise? I know what I would choose if I were to have any choice whether, if I were mad or utterly in the wrong, I would prefer…a) to be praised by all men or, b) if I were steadily and fully confident in the truth, would prefer to be blamed by all. However, I wish I were unwilling that the approval of others should add anything to my joy for any good I have. Nevertheless, I admit that it does increase it; and, more than that, criticism diminishes it.

Gratified by Praise

If, when I'm disturbed over this wretchedness of mine, an excuse presents itself to me, it renders me uncertain. You have imposed both restraint and righteousness on me—when to hold back love and when to bestow love. Your desire is for me to love not only You, but also my neighbor, so it often turns out that when I'm gratified by intelligent praise I seem to be gratified by the competence or insight of my neighbor. On the other hand, I'm sorry for the defect in him when I hear him criticize either what he doesn't understand or what is good.

I'm sometimes grieved at the praise I get, either when those things that displease me in myself are praised in me, or when lesser and trifling goods are valued more highly than they should be. How do I know whether I feel this way because I'm unwilling that he who praises me should differ from me concerning myself? Not because I am moved with any consideration for him, but because the good things that please me in myself are more pleasing to me when they also please another. For in a way, I'm not praised when my judgment of myself is not praised, since either those things that are displeasing to me are praised, or those things that are less pleasing to me are more praised. Am I not, then, quite uncertain of myself in this respect?

Behold, O Truth, it's in You that I see that I ought not to be moved at my own praises for my own sake, but for the sake of my neighbor's good. Whether this is actually my way, I truly don't know. On this score I know less of myself than You do. I beseech You now, O my God, to reveal myself to me as well, so that I may confess to my brethren, who are to pray for me in those matters where I find myself weak.

Let me once again examine myself more diligently. If, in my own praise, I'm moved with concern for my neighbor, why am I less moved if some other man is unjustly criticized than when it happens to me? Why am I more irritated at that reproach which is cast on me than at one that is with equal injustice cast upon another in my presence? Am I ignorant of this as well? Or is it still true that I'm deceiving myself and don't keep the truth before You in my heart and tongue? Put such madness far from me, O Lord, lest my mouth be to me the oil of sinners, to anoint my head.

Chapter 38—Boastful Pride

"I am poor and needy."[375] Still, I'm better when in secret I displease myself and seek Your mercy until what is lacking in me is renewed and made complete for that peace which the eye of the proud does not know. The reports that come from the mouth and from actions known to men have in them a dangerous temptation to the love of praise. This love builds up a certain complacency in one's own excellence and then goes around collecting solicited compliments. It tempts me, even when I inwardly rebuke myself for it, and this precisely because it is rebuked. For a man may often revel in the contempt of boastful pride—in this case it's no longer the contempt of boastful pride in which he glories, for he doesn't truly despise it when he inwardly glories in it.

Chapter 39—Hedonism Condemned

There is within us yet another evil arising from the same sort of temptation. By it men become empty who please themselves in themselves, though they don't please or displease or aim at pleasing others. However, in pleasing themselves they displease You very much, not merely taking pleasure in things that are not good as if they were good, but taking pleasure in Your good things as if they were their own. Often, they treat pleasant things as if they were Yours but as if they had received them through their own merit.

In these and similar perils, You perceive the agitation of my heart. I would rather feel my wounds being cured by You than not inflicted by me on myself.

Chapter 40—God is Ever Present

Where have You not accompanied me, O Truth? You have taught me both what to avoid and what to desire, when I have submitted to You what I could understand about matters here below, and sought Your counsel about them.

With my external senses I've viewed the world, as I was able, and have noticed the life that my body derives from me and from these senses of mine. From that stage I advanced inwardly into the recesses of my memory—the manifold chambers of my mind, so marvelously full of unmeasured wealth. I reflected on this and was afraid. I didn't understand any of these things without You and found You to be none of them. Nor did I myself discover these things. I went over them all and worked to distinguish and value everything according to its dignity. I accepted some things on the report of my senses and questioned others that I thought were related to my inner self, distinguishing and numbering the reporters themselves. I labored in that vast storehouse of my memory, investigating some things, depositing other things, and taking out still others.

I wasn't myself when I did this, that is, in the ability of mine by which I did it. Nor was it You, for You are that never failing light from which I took counsel about everything—whether they were what they were, and what was their real value. In all this I heard You teaching and commanding me. This I often do, which is a delight to me, and as far as I can get relief from my necessary duties, I resort to this kind of pleasure. However, in all these things that I review when I consult You, I still don't find a secure place for my soul except in You. It's only in You that my scattered members may be gathered together and nothing of me escape from You.

Sometimes You introduce me to a rare and inward feeling, an inexplicable sweetness. If this were to come to perfection in me I don't know to what point life might then arrive. But still, by these wretched weights of mine, I relapse into these common things and am sucked in by my old customs and held. I sorrow much, yet I'm still closely held. To this extent, then, the burden of habit presses me down. I can exist in this fashion but don't wish to do so. In that other way I wish I were, but cannot be—in both ways I am wretched.

CHAPTER 41—GRIEVING OVER GREED

I have considered the infirmities of my sins under the headings of the three major "lusts," and have called Your right hand to my aid. With a wounded heart I've seen Your brightness, and having been beaten back I cried: Who can attain to this? "I am cut off from before Your eyes."[376] You are the Truth, who presides over all things, but because of my greed, I didn't wish to lose You. I wished also to possess a lie—just as no one wishes to lie in such a way as to be ignorant of what is true—but by this I lost You. You will not agree to be enjoyed along with a lie.

Chapter 42—The Need for a Mediator

Whom could I find to reconcile me to You? Should I have approached the angels? What kind of prayer? What kind of rites? Many who were striving to return to You and were not able of themselves have tried this and have fallen into longing for curious visions. They deserve to be deceived. Being exalted, they sought You in their pride of learning, and thrust themselves forward rather than beating their breasts.[377] So, by a likeness of heart, they drew to themselves the princes of the air,[378] these conspirators and companions in pride deceived them by the power of magic. Thus they sought a mediator by whom they might be cleansed, but there was none. For the mediator they sought was the devil, disguising himself as an angel of light.[379] And he allured their proud flesh the more because he had no fleshly body.

They were mortal and sinful, but You, O Lord, to whom they arrogantly sought to be reconciled, are immortal and sinless. But a mediator between God and man ought to have something in him like God and something in him like man—lest in being like man he should be far from God, or if only like God he should be far from man, and so should not be a mediator. That deceitful mediator, then, by whom, by Your secret judgment, human pride deserves to be deceived, had one thing in common with man, his sin. In another respect, he would seem to have something in common with God, for not being clothed with the mortality of the flesh, he could boast that he was immortal. However, since "the wages of sin is death,"[380] what he really has in common with men is that, together with them, he is condemned to death.

CHAPTER 43—JESUS CHRIST THE MEDIATOR

The true Mediator, whom You have revealed to the humble and sent to them, so that through His example they also might learn the same humility, that "Mediator between God and man, the man Christ Jesus,"[381] appeared between mortal sinners and the immortal Just One. He was mortal as men are mortal. He was righteous as God is righteous. Because the reward of righteousness is life and peace, He could, through His righteousness united with God, cancel the death of justified sinners, which He was willing to have in common with them.

He was manifested to holy men of old, to the end that they might be saved through faith in His Passion to come, even as we through faith in His Passion which is past. As man He was Mediator, but as the Word He was not something in between the two. He was equal to God, and God with God, and, with the Holy Spirit, one God.

Jesus Secured the Victory

How have You loved us, O good Father. You did not spare Your only Son, but delivered Him up for us wicked ones![382] How have You loved us. He who did not count it robbery to be equal with You "became obedient unto death, even the death of the cross!"[383] He alone was "free among the dead."[384] He alone had power to lay down His life and power to take it up again, and for us He became to You both Victor and Victim—Victor because He was the Victim. For us, He was to You both Priest and Sacrifice, and Priest because He was the Sacrifice.

Out of slaves, He makes us Your sons, because He was born of You and served us. Rightly, then, is my hope fixed strongly on Him, that You will "heal all my diseases"[385] through Him, who sits at

Your right hand and makes intercession for us.[386] Otherwise I would utterly despair, for my infirmities are many and great—indeed, they are very many and very great. But Your medicine is still greater. Otherwise, I might think that Your Word was removed from union with man and despair, had it not been that He was "made flesh and dwelt among us."[387]

Terrified by my sins and the load of my misery, I considered hiding in the wilderness. But You forbade me, and You strengthened me, saying that "He died for all, that those who live should live no longer for themselves, but for Him who died for them and rose again."[388]

Behold, O Lord, I cast all my care on You, that I may live and "behold wondrous things out of Your law."[389] You know my incompetence and my infirmities. Teach me and heal me. Your only Son "in whom are hid all the treasures of wisdom and knowledge"[390] has redeemed me with His blood. Prevent the proud from speaking evil of me, because I keep my ransom before my mind, and eat and drink and share my food and drink. Being poor, I desire to be satisfied from Him, together with those who eat and are satisfied. "Be exalted, O LORD, in Your own strength!

We will sing and praise Your power."[391]

BOOK ELEVEN

The Time of Creation

Augustine discusses the eternal Creator and the Creation in time. He ties together his memory of his past life, his present experience, and his ardent desire to comprehend the mystery of creation. This leads him to questions about the mode and time of creation. He ponders the mode of creation and shows that it involved no alteration in the being of God. He then considers the question of the beginning of the world and time and shows that time and creation are co-temporal. But what is time? To this Augustine devotes a brilliant analysis of the subjectivity of time and the relation of all temporal process to the abiding eternity of God.

Chapter 1–Stir up my Love

Is it possible, O Lord, that, since You are in eternity, You are ignorant of what I am saying to You? Do You see an event in time at the time it occurs? If not, then why am I recounting such things to You? Certainly not to acquaint You with them through me, but that through them I may stir up my own love and the love of my readers toward You. Then all will say, "Great is the Lord and greatly to be praised." I've said this before and repeat it again here: "For love of Your love I do it."

We pray and yet Truth tells us, "your Father knows the things you have need of before you ask Him."[392] Therefore, we lay bare our feelings before You, so that through confessing our plight to You and Your mercies toward us, You may go on to free us altogether. You have already begun to do this, so that we may cease to be wretched in ourselves and blessed in You.

You have called us to be poor in spirit, meek, mourners, hungering and thirsting for righteousness, merciful and pure in heart.[393] Thus I've told You many things as I could find the ability and will to do so. It was Your will in the first place that I should confess to You, O Lord my God, for "You are good and Your mercy endures forever."[394]

CHAPTER 2—REVEAL THE SECRETS OF YOUR WORD, GOD

How long would it take to write enough of Your exhortations, of Your terrors, comforts and leadings by which You brought me to preach Your Word and administer Your sacraments to Your people? Even if I could do this sufficiently, the drops of time[395] are very precious to me. I've been burning with the desire to meditate on Your law for a long time, and to confess in Your presence my knowledge and ignorance of it—from the first streaks of Your light in my mind and the remaining darkness, until my weakness is swallowed up in Your strength. I don't want the hours that I can wrench free from the necessary things of life to be invested in anything other than You.

O Lord my God, hear my prayer and let Your mercy attend my desire. It doesn't burn for itself alone but to serve the cause of brotherly love as well. You see in my heart that this is so. Let me offer the service of my mind and my tongue, and give to me what I may in turn offer back to You. "I am needy and poor," but You are rich to all who call upon You, who, in Your freedom from care, cares for me.

Trim all rashness and lying away from my lips, both inwardly and outwardly. Let Your Scriptures be my pure delight. Let me not be deceived in them, nor deceive others from them.

O Lord, hear my cry! O Lord my God, light of the blind and the seeing, strength of both the weak and the strong, hearken to my soul and hear it crying from the depths.[396] Unless Your ears attend me even in the depths, where could I go? To whom could I cry?

Perfect Me, O Lord

"The day is Yours, and the night also is Yours,"[397] and at Your bidding, moments fly by. Grant me in these moments time for my meditations on the hidden things of Your law, and do not close the door of Your law against me when I knock. You have not willed that the deep secrets of those pages should have been written in vain. Those forests are not without their stags, which, though they remain hidden, forage and walk, feed and lay down to rest.

Perfect me, O Lord, and reveal Your secrets to me. Your voice is my joy, which surpasses an abundance of delights. Give me what I love, for I do love it. This too is Your gift. Therefore, do not abandon Your gifts and do not despise Your "grass" which thirsts for You.[398]

Let me confess to You everything that I've found in Your books "That I may proclaim with the voice of thanksgiving, and tell of all Your wondrous works."[399] Let me drink from You "that I may see wondrous things out of Your law."[400] Let me see from the very beginning when You made heaven and earth all the way to the everlasting reign of Your Holy City with You.

O Lord, have mercy on me and hear my petition. My prayer is not for earthly things such as…

- Gold
- Silver
- Precious stones
- Gorgeous apparel
- Honors
- Power
- Fleshly pleasures
- Bodily necessities for this life of our pilgrimage

All of these are "added" to those who seek Your Kingdom and Your righteousness.[401]

Observe, O God, from where my desire comes. The unrighteous have told me of delights but not such as those in Your law, O Lord. Behold, this is the spring of my desire. See, O Father, look and see—and approve! Let it be pleasing in Your mercy's sight that I should find favor with You.

Let the secret things of Your Word be opened to me when I knock. I beg this of You by our Lord Jesus Christ, Your Son, the Man of Your right hand, the Son of Man—Jesus, whom You made strong for Your purpose as Mediator between You and us, and through whom You sought us when we were not seeking You, but did seek us so that we might seek You. Jesus is Your Word through whom You made all things, and me among them. He is Your only Son, through whom You have called Your faithful people to adoption, and me among them. I beseech You through Him who sits at Your right hand and makes intercession for us, "in whom are hidden all the treasures of wisdom and knowledge."[402] It is He that I seek in Your books. Moses wrote of Him—he says so himself—the Truth tells us so as well.

CHAPTER 3—SEEKING TRUTH IN GOD'S WORD

Let me hear and understand how in the beginning You made heaven and earth.[403] Moses wrote of this and passed on—moving from You to You—and he is now no longer before me. If he were, I would take hold of him and solemnly ask him in Your name if he would reveal these mysteries to me. Then, I would open my ears to hear every word that came out of his mouth. If he spoke in Hebrew, the words would beat on my senses in vain and nothing would touch my mind because I don't understand Hebrew. However, if he spoke in Latin, I would understand what he said.

How, then, would I know if what Moses said was true? If I knew even this much, would it be that I knew it from him? Within me, deep inside the chambers of my thought, Truth itself—which is neither Hebrew, Greek, Latin, nor barbarian and is without any organs of voice and tongue, and without the sound of syllables— would say, "He speaks the truth." This would assure me.

Then I would confidently say to that man of Yours, "You speak the truth."[404] However, since I cannot inquire of Moses, I come to You, O Truth, from whose fullness Moses spoke truth. I ask You, my God, to forgive my sins, and as You gave Moses the gift to speak these things, grant unto me the gift to understand them.

CHAPTER 4—EARTH AND HEAVEN

Look around and see the heavens and the earth. They cry aloud that they were made, for they change and vary. Whatever there is that has not been made and yet has being, has nothing in it that was not there before. This having something not already existent is what it means to be changed and varied. Therefore, heaven and earth plainly speak that they did not make themselves:

> *We are, because we have been made; we did not exist before we came to be so that we could have made ourselves!*

The voice with which earth and heaven speak is simply their visible presence. It was You, O Lord, who made these things. Therefore...

- You are beautiful, so they are beautiful.
- You are good, so they are good.
- You are, so they are.

However, they're not as beautiful, nor as good, nor as truly real as You are, their Creator. Compared with You, they are neither beautiful nor good, nor do they even exist. These things we know, thanks to You, yet our knowledge is ignorance when it is compared with Yours.

CHAPTER 5—QUESTIONS ABOUT THE ORIGIN OF CREATION

How did You make the heavens and the earth? What tool did You use for such a mighty work as this? The act of creation was not accomplished like a human worker fashioning matter from matter. He does this according to the desires of his mind, and is able somehow to impose on it a form that his mind perceived in itself by its inner eye. Yet how would he even be able to do this if You hadn't made that mind?

The craftsman imposes the form on something already existing and having some sort of being, such as clay, stone, wood, gold, or such. However, where would these things come from if You had not furnished them? You made the artisan's body and You made his mind, which directs his limbs. You also made the matter from which he makes things, and You created the capacity by which he understands his art and sees within his mind what he can do with the things before him. You gave the artist his bodily senses by which he may communicate from mind to matter what he proposes to do and report back to his mind what has been done. This so the mind can consult with the Truth that presides over it as to whether what is done is well done.

All these things praise You, Creator of all. But how did You make them? How, O God, did You make the heavens and earth? For truly, neither in heaven nor on earth did You make heaven and earth. Nor did You make them in the air or in the waters, since all of these also belong to the heaven and the earth. Nowhere in the entire world did You make the entire world—there was no place where it could be made before it was made. Furthermore, You held nothing in Your hand from which to fashion the heaven and the earth,[405] for where could You have gotten what You had not made in order to make something with it?

Does anything at all exist except because You are? You spoke and they were made,[406] and by Your Word You made them all.

CHAPTER 6—THE VOICE OF CREATION

How did You speak? Was it in the same manner in which the voice came from the cloud saying, "This is my beloved Son"?[407] That voice sounded forth and died away—it began and ended. The syllables sounded and passed away, the second after the first, the third after the second, and so forth, till the very last after all the rest, and silence after the last. From this it's clear and plain that it was the action of a creature, itself in time, which sounded that voice, obeying Your eternal will.

What these words were that were formed at that time the outer ear conveyed to the conscious mind, whose inner ear lay attentively open to Your eternal Word. The mind compared those words, which sounded in time with Your eternal word sounding in silence and said:

> *This is different, quite different! These words are far below me; they are not even real, for they fly away and pass, but the Word of my God remains above me forever.*

If, then, in words that sound and fade away You said that heaven and earth should be made, and thus made heaven and earth, then there was already some kind of physical creature before heaven and earth by whose motions in time that voice might have had its occurrence in time. However, there was nothing physical before the heaven and the earth. If there was, then it's certain that without a time-bound voice, You created whatever it was out of which You made the time-bound voice, by which You said, "Let the heaven and the earth be made!" For whatever the voice was made of simply didn't exist until You made it. Was it decreed by Your Word that a body might be made from which such words might come?

Chapter 7—The Word is Co-eternal with God

You do call us, then, to understand the Word. This is the God who is God with You, which is spoken eternally and by which all things are spoken eternally. For what was first spoken was not finished, and then something else spoken until the whole series was done, but all things were spoken at the same time and forever. Otherwise, we would have time and change, but not a true eternity nor a true immortality.

This I know, O my God, and I give thanks. I know, I confess to You, O Lord, and whoever is not ungrateful for certain truths knows and blesses You along with me. We know, O Lord, this much, that in the same proportion as anything is not what it was, and is what it was not, in that very same proportion it passes away or comes to be. However, nothing in Your Word ever passes away or returns to its place, for it is truly immortal and eternal. Therefore, unto the Word coeternal with You, at the same time and always You say all that You say. Whatever You say shall be made is made, and You make nothing otherwise than by speaking. Still, not all the things that You make by speaking are made at the same time and always.

CHAPTER 8–JESUS–SPOKEN WORD OF GOD

Why is this, O Lord my God? I see it after a fashion, but I don't know how to express it. That is, unless I say that everything that begins to be and then ceases to be begins and ceases when it's known in Your eternal Reason that it ought to begin or cease. All this, in Your eternal Reason, where nothing begins or ceases. This is Your Word, which is also "the Beginning," because it speaks to us.[408] Thus, in the gospel, Jesus spoke through the flesh, which sounded in the outward ears of men. That way, it would be believed and sought for within, being found in the eternal Truth, in which the good and only Master teaches all his disciples.[409]

There, O Lord, I hear Your voice speaking to me, since He who teaches us speaks to us. But He that does not teach us does not really speak to us even when He speaks. Yet who is it that teaches us unless it's the Truth unchangeable? Even when we are instructed by means of the changeable creation, we are thereby led to the Truth unchangeable. There we truly learn as we stand and hear Him, and we rejoice greatly "because of the bridegroom's voice,"[410] restoring us to the source from whence our being comes.

Therefore, unless the Beginning remained unchangeable, there would be no place to which we could return when we had wandered away. But when we return from error, it's through our gaining knowledge that we return. In order for us to gain knowledge He teaches us, since He is the Beginning, and speaks to us.

CHAPTER 9–THE CREATIVE WISDOM OF GOD

In the Beginning, O God, You made heaven and earth through Your Word, Your Son, Your Power, Your Wisdom, Your Truth, all wondrously speaking and wondrously creating. Who can comprehend such things and who shall tell of it? What is it that shines through me and strikes my heart without injury, so that I both shudder and burn? I shudder because I'm unlike it, and burn because I'm like it. Wisdom itself shines through me, clearing away the fog that overwhelms me so that I faint in the darkness and under the burden of my punishment. My strength is brought down in neediness, so I can't endure even my blessings until You heal my infirmities.

O Lord, You have been gracious to all my iniquities. You are the One "who redeems my life from destruction, who crowns me with lovingkindness and tender mercies, who satisfies my mouth with good things so that my youth is renewed like the eagle's."[411]

By this hope we are saved, and through patience we await Your promises. Let him, who is able, hear You when You speak to his inner mind.

I will cry out with confidence because of Your own oracle: "O LORD, how manifold are Your works! In wisdom You have made them all. The earth is full of Your possessions."[412] This Wisdom is the Beginning, and in that Beginning You have made the heavens and the earth.

CHAPTER 10—THE WILL OF GOD COMES BEFORE CREATION

Are people still full of their old carnal nature who ask us:

> What was God doing before He made heaven and earth? For if He was idle and doing nothing, then why did He not continue in that state forever—doing nothing as He had always done?
> If any new motion has arisen in God, and a new will to form a creature, which He had never before formed, how can that be a true eternity in which an act of will

occurs that was not there before? For the will of God is not a created thing, but comes before the creation. This is true because nothing could be created unless the will of the Creator came before it.

Therefore, the will of God pertains to His very Essence. Yet if anything has arisen in the Essence of God that was not there before, then that Essence cannot truly be called eternal. But if it was the eternal will of God that the creation should come to be, why, then, is not the creation itself also from eternity?[413]

CHAPTER 11—TIME AND ETERNITY

Those who say these things don't understand You, O Wisdom of God, O Light of souls. They can't comprehend how the things are made that are made by and in You. They endeavor to comprehend eternal things, but their heart still flits about in the past and future motions of created things, and is still unstable.

Who will hold the heart and fix it so that it may come to rest, and then, by degrees, help it glimpse the glory of that eternity which abides forever. Then, comparing eternity with the temporal process in which nothing abides, see that the two are impossible to compare? These folk would see that a long time doesn't become long, except from the many separate events that occur in its passage, which cannot be simultaneous.

On the other hand, nothing passes away in the Eternal; the whole is simultaneously present. However, no temporal process is entirely simultaneous. Therefore, let the unstable heart of those who confuse time and eternity see that all time past is forced to move on by the incoming future. Let it see that all the future follows from the past and that all, both past and future, is created and issues forth of that which is forever present.

Who will hold the heart of man so that it can be still and see how eternity, which always stands still, is neither future nor past, but expresses itself in the times that are future and past? Can my hand do this, or can the words of my mouth bring about so difficult a thing even by persuasion?

Chapter 12—Deep Questions Merit Responsible Answers

How, then, shall I respond to those who ask: "What was God doing before He made heaven and earth?" I don't answer facetiously, shrugging off the force of the question as a certain one is reported to have done. This one said, "He was preparing hell for those who pry too deep."

It's one thing to see the answer, but it's quite another to laugh at the questioner, so I don't answer like that. I would've willingly answered, "I don't know what I don't know," instead of causing the one who asked a deep question to be ridiculed—especially if such tactics gain praise for a worthless answer.

Rather, I say that You, our God, are the Creator of every creature. If in the term "heaven and earth" every creature is included, I boldly say further: "Before God made heaven and earth, He didn't make anything at all. For if He did, what did He make unless it were a creature?" I wish I knew. Nevertheless, I do know that no creature was made before any creature was made.

Chapter 13—God's Time is Eternally Today

If the roving thought of someone should question if You, the Almighty God, the All-creating and All-sustaining One, the Architect of heaven and earth, did for ages unnumbered abstain from creation before You actually did it, let him awake and realize that he wonders at illusions. What temporal medium could hold the unnumbered ages that didn't pass by, since You are the Author and Creator of all the ages? Or what periods of time would those be that were not made by You? Or how could they have already passed away if they had not already been?

Therefore, since You are the Creator of time, if there was any time before You made heaven and earth, why is it said that You abstained from working? For You made that very time itself, and periods could not pass by before You made the entire temporal creation. However, if there was no time before heaven and earth, how, then, can it be asked, "What were You doing then?" For there was no "then" when there was no time.

Furthermore, You don't precede any given period of time by another period of time. Otherwise, You wouldn't precede all periods of time. You are ever-present eternity, so You precede all times past, and extend beyond all future times, for they are still to come—and when they have come, they will be past. However, "You *are* the same, and Your years will have no end."[414]

Your years neither go nor come, but our years both go and come in order that all separate moments may come to pass. All Your years stand together as one, since they exist in You. Your years past don't exclude the years to come because Your years do not pass away. All these years of ours shall be with You, when all of them shall have ceased to be. Your years are but a day, and Your day is not recurrent, but always today. Your "today" doesn't yield to tomorrow and doesn't follow yesterday. Your "today" is eternity.

Therefore, You generated the Coeternal, to whom You said, "This day I have begotten You."[415] You made all time and before all times You are, and there was never a time when there was no time.

CHAPTER 14—THE PASSAGE OF TIME

Therefore, there was no time when You hadn't made anything, because You hadn't made time itself. Furthermore, there are no times that are coeternal with You, because You abide forever—but if times should abide, they would not be times.

What is time? Who can easily and briefly explain it? Who can even comprehend it in thought or put the answer into words? Yet isn't it true that in conversation we refer to time familiarly and knowingly? Surely we understand time when we speak of it. Likewise, we understand time when we hear another speak of it.

What, then, is time? If no one asks me, I know what it is. However, if I wish to explain time to him who asks, I don't know. Yet I say with confidence that I know that if nothing passed away, there would be no past time. Also, if nothing were still to come, there would be no future time. And again, if there were nothing at all, there would be no present time.

How can it be that there are the two times, past and future, when now the past is no longer and the future is not yet? However, if the present were always present and did not pass into past time, it obviously wouldn't be time but eternity. If time present—if it can be time—comes into existence only because it passes into time past, how can we say that it is, since the cause of its being is its ceasing to be? Therefore, can we not truly say that time is only as it tends toward nonbeing?

CHAPTER 15—PAST, PRESENT, FUTURE

Still we speak of a long time and a short time, but never speak this way except of time past and future. We call a hundred years ago, for example, a long time past. Likewise, we should call a hundred years future a long time to come. But we call ten days ago a short time past, and ten days future a short time to come. In what sense is something long or short that is nonexistent? The past is not now, and the future is not yet, so let's not say, "It is long." Instead, let's say of the past, "It was long," and of the future, "It will be long."

Nevertheless, O Lord, my Light, shall not Your truth make a mockery of man even here? Was that long time past long when it was already past, or when it was still present? It might've been long when there was a period that could be long, but when it was past, it no longer was. That being the case, then that which was not at all could not be long. Therefore, let's not say, "Time past was long," for we'll not discover what it was that was long because it's past, so it no longer exists. Rather, let's say that, "Time present was long, because when it was present it was long." For then it had not yet passed so as not to be, so it was still in a state that could be called long. However, after it passed, it ceased to be long simply because it ceased to be.

Therefore, let's see, O human soul, whether present time can be long, for it has been given you to feel and measure the periods of time. How, then, will you answer me?

Is a hundred years when present a long time? First, let's see whether a hundred years can be present at once. For if the first year in the century is current, then it's present time, and the other ninety and nine are still future. Therefore, they are not yet. However, if the second year is current, one year is already past, the second present, and the remaining future. So if we fix on any middle year of this century as present, those before it are past, those after it are future. Therefore, a hundred years cannot be present all at once.

Let's see, then, whether the year that is now current can be present. If the first month is current, then the rest are future. If the second is current, the first is already past and the remainder isn't yet. Therefore, the current year is not present all at once. And if it's not present as a whole, then the year is not present. Twelve months make up the year, from which each individual month when it's current is itself present one at a time, but the rest are either past or future.

Time Passes in Fleeting Fractions

Therefore, time present, which we found was the only time that could be called "long," has been cut down to the space of scarcely a single day. However, let's examine even that, for one day is never present as a whole. Each day is made up of twenty-four hours, divided between night and day. The first of these hours has the rest of them as future, and the last of them has the preceding as past. Any of those between have those that preceded it as past and those that succeed it as future.

Each hour passes away in fleeting fractions. The part of it that has fled is past and what remains is still future. If any fraction of time is conceived that can't be divided into the most minute momentary point, this alone is what we may call time present. However, this passes so rapidly from future to past that it can't be extended by any delay. If it is, it's then divided into past and future. But the present has no extension[416] whatever.

Where, therefore, is that time which we may call "long"? Is it future? Actually we don't say of the future, "It is long," for it hasn't yet come to be, so as to be long. Instead, we say, "It will be long."

When will it be? For since it's future, it'll not be long, because what may be long isn't yet. Long will be long only when it passes from the future which is not as yet, and will have begun to be present so that there can be something that may be long. Nevertheless, in that case, time present cries aloud, in the words we have already heard, that it cannot be "long."

CHAPTER 16—INTERVALS OF PERCEPTION

Nevertheless, O Lord, we do perceive intervals of time and we compare them with each other—some are longer and others are shorter. We even measure how much longer or shorter this time may be than that time. We also say that this time is twice as long, or three times as long, while this other time is only just as long as that other.

We measure the passage of time when we measure intervals of perception. But who can measure times past which now are no longer, or times future which are not yet—unless perhaps someone will dare to say that what does not exist can be measured? Therefore, while time is passing, it can be perceived and measured, but when it's past, it can't, since it is not.

CHAPTER 17—TIMES PRESENT AND TIMES PAST

O Father! I'm seeking the truth, not affirming it. So direct and rule me O my God.

Who is there who will tell me that there are not three times—time past, time present, and time future? Who can say that there is only time present because the other two don't exist? Or do they also exist, but when, from the future, time becomes present, it proceeds from some secret place, and when, from times present, it becomes past, it recedes into some secret place?

Where have those men that foretold the future seen what they foretold if it didn't yet exist? For what doesn't exist can't be seen. Likewise, those who tell of things past could not speak of them as if they were true if they didn't see them in their minds. These things could in no way be discerned if they didn't exist. Therefore, there are times present and times past.

Chapter 18—Foretelling the Future

Grant me permission, O Lord, to seek even further. O my Hope, let not my purpose be confounded, for if there are times past and future, I wish to know where they are. However, if I've not yet succeeded in this, I still know that wherever they are, they are not there as future or past, but as present. If they are there as future, they are there as "not yet." If they are there as past, they are there as "no longer." Therefore, wherever they are and whatever they are, they exist only as present.

Although we tell of past things as true, they are drawn out of the memory. Not the things themselves, which have already passed, but words constructed from the images of the perceptions that were formed in the mind. They're like footprints in their passage through the senses.

My childhood, for instance, which is no longer, still exists in time past, which does not now exist. However, when I call to mind its image and speak of it, I see it in the present because it's still in my memory. Whether there be a similar explanation for the foretelling of future events—seeing the images of things that are not yet as if they already exist—I confess, O my God, I don't know. This I do know: We generally think ahead about our future actions, and this premeditation is in time present. However, the action which we premeditate is not yet, because it is still future. When we've started the action and begun to do what we were premeditating, then that action will be in time present, because then it is no longer in time future.

Nothing can be seen except what exists. However, the secret foreseeing of future events happens. What exists now is not future, but present. Therefore, when the one foretelling says that future events are seen, it can't see the events themselves, for they don't yet exist—they're still in time future. Perhaps, instead, their causes and their signs are seen, which already do exist. Therefore, to those already beholding these causes and signs, they are not future, but present, and from them future things are predicted because they are conceived in the mind. These conceptions of the mind exist in the present, so those who predict future things see the conceptions in time present.

For example: I see the dawn and predict that the sun is about to rise. What I see is in time present, but what I predict is in time future. Not that the sun is future, for it already exists, but the sun rising is future, because it is not yet. However, I couldn't predict even its rising, unless I had an image of it in my mind, as I do even now as I speak. But the dawn that I see in the sky is not the rising of the sun, though it does precede it, nor is it a conception in my mind. These two, then, the dawn and the future rising of the sun, are seen in time present so that the event, which is in time future, may be predicted.

Future events, therefore, are not yet, and if they're not yet, they don't exist. If they don't exist, they can't be seen at all, but they can be predicted from things present, which now are and are seen.

CHAPTER 19—REVELATION OF FUTURE EVENTS

Now, O Ruler of Your creatures, what is the mode by which You teach souls those things that are still future? For You have taught

Your prophets. How do You, to whom nothing is future, teach future things, or rather teach things present from the signs of things future? What doesn't exist certainly cannot be taught. This way of Yours is too far from my sight and too great for me, I cannot attain to it.[417] Nevertheless, I'll be enabled by You, when You will grant it, O sweet Light of my secret eyes.

Chapter 20—Three Times—Present

Even now it's plainly evident that there are neither times future nor times past. Thus it's not properly said that there are three times, past, present, and future. Perhaps it might be said rightly that there are three times as such:

1. A time present of things past.

2. A time present of things present.

3. A time present of things future.

These three do coexist somehow in the soul, for otherwise I couldn't see them. The time present of things past is memory. The time present of things present is direct experience. The time present of things future is expectation.[418] If we are allowed to speak of these things as such, I see three times, and grant that there are three.

Let it continue to be said, then, as our misapplied custom has it: "There are three times, past, present, and future." I'll not be troubled by it. Nor will I argue or object, provided that what is said is understood, so that neither the future nor the past is said to exist now. There are but few things we speak about properly and many more that we don't, though we understand one another's meaning.

Chapter 21–The Difficulty of Measuring Time

As I stated before, we measure periods of time as they pass so that we can compare this time to that one by length, and so on for the other fractions of time that we can count by measuring.

We measure periods of time as they pass. If anyone asks, "How do you know this?" I can answer: "I know because we measure. We could not measure things that don't exist, and things past and future don't exist." But how do we measure present time since it has no extension? It's measured while it passes, but when it's passed it's not measured, because measurement of nothing is impossible.

Where does it come from, how does it come, and where does it pass while being measured? Where from but the future? Which way, except through the present? Where does it go, but into the past? Therefore, from what is not yet, through what has no length, it passes into what is now no longer.

However, what do we measure, unless it's a time of some length? For we cannot speak of single, double, triple, equal, and all the other ways in which we speak of time, except in terms of the length of the periods of time. But in what "length," then, do we measure passing time? Is it in the future, from which it passes over? But what does not yet exist cannot be measured. Or, is it in the present, through which it passes? But what has no length we cannot measure. Or is it in the past into which it passes? But what is no longer, we cannot measure.

Chapter 22–To Understand Time

O Lord my God, my soul burns to understand this most intricate problem. O good Father, I beseech You through Christ; don't close off both the familiar and the obscure from my desire.

Don't bar my desire from entering into them, but let their light dawn by Your enlightening mercy.

O Lord, whom else could I ask about these things? Who better to confess my ignorance of them than to You? These studies of mine, in which I greatly desire to understand Your Scriptures, are not a bore. Therefore, give me what I love, for I do love it with the love You have given me. O Father, You truly know how to give good gifts to Your children, so give this to me. Grant it, since I have sought to understand. I'll work hard until You open it. I implore You, through Christ and in His name, the Holy of Holies, let no man interrupt my quest.

"I have believed, and therefore do I speak."[419] This is my hope, and for this I live: That I may contemplate the joys of my Lord.[420] Behold, You have made my days grow old, and they pass away— how I don't know.

We speak of this time and that time, and these times and those times: "How long ago since he said this?" "How long ago since he did this?" "How long ago since I saw that?" "This syllable is twice as long as that single short syllable." These are words we say and hear. By them, we are understood and we understand. They are quite commonplace and ordinary, yet still the meaning of these very same things lies deeply hidden awaiting its discovery.

Chapter 23—The Measurement of Time

I once heard an educated man say that the movement of the sun, moon, and stars constituted time. I didn't agree. Why shouldn't the motions of all bodies constitute time? What if the lights of heaven should cease but a potter's wheel continue to turn. Would there be no time by which we could measure the rotations? Could we not say that it turned at equal intervals, or, if it moved then more slowly and now more quickly, that some rotations were longer and others shorter? While we were saying this, would we not be speaking in time as well? Or would there not be in our words some syllables that were long and others short, because the first took a longer time to sound, and the others a shorter time?

O God, grant men to see in small things the concepts that are common[421] to all things, both great and small. Both the stars and the lights of heaven are "for signs and seasons, and for days and years."[422] This is doubtless the case, but just as I could not say that the circuit of that potter's wheel was a day, neither could that scholar say that there was no time.

I thirst to know the power and nature of time by which we measure the movement of bodies, and say, for example, that this movement is twice as long as that. I ask, because the word "day" refers not only to the length of time that the sun is above the earth separating day from night, but also to the sun's entire circuit from east all the way around to east. It's on this account that we can say, "So many days have passed" (nights included).

Time Measures the Movement of the Sun

Since the day is ended by the motion of the sun and by its passage from east to east, I ask whether the motion itself is the day, or whether the day is the period in which that motion is completed—or both? For if the sun's passage is the day, then there would be a day even if the sun should finish its course in as short a period as an hour. If the motion itself is the day, then it would not be a day if from one sunrise to another there was a period no longer than an hour. But the sun would have to go around twenty-four times to make just one day. If it's both, then that could not be called a day if the sun ran its entire course in the period of an hour.

Nor would it be a day if, while the sun stood still, as much time passed as the sun usually covered during its entire course.

Therefore, I'll not ask any more what is called a day, but rather what time is, for it's by time that we measure the circuit of the sun. By time, we would be able to say that the sun was finished in half the period of time that it customarily takes if it were completed in a period of only twelve hours. If, then, we compare these periods, we could call one of them a single and the other a double period, as if the sun might run its course from east to east, sometimes in a single period and sometimes in a double period.

Let no man tell me that the movement of the heavenly bodies constitutes time. For when the sun stood still at the prayer of a certain man in order that he might gain his victory in battle, it stood still but time went on. For in as long a span of time as was sufficient the battle was fought and ended.[423]

I see, then, that time is a certain kind of extension. But do I see it, or do I only seem to? You, O Light and Truth, will show me.

CHAPTER 24—TIME IS NOT THE MOVEMENT OF AN OBJECT

Do You command me to agree if someone says that time is "the movement of an object?" No! You told me that no object is moved but in time. When an object is moved, I measure by time how long it was moving from the time when it began until it stopped. Likewise, if I didn't see when movement began and it continued to move so I couldn't see it stop, I was unable to measure the movement.

If I look at an object for a long time, I can affirm only that the time is long but not how long it may be. This is because when we say, "How long?" we are speaking comparatively. For example:

"This is as long as that," or, "This is twice as long as that" or other similar ratios. But if we're able to observe the point in space where the object is from and the point to which it is moved, we can say how long the movement took.

Since the motion of an object is one thing, and the norm by which we measure how long it takes is another thing, we cannot see which of these two is to be called time. For though an object is sometimes moved and sometimes stands still, we measure not only its movement but also its rest, and both by time! Thus we say, "It stood still as long as it moved," or, "It stood still twice or three times as long as it moved," or any other ratio which our measuring has either determined or imagined. Therefore, time is not the movement of an object.

CHAPTER 25—IGNORANT OF TIME

I confess to You, O Lord that I am still ignorant as to what time is. Again I confess to You, O Lord, that I know I'm speaking all these things in time, and that I've already spoken of time for a long time, and that "very long" is not long except when measured by the duration of time.

How, then, do I know this, when I don't know what time is? Or, is it possible that I don't know how I can express what I do know? Sadly, I don't even know the extent of my own ignorance.

O my God, in Your presence I don't lie. As my heart is, so I speak. You will light my candle, and You, O Lord my God, will enlighten my darkness.[424]

CHAPTER 26—THE MEASUREMENT OF TIME

Doesn't my soul truly confess to You that I do measure intervals of time? But what is it that I measure, O God, and how is it that I don't know what I measure? I measure the motion of a body by time, but the time itself I don't measure. However, could I truly measure the motion of a body—how long it takes, how long it's in motion from place to place—unless I could measure the time in which it's moving?

How, then, is this time itself measured? Do we measure a longer time by a shorter time, as we measure the length of a crossbeam in terms of cubits?[425] We can say that the length of a long syllable is measured by that of a short syllable and then say that the long syllable is double.

We also measure the length of poems by the length of the lines, and the length of the line by the length of the feet, and the length of the feet by the length of the syllable, and the length of the long syllables by the length of the short ones. We don't measure poems by pages, for in that way we would measure space rather than time. But when we speak the words as they pass by we say:

> It's a long stanza, because it's made up of so many verses. They are long verses because they consist of so many feet. They are long feet because they extend over so many syllables. This is a long syllable because it's twice the length of a short one.

However, no certain measure of time is obtained this way, since it's possible that if a shorter verse is pronounced slowly, it may require more time than a longer one pronounced hurriedly. The same would hold for a stanza, or a foot, or a syllable. From this it appears to me that time is nothing other than extendedness,[426] but extendedness of what I don't know.

This is a marvel to me, because the extendedness may be of the mind itself. What is it that I measure, O God, when I say either, roughly, "This time is longer than that," or precisely, "This is twice as long as that." I know that I'm measuring time. But I'm not measuring the future, for it's not yet. Nor am I measuring the present because no length extends it. Nor am I measuring the past because it no longer is. Therefore, what is it that I'm measuring? Is it time in its passage, but not time past?

CHAPTER 27—THE PAST CONSUMES THE FUTURE

Press on, O my mind, and focus with all your power. God is my Helper: "it is He who has made us, not we ourselves."[427]

Give heed where the truth begins to dawn.[428] Suppose now that a bodily voice begins to sound, and continues to sound, on and on, and then ceases. Now there is silence. The voice is past, and there is no longer a sound. It was future before it sounded and could not be measured because it was not yet. Now it can't be measured because it is no longer. Therefore, while it was sounding, it might have been measured because then there was something that could be measured. But even then it did not stand still, for it was in motion and was passing away. Could it, on that account, be any more readily measured? For while it was passing away, it was being extended into some interval of time in which it might be measured, since the present has no length.

Suppose, though, that the sound could have been measured, then also suppose that another voice had begun to sound and is still sounding with no interruption to break its continued flow. It can be measured only while sounding, because when it has ceased to sound it will be already past and there will be nothing that can be measured.

We Measure Times

Let's measure the sound exactly and say how much it is. But while it's sounding, it can't be measured except from the instant when it began to sound, down to the final moment when it stopped. We measure the time interval itself from a beginning point to an end. This is why a voice that has not yet ended cannot be measured, so that one could say how long or how briefly it will continue. Nor can it be said to be equal to another voice or single or double in comparison to it or anything like this. However, when it has ended, it is no longer. Therefore, how can the sound be measured?

We measure times, though not those which are not yet, nor those which no longer are, nor those which are stretched out by some delay, nor those which have no limit. Therefore, we measure neither times future nor times past, nor times present, nor times passing by, yet we do measure times.

Deus Creator omnium[429] is a verse of eight syllables that alternates between short and long syllables. The four short ones, the first, third, fifth, and seventh, are single in relation to the four long ones, the second, fourth, sixth, and eighth. Each of the long ones is double the length of each of the short ones. I affirm this and report it, and common sense perceives that this indeed is the case. By common sense, then, I measure a long syllable by a short one, and I find that it's twice as long. But when one sounds after another, if the first is short and the latter long, how can I hold the short one and apply it to the long one as a measure? How can I discover that the long one is twice as long, when, in fact, the long one does not begin to sound until the short one ends? That same long syllable I don't measure as present, since I can't measure it until it's ended, but its ending is its passing away.

What is it, then, that I can measure? Where is the short syllable by which I measure? Where is the long one that I am measuring? Both have sounded, have flown away and passed on—they are no longer. Still I measure and confidently answer, as far as a trained ear can be trusted, that this syllable is single and that syllable double. This I couldn't do unless both had passed and were ended. Therefore, I don't measure them, for they exist no longer. However, I measure something in my memory, which remains fixed.

We Measure in our Mind

It's in you, O mind of mine, that I measure periods of time. O my mind, don't shout me down that it exists objectively, and don't overwhelm yourself with the turbulent flood of your impressions. I measure the periods of time in you. I measure as time present the impression that things make on you as they pass by and what remains after they have passed. I don't measure the things themselves that have passed by and left their impression on you. This is what I measure when I measure periods of time. Either, then, these are the periods of time or else I don't measure time at all.

What are we doing when we measure silence and say that this silence has lasted as long as that voice lasts? Don't we project our thought to the measure of a sound as if it were then sounding, so that we can say something concerning the intervals of silence in a given span of time? For, even when both the voice and the tongue are still, we review them in thought just as if we were speaking them aloud and we specify their time spans. Things such as:

- Poems and verses
- Conversation of various kinds
- Various measures of movement

If a man wishes to utter a prolonged sound, and if, in forethought, has decided how long it should be, he has in silence already gone through a span of time, and committed the sound to memory. Thus he begins to speak and his voice sounds until it reaches the predetermined end. His voice has truly sounded and will go on sounding, but what has already finished has already sounded and what remains will still sound. Thus it passes on, until the present intention carries the future over into the past. The past increases by the diminution of the future until by the consumption of all the future all is past.[430]

Chapter 28—The Mind Measures Time

How is the future diminished or consumed when it doesn't yet exist? Or how does the past, which exists no longer, increase, unless in the mind where all this happens there are three functions? The mind expects, it attends, and it remembers, so that what it expects passes into what it remembers by way of what it attends to.

Who denies that future things don't yet exist? Nevertheless, in the mind there is already the expectation of things still future. Who denies that past things now no longer exist? Still there is in the mind the memory of things past. Who denies that time present has no length, since it passes away in a moment? Yet, our attention has a continuity and it's through this that what is present may proceed to become absent. Therefore, future time, which is nonexistent, is not long, but "a long future" is "a long expectation of the future." Nor is time past, which is now no longer, long. A "long past" is "a long memory of the past."

I'm about to repeat a psalm that I know. Before I begin, my attention encompasses the whole, but once I've begun, as much of it that becomes past while I speak is still stretched out in my memory. The span of my action is divided between my memory, which contains what I have repeated, and my expectation, which contains what I am about to repeat. Yet my attention is continually present with me, and through it what was future is carried over so that it becomes past. The more this is done and repeated, the more the memory is enlarged, and expectation is shortened until the entire expectation is exhausted. Then the entire action is ended and passed into memory.

What occurs in the entire psalm occurs also in each individual part and in each individual syllable. This also holds in the even longer action of which that psalm is only a portion. The same holds in the entire life of man, of which all the actions of men are parts. The same holds in the entire age of the sons of men, of which all the lives of men are parts.

CHAPTER 29—FOLLOWING JESUS INTO THE FUTURE

"Because Your loving-kindness is better than life itself,"[431] observe how my life is but a stretching out. Observe, also, how Your right hand has upheld me in so many ways and by so many means in my Lord, the Son of Man. Jesus is the Mediator between You, the One, and us, the many. Through Him I lay hold upon Him in whom I'm also laid hold upon. Through Him I'm gathered up from my old way of life to follow Him and forget what is behind, no longer stretched out but now pulled together again—stretching forth not to what will be and will pass away but to those things that are before me. Now I follow Him, not distractedly, but intently, for the prize of my heavenly calling[432] is in Him, where I may hear the sound of Your praise and contemplate Your delights, which neither come to be nor pass away.

My years are now spent in mourning,[433] but You, O Lord, are my comfort, my eternal Father. Nevertheless, I've been torn between the times, the order of which I don't know. My thoughts, even the inmost and deepest places of my soul, are mangled by turmoil until I shall flow together into You, purged and molten in the fire of Your love.

Chapter 30—Time Requires Space

I will be immovable and fixed in You, and Your truth will be my mold. I will not have to endure the questions of those men who, as if in a morbid disease, thirst for more than they can hold. They ask, "What did God make before He made heaven and earth?" or, "How did it come into His mind to make something when He had never before made anything?" Grant them, O Lord, to consider well what they are saying, and grant them to see that where there is no time they cannot say "never." When, therefore, He is said, "never to have made" something, what is this but to say that it was made in no time at all?

Let these men see that there could be no time without a created world, and let them cease to speak empty words of this kind. Let them also be stretched out to those things which are before them, and understand that You, the eternal Creator of all times, are before all times and that no times are coeternal with You. Nor is any creature, even if there is a creature "above time."

Chapter 31—Only in God is Time Understood

O Lord my God, what a chasm there is in Your deep secret! How far short have the consequences of my sins cast me? Heal my eyes, that I may enjoy Your light. Surely, if there is a mind that so greatly abounds in knowledge and foreknowledge, to which all things past and future are as well known as one psalm is well known to me, that mind would be exceedingly marvelous and altogether astonishing. For whatever is past and whatever is yet to come would be no more concealed from him than the past and future of that psalm were hidden from me when I was chanting it—how much of it had been sung from the beginning and what and how much still remained till the end.

Far be it from You, O Creator of the universe, and Creator of our souls and bodies, that You should merely know all things past and future. You know them far more wonderfully and far more mysteriously. You know them not as the feelings of one singing or hearing a familiar song, in which his feelings are varied and his senses are divided because of his expectation of words still to come and his remembrance of those that are past.

This isn't the way that anything happens to You, who are unchangeably eternal and the eternal Creator of minds. In the beginning, You knew both the heavens and the earth without any change in Your knowledge. Therefore, You made heaven and earth in their beginnings with no division in Your action.[434] Let he who understands this confess to You, and let he who doesn't also confess to You! O God, exalted as You are, Your dwelling place is still the humble in heart! You lift those who are cast down, and those for whom You are the Most High don't fall.

BOOK TWELVE

The Processes of Creation

Augustine now moves to a discussion of the mode of creation and the truth of Scripture. He explores the relation of the visible and formed matter of heaven and earth to the prior medium from which it was formed. This leads to an intricate analysis of "unformed matter" and the primal "possibility" from which God created. Augustine finds a reference to this in the misconstrued Scriptural phrase "the heaven of heavens." Realizing that his interpretation of Gen. 1:1, 2, is not self-evidently the only possibility, Augustine turns to an elaborate discussion of the multiplicity of perspectives in Scriptural interpretation and in the course of this, reviews the various possibilities of true interpretation of his Scripture text. He emphasizes the importance of tolerance where there are plural options, and confidence where basic Christian faith is concerned.

Chapter 1—Knock and it will be Opened

O Lord, my heart is deeply stirred, when in this poor life of mine the words of Your Holy Scriptures pierce it. This is why the poverty of the human intellect expresses itself in an abundance of language: inquiry is more talkative than discovery, demanding takes longer than obtaining, and the hand that knocks is more active than the hand that receives. However, we have these promises, and who shall break them?

> *If God is for us, who can be against us?*[435]
> *Ask, and it will be given to you; seek, and you will find; knock, and it will be opened to you. For everyone who asks receives, and he who seeks finds, and to him who knocks it will be opened.*[436]

These promises are from You, Lord. Therefore, we have no need to fear being deceived because Truth has promised.

Chapter 2—Heaven of Heavens

My tongue humbly confesses to Your exaltation, for You made heaven and earth. You made the heaven that I see and this earth upon which I walk, from which came this "earth" that I carry about me.

O Lord, where is that heaven of heavens about which we hear in the words of the psalm, "The heaven of heavens is the Lord's, but the earth he hath given to the children of men"?[437] Where is the heaven that we cannot see, in relation to which all that we can see is earth? For the entire physical creation is beautifully formed, though not everywhere in its entirety, and our earth is the lowest of these levels.

Nevertheless, compared with that heaven of heavens, even the heaven of our own earth is only earth. It's not unreasonable to call both earth and sky "earth" when compared with that indescribable heaven which is the Lord's and not for the sons of men.

Chapter 3—The Cradle of Creation

Truly this earth was invisible and unformed,[438] and there was an inexpressibly profound abyss[439] above in which there was no light since it had no form. Lord, You commanded it written, "darkness was on the face of the deep."[440] What is darkness except the absence of light? For if there had been light, where would it have been except by being over all, showing itself rising aloft and giving light? Therefore, where there was as yet no light, why was it that darkness was present, unless it was that light was absent?

Darkness, then, was heavy upon the deep, because the light from above was absent…just as there is silence where there is no sound. What is it to have silence anywhere but simply not to have sound? O Lord, haven't You taught this soul which confesses to You, that before You formed and separated this formless matter there was *nothing*: no color, no figure, no body, no spirit? Yet it wasn't absolutely nothing that it was a certain formlessness without shape.

Chapter 4—Formlessness of Primordial Matter

Some form of common speech must be used so those who are slow to learn may comprehend that formlessness. But what can be found anywhere in the world nearer to a total formlessness than the earth and the abyss? Because of their being on the lowest level, they are less beautiful than the other, higher parts, which are translucent and shining.

Therefore, I ponder the formlessness of matter. You created without shapely form that with which to make this shapely world, fittingly indicated to men by the phrase, "The earth invisible and unformed."

Chapter 5—Thoughts on Unformed Matter

Our human thought seeks something for the senses to fasten to in this concept of unformed matter. In so doing, we may be attempting to either know by being ignorant, or by knowing how not to know. Thoughts of this nature may say:

> It's not an intelligible form, such as life or justice, since it's the material for bodies; nor is it a former perception, for there is nothing in the invisible and unformed, which can be seen and felt.

Chapter 6—Comprehending the Unformed

O Lord, I must confess to You by my mouth and my pen all that You have taught me concerning this unformed matter. However, when I first heard of it and didn't understand—those who told me didn't understand either—I imagined this matter had countless and varied forms. I didn't comprehend it correctly. In my mind, I imagined all sorts of foul and horrible "forms," but they were "forms" nonetheless.

I still called this matter formless, not because it was unformed, but because it had a kind of form that my mind turned away from. It was bizarre and out of place, and caused confusion in my human weakness. What I did imagine as unformed was so, not because it was deprived of form, but only as it compared with more beautiful forms. Then reason persuaded me, saying that I ought to remove all vestiges of form whatsoever if I wished to imagine matter that was entirely unformed...this I couldn't do. I could more readily imagine that what was deprived of all form simply didn't exist than I could of anything between form and nothing—something which was neither formed nor nothing, something that was unformed and nearly nothing.

The Changeability of Changeable Things

Therefore, my mind stopped questioning my spirit, filled as it was with the images of formed bodies, changing and varying them according to its will. So I applied myself to the objects themselves and looked more deeply into their changeability, by which they cease to be what they had been and begin to be what they were not. This transition from form to form I regarded as involving something like a formless condition, though not actual nothingness.[441]

I desired to know, not to guess. So, if I were to confess to You all the various knots You have untied for me about this question, who among my readers could endure to grasp the entire account? Nevertheless, my heart will not cease to give honor to You or to sing Your praises concerning those things which it is unable to express.

The changeability of changeable things carries with it the possibility of all the forms into which changeable things can be changed. But what is this changeability? Is it soul? Is it body? Is it the external appearance of soul or body? Could it be said, "Nothing was something," and "That which is, is not"? If this were possible, I would declare that this was it, and in some such manner it must have been in order to receive these visible and composite forms.[442]

CHAPTER 7—CREATED OUT OF NOTHING

Where and how was this, unless it came from You, because all things are from You, in so far as they are? However, the farther something is from You, the more unlike You it is—and this isn't a matter of distance or place.

You, O God, aren't one thing in one place and another thing in another place, but the Selfsame, and the Selfsame, and the Selfsame. You are "Holy, Holy, Holy, Lord God Almighty."[443] So it was that in the beginning, and through Your Wisdom which is from You and born of Your substance, You created something out of nothing.[444]

You created the heavens and the earth, but not out of Yourself, because then they would be equal to Your only Son and thereby to You. There is no sense in which it would be right that anything should be equal to You that was not of You. However, what else besides You was there out of which You might create these things, O God, one Trinity, and trine Unity? Therefore, You created the heavens and the earth—something great and something small—out of nothing, for You are Almighty and Good. You are able to make all things good, even the great heaven and the small earth.

You are, and there was nothing else from which You created heaven and earth, these two things, one near You, the other near to nothing. The one to which only You are superior, the other to which nothing is inferior.

CHAPTER 8—THE FIRMAMENT BETWEEN WATER AND THE WATERS

That heaven of heavens was Yours, O Lord. However, the earth, which You gave to the sons of men to be seen and touched, wasn't in the same form then as it is now when we see and touch it. Then it was invisible and unformed, and there was an abyss over which there was no light. The darkness was truly <u>over</u> the abyss, more than just <u>in</u> the abyss. This abyss of waters, which now is visible, has in its depths a certain light appropriate to its nature, and perceptible to fishes and other creatures that move about on the bottom. But then, the entire abyss was almost nothing, since it was still altogether unformed. Yet even there, was something that had the possibility of being formed.

O Lord, You made the world out of unformed matter, and the abyss that You made out of nothing, You made into almost nothing. From it, then, You made these great things that the sons of men marvel at.

The physical heaven is truly marvelous—this firmament between the water and the waters. You made it on the second day after the creation of light, saying, "Let it be done," and it was done.[445] This firmament, that is, the heaven of this earth and sea which You made on the third day, You called heaven, which gives a visible shape to the unformed matter which You had made before all the days. Before any day existed, You had already made a heaven—the heaven of this heaven, for in the beginning You made heaven and earth.

However, the earth itself was unformed matter. It was invisible and unformed, and darkness was over the abyss. Out of this invisible and unformed earth, this formlessness which is almost nothing, You then made all these things of which the changeable world consists. However, it doesn't fully consist in itself,[446] because its very changeableness appears in that its times and seasons can be observed and numbered. Periods of time are measured by the changes of things, while the forms, whose matter is the invisible earth of which we have spoken, are varied and altered.

CHAPTER 9—CREATION BEFORE EARTH

Therefore, when the Spirit, the Teacher of Moses, mentions that, "in the beginning You made heaven and earth," He says nothing about times and is silent as to the days. Clearly, the heaven of heavens that You created in the beginning is in some way an intellectual creature, although in no way coeternal with You, O Trinity. Nonetheless, it partakes in Your eternity. Because of the sweetness of its happy contemplation of You, it is greatly restrained in its own changeability and clings to You with no lapse from the time in which it was created, surpassing the rolling changes of time. However, this shapelessness—this earth invisible and unformed—wasn't numbered among the days itself. For where there is no shape or order there is nothing that either comes or goes, and where this does not occur there certainly are no days, nor any change of duration.

CHAPTER 10—YOU SPOKE LIFE INTO MY DARKNESS

O Truth, O Light of my heart, let not my own darkness speak to me! I had fallen into that darkness and by it was darkened. Nevertheless, even in its depths, I came to love You. I went astray, but still I remembered You. I heard Your voice behind me, bidding me to return, though I could scarcely hear You through the roar of my unruly passions.

Behold, now I'm returning to You, burning and thirsting after Your fountain. Let no one hinder me, for here I will drink and so have life. Let me not be my own life, because of myself I have lived badly. I was death to myself, but in You I have revived. Speak to me, and converse with me. I believe Your books, the words of which are very deep.

Chapter 11—Creation Clings to its Creator

O Lord, with a strong voice in my inner ear, You've already told me that You are eternal and alone have immortality. You aren't changed by any shape or motion, and Your will isn't altered by temporal process—no will that changes is immortal. This is clear to me, in Your sight, but let it become more and more clear, I pray. Let me abide soberly under Your wings in that light.

Lord, You've also told me, with a strong voice in my inner ear, that You created all natures and all substances that aren't what You are Yourself, yet they do exist. Only that which is nothing at all is not from You. Furthermore, any movement of the will away from You, who is, toward something that only exists in a lesser degree is an offense and a sin. Nobody's sin either hurts You or disturbs the order of Your rule, either first or last. All this, in Your sight, is clear to me. Let it become clearer and clearer, I pray, and in that light let me abide soberly under Your wings.

Likewise, You've told me, with a strong voice in my inner ear, that this creation—who delights only in You—is not coeternal with You. With persevering purity it draws its support from You, and nowhere, ever betrays its own changeability, because You are ever present with it. Additionally, creation clings to You with its entire affection, having no future to expect and no past that it remembers; it is varied by no change and is extended by no time.

The House of the Lord

Your creation is blessed in You, its everlasting Inhabitant and its Light. I can't find a term that I would judge more fitting for "the heaven of the heavens of the Lord" than "Your house." It contemplates Your delights with no inclination toward anything else and with a pure mind in most harmonious stability, joins all together in the peace of those saintly spirits who are citizens of Your city in those heavens that are above this visible heaven.

From this let the soul that has wandered from You understand (as much as it can) how far above all times You are in Your eternity. Let it understand that Your house has never wandered away from You, and though not coeternal with You, it continually and unfailingly clings to You, suffering no change of time. This, in Your sight, is clear to me. O God, may it become clearer and clearer to me, I pray, and in this light may I soberly abide under Your wings.

I don't know what kind of formlessness there is in the mutations of these last and lowest creatures. Who will tell me, unless it's someone who, in the emptiness of his own heart, wanders about drunk in his own imaginations? Who, except such a one, would tell me whether, if all form was diminished and consumed, formlessness alone would remain, through which a thing was changed and turned from one species into another, so that sheer formlessness would then be characterized by temporal change? Surely this couldn't be, because without motion there is no time, and where there is no form there is no change.

Chapter 12—The Ordered Process of Motion and Form

These things I've considered as You've given me ability, O my God. You excite me to knock and open to me when I do, therefore, I seek understanding. Two things I find which You have made, not within intervals of time, although neither is coeternal with You. One of them is so formed that, with no wavering in its contemplation and no interval of change—changeable but not changed—it may fully enjoy Your eternity and immutability. The other is so formless that it couldn't change from one form to another (either of motion or of rest), so time has no hold upon it. However, You didn't leave this formless. Before any "day" in the beginning, You created heaven and earth—these are the two things of which I spoke.

However, "the earth was invisible and unformed, and darkness was over the abyss." By these words earth's formlessness is indicated to us. That way, those who can't fully understand total formlessness without arriving at nothing may in small steps be led forward. From this formlessness a second heaven might be created and a second earth. This one visible and well formed, with the ordered beauty of the waters, and whatever else is recorded as created (though not without days) in the formation of this world. All this because such things are so ordered that in them the changes of time may take place through the ordered processes of motion and form.

Chapter 13—Heaven Formed Prior to Earth

Meanwhile, O my God, this is what I understand Your Scriptures to say: "In the beginning God made the heaven and the earth, but the earth was invisible and unformed, and darkness was over the abyss." Scripture doesn't say on what day You created these things. So for the time being, I understand "heaven of heavens" to mean the intelligible heaven, where to understand is to know all at once—not "in part," not "darkly," not "through a glass," but as a simultaneous whole, in full sight, "face to face."[447] It's not this thing now and then another thing, but knowledge all at once with no temporal change.

By the invisible and unformed earth, I understand it's that which suffers no temporal change. Temporal change customarily means having one thing now and another later. However, where there is no form, there can be no distinction between this and that.

Therefore, by means of these two notions—one thing well formed in the beginning, heaven (the heaven of heavens), and another thing wholly unformed, earth (invisible and unformed)—I'm able to understand why Your Scripture said, with no mention of days, "In the beginning God created the heaven and the earth." For it immediately indicated which earth it was speaking about. When, on the second day, the firmament is recorded as having been created and called heaven, this suggests to us which heaven it was that he was speaking about earlier, without specifying a day.

Chapter 14—The Marvel of God's Revelation

Marvelous is the depth of Your revelations, O God. Their surface is before us, inviting the little ones, and yet wonderful is their depth. O my God, marvelous is their depth! It's a fearful thing to look into them, because they invoke awesome honor and tremors of love.

Enemies of Your revelation I vehemently hate. Oh, if You would slay them with Your two-edged sword, so that there would be no enemies! I prefer that they be slain to themselves, that they might live to You.

There are others who are not critics of the book of Genesis, but praise it. They declare that, "The Spirit of God who wrote these things by his servant, Moses, did not wish these words to be understood in this way. God's desire is to have it understood as we say, not as you say." To them, O God of us all, with You being the judge, I give answer.

CHAPTER 15—OBJECTORS ANSWERED

This, O God, is my answer:

> Will you say that what Truth tells me about the very eternity of the Creator is false? He speaks with a loud voice in my inner ear, so I know that His essence is changed in no respect by time and that His will is not distinct from His essence. Thus, He doesn't will one thing now and another later, but He wills once and for all everything that He wills. He doesn't will again and again, this no more but now that, nor does He will afterward what He didn't will before. Neither does He cease to will what He had willed before. Such a will would be mutable (changeable) and no mutable thing is eternal. But our God is eternal.
>
> Again, Truth tells me in my inner ear that the expectation of future things is turned to sight when they've come to pass, and this same sight is turned into memory when they've passed. Moreover, all thought that varies is mutable, and nothing mutable is eternal. But our God is eternal.

These things I sum up and put together. I conclude that my God, the eternal God, has not made any creature by any new will, and His knowledge doesn't admit anything transitory.

What, then, will you say to this, you objectors? Are these things false?

"No," they say.

What then? Is it false that every entity already formed and all matter capable of receiving form is from Him alone who is supremely good, because He is supreme?

"We do not deny this, either," they say.

What then? Do you deny this: that there is a certain magnificent created order that clings with such a pure love to the true and truly eternal God that, although it's not coeternal with Him, it doesn't separate itself from Him. Nor does it flow away into any mutation of change or process but abides in true contemplation of Him alone?

If You, O God, show Yourself to him who loves You as You have commanded, and are sufficient for him, then such a one will neither turn himself away from You, nor turn away toward himself.

This is "the house of God." It's not an earthly house and is not made from any celestial matter. This is a spiritual house, nourished in Your eternity and without blemish forever. You have made it steadfast forever and ever, and have given it a law that will not be removed. Still, it's not coeternal with You, O God, since it is not without beginning—it was created.

Wisdom Came Before All

We can find no <u>time</u> before creation, because wisdom was created before all things.[448] Wisdom is absolutely coeternal and equal with You, O God, and through Wisdom all things were created in the beginning. This is truly the created Wisdom, namely, the intelligible nature, which in its contemplation of light, is light. This is also called wisdom, even if it is a created wisdom. But the difference between the Light that lightens and that which is enlightened is as great as is the difference between the Wisdom that creates and that which is created.

Likewise we see the difference between the Righteousness that justifies and the righteousness that is made by justification. We are called Your righteousness as Paul, Your servant says: "That we might be made the righteousness of God in Him."[449] Therefore, a certain created wisdom was created before all things—it's the rational and intelligible mind of that pure city of Yours. It's our mother that is above and free,[450] "eternal in the heavens."[451] But in what heavens except those which praise You, the "heaven of heavens?" This also is the "heaven of heavens" which is the Lord's. We find no time before it, since what has been created before all things also precedes the creation of time. Still, the eternity of the Creator himself is before it, from whom it took its beginning as created, though not in time (since time as yet was not), even though time belongs to its created nature.

So it is that the intelligible heaven came to be from You, our God, but in such a way that it is quite another being than You— it's not the Selfsame. Yet we discover that not only is time not before it, but time isn't even in it, thus making it able to behold Your face forever and not ever be turned aside. Therefore, heaven is varied by no change at all. Nevertheless, there is still that changeability in virtue in which it could become dark and cold, if it were not cleaving to You with a supernal love.

The House of God

O house full of light and splendor! "LORD, I have loved the habitation of Your house,

And the place where Your glory dwells."[452] In my wandering let me sigh for you. I ask this of He who made you, that He would also possess me in you, seeing that He made me as well. "I have gone astray like a lost sheep,"[453] but on the shoulders of my Shepherd, I hope to be brought back to the house of God.

> What will you say to me now, you objectors? You still believe that Moses was the holy servant of God, and that his books were the oracles of the Holy Spirit. Isn't this the 'house of God' that you vainly seek for temporal change? You will not find it there. It rises above all extension and every revolving temporal period to what is forever good and clings fast to God.

"It is so," they reply.

> What, then, about those things that my heart cried out to my God, when it heard the voice of His praise? What, then, do you contend is false in them? Is it because matter was unformed, and since there was no form there was no order? But where there was no order there could have been no temporal change. Yet even this 'almost nothing,' since it was not altogether nothing, was truly from Him from whom everything that exists is, no matter what its state.

They reply, "This also we don't deny."

Chapter 16—Let God be the Judge

I would like to discuss further in Your presence, O my God, with those who admit that all these things Your Truth has spoken to my mind are true. Let those who deny these things bark and drown their own voices with as much racket as they please. I'll endeavor to persuade them to be quiet and to permit Your Word to reach them. However, if they're unwilling and reject me, I ask of You, O my God, that You would not be silent to me.[454] Speak truly in my heart. If only You would do so, I would send them away, blowing up the dust and raising it in their own eyes.

As for me, I'll enter the inward closet of my heart and sing songs of love to You, groaning with sounds unspeakable by this body.[455] I will remember Jerusalem, my mother,[456] with my heart uplifted to her and to You O God, Ruler of the source of Light, its Father, Guardian, and Husband. You, O God, are its pure and strong delight, its solid joy and all its goods inexpressible—and all of this at the same time, since You are the one supreme and true Good!

I will not be turned away until You have brought back together all that I am from this dispersion and deformity to the peace of that dearest mother, Jerusalem. She is where the first fruits of my spirit are to be found and from which all these things are promised to me, which You conform and confirm forever. However, as for those who don't declare the truth, but still honor Your Scripture set before us by Moses, who place it on the summit of authority yet oppose us in some particulars, I say: "Be You, O God, the judge between my confessions and their opposition."

Chapter 17—Physical or Spiritual Creation

For these naysayer declare:

> Even if these things are true, still Moses did not refer
> to these two things when he said, by divine revelation, 'In
> the beginning God created the heaven and the earth.' By
> the term 'heaven' he did not mean that spiritual or intel-
> ligible created order which always beholds the face of
> God. And by the term 'earth' he was not referring to
> unformed matter.

I then ask, "What then do these terms mean?"

They reply:

> Moses meant what we mean, and is what he said in
> those terms.

Again I ask, "What is that?"

Their reply:

> By the terms of heaven and earth, Moses wished first
> to indicate universally and briefly the entire visible world.
> After this, by an enumeration of the days, he could point
> out, one by one, all the things that it has pleased the Holy
> Spirit to reveal in this way. For the people to whom he
> spoke were unlearned and carnal, so that he judged it
> prudent that only those works of God which were visible
> should be mentioned to them.

However, they do agree that the phrases, "The earth was
invisible and unformed," and "The darkened abyss," may not
inappropriately be understood to refer to this unformed matter.
Also, as it is subsequently related, out of this all the visible things
that are known, all were made and set in order during those
specified "days."

What if another one said:

> This same formlessness and chaos of matter was first mentioned by the name of heaven and earth because, out of it, this visible world—with all its entities that clearly appear in it and that we refer to by the name of heaven and earth—was created and perfected?

What if still another should say:

> The invisible and visible nature is quite fittingly called heaven and earth. Thus, the entire creation that God has made in His wisdom, in the beginning, was included under these two terms. However, since all things have been made from nothing, and because they are a different reality from God, and because in them all is a certain changeability, then the common matter of all things, both invisible and visible from which heaven and earth were to be created, was spoken of in the same terms by which the invisible and unformed earth and the darkness over the abyss would be called.
>
> However, there was a difference: the invisible and unformed earth must be understood as having physical matter before it had any form or shape, but the darkness over the abyss was <u>spiritual</u> matter, before its unlimited fluidity was harnessed, and before it was enlightened by Wisdom.

If another wished, he might also say:

> The entities already perfected and formed both invisible and visible, aren't signified by the terms 'heaven and earth,' when it reads, 'In the beginning God created the heaven and the earth.' Instead, the unformed beginning of things, the matter capable of receiving form

and being made was called by these terms, because the chaos was contained in it and was not yet distinguished by qualities and forms. These have now been arranged in their own orders and are called heaven and earth: the former a spiritual creation, the latter a physical creation.

CHAPTER 18—INTERPRETING SCRIPTURE

When all these things have been said and considered, I am unwilling to contend about words, for such contention is profitable for nothing but the subverting of the hearer.[457] However, the law is profitable for edification if one uses it lawfully. Scripture declares: "Now the purpose of the commandment is love <u>from</u> a pure heart, <u>from</u> a good conscience, and <u>from</u> sincere faith."[458] The Master knew this well, because it was on these two commandments that He hung all the Law and the Prophets.[459]

How would it harm me, O my God, if while passionately confessing these things, I interpreted the meaning of the sacred writer differently than another man does? Many different things may be understood from these words, all of which may be true!

All of us who read are seeking to understand what the author of Scripture wished to convey, and since we believe that he spoke the truth, we dare not suppose that he has written anything that we either know or suspect to be false. Therefore, since we're all trying to understand what the writer of Holy Scripture understood, what harm is done if a man understands what You reveal to him to be true, though the author didn't understand this aspect of the truth, but understood the truth in a different meaning?[460]

CHAPTER 19—AFFIRMATIONS OF TRUTH REGARDING CREATION[461]

These truths are evident from the foregoing affirmations:

- You created the heavens and the earth, O Lord.

- "The beginning" is Your wisdom in which You created all things.

- This visible world has its own great division (the heaven and the earth) and these two terms include all entities that have been made and created.

- Everything changeable confronts our minds with a certain lack of form, whereby it receives form, or whereby it's capable of taking form.

- That which clings to the changeless form so closely, that, though mutable is not changed, is not subject to temporal process.

- Formlessness, which is almost nothing, cannot have temporal change in it.

- Matter from which something is made can, in a manner of speaking, be called by the same name as the thing that is made from it. Thus, that formlessness of which heaven and earth were made might be called "heaven and earth."

- Of all things having form, nothing is nearer to the unformed than the earth and the abyss.

- Not only every created and formed thing but also everything capable of creation and of form were created by You, from whom all things are.[462]

- Everything that is formed from what is formless was formless before it was formed.

CHAPTER 20—DIFFERING INTERPRETATIONS OF "IN THE BEGINNING..."

These truths are not doubted by those to whom You have granted insight and who believe undeniably that Your servant Moses spoke in the spirit of truth. However, from them more than one understanding of "In the beginning God created the heaven and the earth" can be derived. For example:

- One man interprets the Scripture thus, "In His Word, coeternal with Himself, God made both the intelligible and the tangible, the spiritual and the physical creation."

- Another interprets it thus, "In His Word, coeternal with Himself, God made the universal mass of this physical world, with all the observable and known entities that it contains."

- Still another finds a different meaning, "In His Word, coeternal with Himself, God made the unformed matter of the spiritual and physical creation."

- Another man declares, "In His Word, coeternal with Himself, God made the unformed matter of the physical creation, in which heaven and earth were as yet indistinguishable; but now that they have come to be separated and formed, we can now perceive them both in the mighty mass of this world."

- Another says, "In the very beginning of creating and working, God made that unformed matter which contained, undifferentiated, heaven and earth, from which both of them were formed, and both now stand out and are observable with all the things that are in them."

Chapter 21—Different Understandings of "Invisible and Unformed"

Again, interpretations of the Scripture, "But the earth was invisible and unformed and darkness was over the abyss" can differ:

- One man interprets it to mean, "That physical entity which God made was as yet the formless matter of physical things without order and without light."

- Another that it means, "This totality called heaven and earth was as yet unformed and lightless matter, out of which the physical heaven and the physical earth were to be made, with all the things in them that are known to our physical senses."

- Again, another says, "This totality called heaven and earth was as yet an unformed and lightless matter, from which were to be made that intelligible heaven (which is also called 'the heaven of heavens') and the earth (which refers to the entire physical entity, under which term may be included this physical heaven), that is, He made the intelligible heaven from which every invisible and visible creature would be created."

- Another says that, "The Scripture does not refer to that formlessness by the term 'heaven and earth' because that formlessness itself already existed. This it called the invisible 'earth' and the unformed and lightless 'abyss,' from which God made the heaven and the earth (namely, the spiritual and the physical creation)."

- Still another says, "There was already an unformed matter from which, as the Scripture had already said, God made heaven and earth, namely, the entire physical mass of the world, divided into two very great parts, one superior, the other inferior, with all those familiar and known creatures that are in them."

CHAPTER 22—THE DIALOGUE CONTINUES

Suppose that someone tried to argue against these last two opinions as follows:

If you will not admit that this formlessness of matter appears to be called by the term 'heaven and earth,' then there was something that God had not made out of which He made heaven and earth. Scripture has not told us that God made this matter, unless we understand that it is implied in the term 'heaven and earth' (or the term 'earth' alone) when it is said, 'In the beginning God created the

*heaven and earth.' Thus, in what follows, 'the earth was
invisible and unformed,' even though it pleased Moses to
so refer to unformed matter, we can only understand by
it that which God Himself has made, as it stands written
in the previous verse, 'God made heaven and earth.'*

Those who maintain either one or the other of these two
opinions, which we have set out above, will answer to such objections:

*We don't deny that God, from whom all things are,
created this unformed matter and all things are very good.
We hold that what is created and endowed with form is a
higher good, and also hold that what is made capable of
being created and endowed with form, though it is a lesser
good, is still a good.*

*However, Scripture has not specifically said that God
made this formlessness any more than it has declared the
same specifically of many other things, such as the
'cherubim' and 'seraphim,' and 'thrones,' 'dominions,'
'principalities,' and 'powers,'[463] though it's clear that
God made them all.*

*If in the phrase 'He made heaven and earth' all things
are included, what are we to say about the waters upon
which the Spirit of God moved? For if they are understood as included in the term 'earth,' then how can
unformed matter be meant by the term 'earth' when we
see the waters so beautifully formed? Or, if it's taken
thus, why, then, is it written that out of the same
formlessness the firmament was made and called heaven,
and yet is it not specifically written that the waters were
made? For these waters, which we perceive flowing in so
beautiful a fashion, are not formless and invisible. But if
they received that beauty at the time God said of them,
'Let the waters which are under the firmament be*

gathered together,'[464] *thus indicating that their gathering together was the same thing as their reception of form, what, then, is to be said about the waters that are* <u>above</u> *the firmament? If they are unformed, they do not deserve to have a seat so honorable, and yet it is not written by what specific word they were formed.*

If, then, Genesis is silent about anything that God has made, which neither sound faith nor unerring understanding doubts that God has made, let not any sober teaching dare to say that these waters were coeternal with God because we find them mentioned in the book of Genesis but do not find it mentioned when they were created.

If Truth instructs us, why not interpret that unformed matter which the Scripture calls the earth—invisible and unformed—and the lightless abyss as having been made by God from nothing, and thus understand that they are not coeternal with Him, although the narrative fails to tell us precisely when they were made?"

Chapter 23—Seek Truth

I've heard and considered these theories as well as my weak apprehension allows, and I confess my weakness to You, O Lord, though already You know it. So I see that two categories of disagreement may arise when signs relay anything, even it the reporter is trustworthy:

- Disagreement about the truth of the things involved

- Disagreement about the meaning of the one who reports them

It's one thing to ask what is true about the formation of the Creation, but quite another to ask what Moses wished for the reader to understand from the words. As for the first question, let all those depart from me who imagine that Moses spoke things that are false. However, let me be united with them in You, O Lord, and delight myself in You with those who feed on Your truth in the bond of love. Let's approach together the words of Your book and make diligent inquiry in them for Your meaning through the meaning of Your servant by whose pen You have given them to us.

CHAPTER 24—CONFIDENT IN GOD'S WORD

Surrounded by so many truths that occur to the interpreters of these words (understood as they can be in different ways), who can discover the single interpretation that Moses wished to convey?

O God, I'm Your servant, and I've vowed in this book an offering of confession to You.[465] Therefore, I pray that by Your mercy I may honor my vow to You. Could I assert that Moses meant nothing more than my interpretation when he wrote, "In the beginning God created the heaven and the earth," as confidently as I can assert that You in Your unchangeable Word have created all things, invisible and visible? No, I can't, because I can't be certain as to what Moses' actual meaning was. Moses' thoughts might have been focused on the very beginning of creation when he said, "In the beginning." Likewise, he may have wished it understood that "heaven and earth" refers to no formed and perfect entity, whether spiritual or physical, but each of them only newly begun and still formless.

Whichever of these possibilities has been mentioned, I can see the truth of each. However, which one he actually intended to express in these words I don't clearly see. But whether it was one of these, or some other meaning that I haven't mentioned, that

Moses saw in his mind when he used these words, I have no doubt that he saw it truly and expressed it suitably.

Chapter 25—Seek Common Ground

Let no man trouble me now by saying, "Moses didn't mean what <u>you</u> say, but what <u>I</u> say." However, if he asks me, "How do you know that Moses meant what you deduce from his words?" I must respond calmly and reply as I have already done, or even more fully if he happens to be untrained. But if he persists in putting forth only his interpretation, pour Your soothing balm into my heart, O God, that I may patiently bear with him! It's not because they're godly men and have seen in the heart of Your servant what they say, but rather they are proud men and have not considered Moses' meaning, but only love their own—and that not because it's true but because it's theirs. Otherwise they could equally love another true opinion, as I love what they say when what they speak is true—not because it's theirs but because it's true.

If these men love an opinion because it's true, it becomes both theirs and mine, since it's the common property of all lovers of the truth. But I neither accept nor approve when they contend that Moses didn't mean what I say but only what they say. Even if it were so, such rashness is born not of knowledge, but of offensive boldness. It comes not from vision but from pride.

Therefore, O Lord, Your judgments should be held in awe, because Your truth is neither mine nor his nor anyone else's. Your truth belongs to all whom You have openly called to share it in common. You have warned us not to possess it as our own special property, for if we do we lose it. If anyone appropriates to himself what You have bestowed on all to enjoy, desiring for himself what belongs to all, he is forced away from what is common to all, to what is his very own, indeed—falsehood. For he who tells a lie speaks of his own thought.[466]

Remain Steadfast in God's Word

Listen, O God, best judge of all! O Truth itself, listen to what I say to this disputant. Hear it, because I say it in Your presence and before my brethren who use the law rightly to express love. Hear and give heed to what I shall say to him, if it pleases You.

I would return this brotherly and peaceful word to him:

> *If we both see that what you say is true, and if we both say that what I say is true, where is it, I ask you, that we see this? Certainly, I don't see it in you, and you don't see it in me, but both of us see it in the unchangeable truth itself, which is above our minds.*[467]

If, then, we agree about the true light of the Lord our God, why do we disagree about the thoughts of our neighbor, which we cannot see as clearly as the unchangeable Truth is seen? If Moses himself had appeared before us and said, "This is what I meant," it wouldn't be so that we could see it but so that we would believe him. Therefore, let us not "go beyond what is written and be puffed up for the one against the other."[468] Instead, let's "love the Lord our God with all our heart, with all our soul, and with all our mind, and our neighbor as ourself."[469]

Unless we believe that whatever Moses meant in these books he meant to be ordered by these two precepts of love, we make God a liar. Likewise, if we judge the soul of His servant in any way other than how He has taught us. Therefore, in the face of so great an abundance of true opinions that can be taken from these words, see how foolish it is to rashly affirm that Moses specifically intended only one interpretation. And then, with destructive contention, see how foolish it is to violate love itself, on behalf of which he said all the things we are endeavoring to explain!

CHAPTER 26—MY DESIRE TO COMMUNICATE EFFECTIVELY

O my God, You are the exaltation of my humility and my rest from labor. You hear my confessions and forgive my sins, and since You command me to love my neighbor as myself, I can't believe that You would give Moses a lesser gift than I desire for myself.

Had I been Moses and been ordered by You to write the book of Genesis, I surely would have asked for the power of expression and art of arrangement to be given me. That way, those who don't yet understand <u>how</u> God created would not reject my words as beyond their power to comprehend. Furthermore, I would wish that those who do understand would find fully contained in the concise speech of Your servant whatever truths they had arrived at in their own thought. And if, in the light of the Truth, some other man saw some further meaning, that it would be found congruent to my words as well.

CHAPTER 27—THE COMPLEXITIES OF CREATION

Just as a spring dammed up is more plentiful and affords a larger supply of water for more streams over wider fields than any single stream led off from the same spring over a long course, so also is the narration of Your minister. It is intended to benefit many who are likely to discuss it and, with an economy of language, overflows into various streams of clear truth from which everyone may draw for himself that particular truth about their topic of interest.

When some people read or hear the words, "In the beginning God created…" they think that God, like a man or some sort of huge body and by some new and sudden decision, produced outside Himself and beyond a certain distance two great bodies, one above and the other below, within which all created things were to be contained. And when they hear, "God said, 'Let such and such be done,' and it was done," they think of words begun and ended, sounding in time and then passing away, followed by the coming into being of what was commanded. They think of other things in the same way as their familiarity with the world suggests to them.

These people are still immature. They have their faith built up healthfully and come to possess and hold as certain the conviction that God made everything their senses perceive around them in such marvelous variety. If one despises these words as if they were trivial, and with proud weakness stretches himself beyond his fostering cradle, he will, sadly, fall away. Have pity, O Lord God, lest those who pass by trample on the young bird.[470] Send Your angel to restore it to its nest, so that it may live until it can fly.

CHAPTER 28—REJOICE IN THE LIGHT OF GOD'S TRUTH

Others, to whom the words, "In the beginning God created…" are no longer in a nest but, rather, a shady thicket. They spy the fruits concealed therein and fly around rejoicing. They search among the fruit and pluck them with cheerful chirpings. For when they read or hear these words, O God, they see that all times past and times future are transcended by Your eternal and stable permanence. They also see that there is no temporal creature that is not of Your making.

O God, by Your will, since it is the same as Your being, You have created all things. Not by any mutation of will and not by any will that previously was nonexistent, and not out of Yourself, but in Your own likeness. You made from nothing the form of all things. This was an unlikeness which was capable of being formed by Your likeness through its relation to You, the One, as each thing has been given form appropriate to its kind according to its preordained capacity. Thus, all things were made very good, whether they remain around You or whether, removed in time and place by various degrees, they cause or undergo the beautiful changes of natural process.

These men see these things and rejoice in the light of Your truth to whatever degree they can.

Again, one of these men[471] directs his attention to the verse, "In the beginning God made the heaven and the earth," and he beholds Wisdom as the true "beginning," because it also speaks to us. Another man directs his attention to the same words, and by "beginning" he understands simply the commencement of creation, and interprets it thus: "In the beginning he made," as if it were the same thing as to say, "At the first moment, God made...."

Pursue True Meaning

Among those who interpret "In the beginning" to mean that in Your wisdom You have created the heaven and earth, one believes that the matter out of which heaven and earth were to be created is what is referred to by the phrase "heaven and earth." But another believes that these entities were already formed and distinct. Still another will understand it to refer to one formed entity—a spiritual one, designated by the term "heaven"—and to another unformed entity of physical matter, designated by the term "earth."

However, those who understand the phrase "heaven and earth" to mean the yet unformed matter from which the heaven and the earth were to be formed do not take it in a simple sense. One man regards it as that from which the intelligible and tangible creations are both produced, while another only as that from which the tangible, physical world is produced, containing in its vast bosom these visible and observable entities. Nor are they in simple accord who believe that "heaven and earth" refers to the created things already set in order and arranged. One believes that it refers to the invisible and visible world, while another, only to the visible world, in which we admire the luminous heavens, the darkened earth, and all the things that they contain.

Chapter 29—First Matter, Then Things

The man who understands "In the beginning God made" as if it meant, "At first God made," can truly interpret the phrase "heaven and earth" as referring only to the "matter" of heaven and earth, namely, of the prior universal, which is the intelligible and physical creation. For if he would try to interpret the phrase as applying to the universe already formed, then it might rightly be asked of him, "If God first made this, what then did he do afterward?" After the universe, he will find nothing. But then he must, however unwillingly, face the question, "How is this the first if there is nothing afterward?"

However, when he said that God made matter first formless and then formed, he is not being absurd if he is able to discern what precedes by eternity, and what proceeds in time—what comes from choice, and what comes from origin. God is before all things in eternity. In the temporal process, the flower is before the fruit, in the act of choice, the fruit is before the flower, and in the case of origin, sound is before the tune. Of these four relations, the first and last that I have referred to are understood, though with much difficulty. The second and third are very easily understood.

It's an uncommon and lofty vision, O Lord, to behold Your eternity unchangeably making changeable things, and thereby standing always before them. Whose mind is astute enough to be able to discover how the sound comes before the tune? For a tune is a formed sound, and an unformed thing may exist. However, a thing that does not exist cannot be formed. Likewise, matter is prior to what is made from it. It's not prior because it makes its product, for it is itself made, and its priority is not that of a time interval. For in time we don't first utter formless sounds without singing, and then adapt or fashion them into the form of a song, like forming wood or silver into a chest or vessel. Such materials precede in time the forms of the things that are made from them.

The Example of Song

However, in singing this isn't so, because when a song is sung, its sound is heard at the same time. There is not first a formless sound, which afterward is formed into a song, but as soon as it has sounded it passes away, making it impossible to find anything to gather up and shape. Therefore, the song is absorbed in its own sound and the "sound" of the song is its "matter."

Nevertheless, the sound is formed in order that it may be a tune. This is why the matter of the sound is prior to the form of the tune. It's not "before" in the sense that it has any power of making a sound or tune. Nor is the sound itself the composer of the tune. Rather, the sound is sent forth from the body and is ordered by the soul of the singer, so that from it he may form a tune. Nor is the sound first in time, for it is given forth together with the tune. Nor is it first in choice, because a sound is no better than a tune, since a tune is not merely a sound but a beautiful sound. But it is first in origin, because the tune is not formed in order that it may become a sound, but the sound is formed in order that it may become a tune.

From this example, let him who is able to understand see that the matter of things was first made and was called "heaven and earth" because out of it the heaven and earth were made. This primal formlessness was not made first in time, because the form of things gives rise to time. But now, in time, it is intuited together with its form. However, nothing can be related of this unformed matter unless it is regarded as if it were the first in the time series though the last in value. Things formed are certainly superior to things unformed, and all is preceded by the eternity of the Creator. That way, from nothing there might be made that from which something might be made.

CHAPTER 30—PAY HONOR TO MOSES

Let Truth itself bring harmony in this discord of true opinions, and may God have mercy on us all, that we may use the law rightly to the end of the commandment which is pure love. Thus, if anyone asks me which of these opinions was the meaning of Your servant Moses, these would not be my confessions if I didn't confess to You that I don't know. Yet I do know that those opinions are true—with the exception of the carnal ones—about which I have said what I thought was proper.

Those little ones of good hope are not frightened by the words of Your Book, for they speak of high things in a lowly way and of a few basic things in many varied ways. However, let all of us, whom I acknowledge to see and speak the truth in these words, love one another and also love You, our God, O Fountain of Truth. This we will do if we thirst not after pride but for the Fountain of Truth. Let's honor Moses as full of the Spirit and as dispenser of this

Scripture. That way, we'll believe that when You revealed Yourself to him and he wrote, that what he intended will minister both for the light of truth and to the increase of our fruitfulness.

Chapter 31—Moses Apprehended the Truth He Wrote

Thus, when one man says, "Moses meant what I mean," and another says, "No, he meant what I do," I think that I speak more faithfully when I say, "Why could he not have meant both if both opinions are true?" Furthermore, if there could be still a third truth or a fourth one, and if anyone should seek a truth quite different in those words, why would it not be right to believe that Moses saw all these different truths? After all, it's God that tempers the Holy Scriptures to the understanding of many different people, who should see truths in it even if they are different.

Certainly—and I say this fearlessly and from my heart—if I were to write anything on such a supreme authority, I would prefer to write it so that whatever truth is apprehended, my words would echo in several minds rather than set down one true opinion so clearly on one point that the rest are excluded, even though they contained no falsehood.

Therefore, I'm unwilling, O my God, to be so headstrong as not to believe that Moses has received at least this much from You. Surely when he was writing these words, he saw fully and understood all the truth we've been able to find in them. In fact, I'm sure that he understood more than we've been able to discern and are not yet able to discover, though it's there waiting to be found.

Chapter 32—Say What You Mean

O Lord, You are God and not flesh and blood.

Finally, if any man sees anything less, can anything lie hidden from "Your good Spirit?" He will "lead me in the land of uprightness,"[472] which You, through Moses' words, were revealing to future readers, even though he fixed on only one of the many interpretations that might have been found. If this is so, let's agree that the meaning he saw is more exalted than the others.

However, to us, O Lord, either point out the same meaning or any other true one as it pleases You. Whether You make known to us what You did to Moses or some other meaning by the agency of the same words, still You feed us and let error not deceive us.

Behold, O Lord, my God, how much we have written concerning these few words—how much, indeed! What strength of mind, what length of time, would suffice for all Your books to be interpreted in this manner?[473] Therefore, allow me in these concluding words to confess more briefly to You and select some true, certain, and good sense that You will inspire—although many meanings offer themselves and many indeed are possible.[474]

This is the faith of my confession, that if I could say what Your servant meant, it is truest and best. For that I must strive. However, if I don't succeed, may it be that I shall say at least what Your Truth wished to say, just as Moses did.

BOOK THIRTEEN

The Mysteries of Creation

An exploration of the mysteries and allegories of the days of creation. Augustine undertakes an interpretation of Gen. 1:2-31 in a mystical and allegorical fashion in order to exhibit the great depth and meaning of God's power, wisdom and love. He is also interested in developing his theories of biblical interpretation on his favorite topic: creation. Augustine finds the Trinity in the account of creation and ponders the work of the Spirit moving over the waters. He finds the allegory of the Holy Scripture in the firmament, and in the dry land and bitter sea he finds the division between the people of God and the conspiracy of the unfaithful. Augustine develops the theme of man being made in the image and likeness of God. He brings his survey to a climax and his confessions to an end with a meditation on the goodness of all creation and the promised rest and blessedness of the eternal Sabbath, on which God, who is eternal rest, "rested."

Chapter 1—My Being is Found in God

I call on You, my God and my Mercy, who made me and did not forget me, though I was forgetful of You. I call You into my soul, which You prepared to receive You by the desire which You inspired in it. Don't forsake me when I call on You, O God. You anticipated me before I called and repeatedly urged me to hear from afar and turn to call upon You.

O Lord, You have blotted out all my evil deserts, not punishing me for what my hands have done. You have anticipated all my good deserts so as to reward me for what Your hands have done—the very hands that made me.

Before I was, You were, and I was not anything at all that You should grant me being. But see how I exist by reason of Your goodness, which has made provision for all that You made me to be and all that You made me from. You didn't stand in need of me, nor am I the kind of good entity which could be a help to You, my Lord and my God. It's not that I may serve You as if You were fatigued in working, or as if Your power would be less if it lacked my assistance. Nor is the service I pay You like the cultivation of a field, so that You would go untended if I didn't tend You. Instead, it's that I may serve and worship You and so draw my well-being from You. For it's from You that my capacity for well-being comes.

Chapter 2–God's Goodness Enables Life

Indeed, it's from the fullness of Your goodness that Your creation exists at all. You sustain it so that the created good might not fail to be, even though it profits You nothing. Creation is nothing of You nor equal to You, since its created existence comes from You.

For what did the heaven and earth, which You made in the beginning, ever deserve from You? Let these spiritual and physical entities, which You made in Your wisdom, declare what they merited at Your hands. An unformed spiritual entity is more excellent than a formed physical entity. And the physical, even when unformed, is more excellent than if it were simply nothing at all. Still, these formless entities are held in their state of being by You, until they are recalled to Your unity and receive form and being from You, the one sovereign Good. What have they deserved of You, since they would not even be unformed entities except from You?

What has physical matter deserved of You, even in its invisible and unformed state, since it wouldn't exist at all if You had not made it? If it didn't exist, it couldn't merit its existence from You.

The Spiritual Creation

What has that formless spiritual creation deserved of You, that it should flow with no light like the abyss? It's so unlike You and wouldn't exist at all had it not been for the Word which made it, and illumined by that Word, been made light, though not as Your equal but only as an image of that Form of Light which is equal to You. For, in the case of a body, its being is not the same thing as its being beautiful, or else it could not then be a deformed body. Likewise, in the case of a created spirit, living is not the same state as living wisely, or else it could then be immutably wise. However, the true good of every created thing is always to cling fast to You. Otherwise, in turning away from You, it would lose the light it had received in being turned by You, and so relapse into a life like that of the dark abyss.

As for we who are a spiritual creation by virtue of our souls, when we turned away from You, O Light, we were in that former life of darkness. We toiled amid the shadows of our darkness until, through Your only Son, we become Your righteousness,[475] like the mountains of God. For we, like the great abyss,[476] have been the objects of Your judgments.

Chapter 3—God Is—Without Complication

You said in the beginning of the creation, "Let there be light: and there was light." I interpret that to refer to the spiritual creation, because it already had a kind of life which You could illuminate. However, since it had not merited from You that it should be a life capable of enlightenment, it didn't merit from You that it should be enlightened when it already began to exist. Neither could its formlessness please You until it became light. It became light, not because of the bare fact of existing, but by the act of turning its face to the light, which enlightened it, and by cleaving to it. Thus the spiritual creation owed the fact that it lived, and lived happily, to nothing whatsoever but Your grace, since it had been turned, by a change for the better, toward that which cannot be changed for either better or worse.

You alone are, because You alone are without complication. For You it's not one thing to live and another thing to live in blessedness—You are Your own blessedness.

CHAPTER 4—GOD CREATED OUT OF HIS ABUNDANCE

Therefore, what would have been lacking in Your good, which You Yourself are, even if these things had never been made or had remained unformed? You didn't create them out of any lack but out of the abundance of Your goodness. You ordered them and turned them toward form,[477] but not because Your joy had to be perfected by them. You are perfect, and their imperfection is displeasing. Therefore, they were perfected by You and became pleasing to You—but not as if You were before that imperfect and had to be perfected in their perfection.

Your good Spirit moved over the face of the waters[478] but wasn't held up by them as if resting on them. For those in whom Your good Spirit is said to rest He actually causes to rest in Himself. However, Your incorruptible and unchangeable will, in itself all-sufficient for itself, moved over that life which You had made—in which living isn't at all the same as living happily—because that life still lives even as it flows in its own darkness. That life remains to be turned to Him who made it, and to live more and more like "the fountain of life," and in His light "to see light,"[479] and to be perfected, enlightened, and blessed.

CHAPTER 5—FATHER, SON, AND HOLY SPIRIT—CREATOR OF ALL

The Trinity appears to me in an enigma in the biblical account of creation. You are the Trinity, O my God, since You, O Father created the heaven and the earth in the beginning of our wisdom, that is, in Your wisdom born of You, equal and coeternal with You, Your Son.

We've said many things about the heaven of heavens, about the earth invisible and unformed, and about the shadowy abyss. We've also discussed the aimless flux of the abyss being spiritually deformed unless it's turned to Him from whom it has its life (such as it is), and by His Light become a life suffused with beauty. We've seen that it would be a [lower] heaven and a [higher] heaven, which afterward was made between water and water.[480]

I came to recognize, in the name of God, the Father who made all these things, and in the term "the Beginning" to recognize the Son, through whom He made all these things. Since I believed that my God was the Trinity, I sought still further in his Holy Word, and, behold, "Your Spirit moved over the waters." Therefore, I see the Trinity, O my God: Father, Son, and Holy Spirit, the Creator of all creation!

CHAPTER 6—THE HOLY SPIRIT IN CREATION

But why, O truth-speaking Light? To You I lift up my heart, let it not teach me worthless ideas. Disperse its shadows and tell me, I pray, by that Love which is our mother, the reason why Your Scripture at long last referred to Your Spirit, but only after the reference to heaven, to the invisible and unformed earth, and the darkness over the abyss? Was it because it was appropriate that He should first be shown to us as "moving over"? If so, this couldn't have been said unless something had already been mentioned over which Your Spirit could be understood as "moving". Didn't He "move over" the Father and the Son? He couldn't properly be said to be "moving over" if He were "moving over" nothing. Thus, what He was "moving over" had to be identified before He could then be mentioned. Nevertheless, why wasn't it fitting that He be introduced in some other way than in this context of "moving over"?

CHAPTER 7—RESCUED BY GOD'S LOVE

Let him who is able, follow Paul, Your apostle, with his understanding when he says, "the love of God has been poured out in our hearts by the Holy Spirit who was given to us."[481] It was he who teaches us about spiritual gifts[482] and shows us a more excellent way of love. It was he who bows his knee unto You for us, that we may come to the surpassing knowledge of the love of Christ.[483] Thus, from the beginning, he who is above all was "moving over" the waters.

To whom shall I tell this? How can I speak of the weight of unholy lust that drags us downward into the deep abyss, and of the love, which lifts us up by Your Spirit who moved over the waters? To whom shall I tell this? And how shall it be told? For lust and love are not certain "places" into which we are plunged and out of which we are lifted again. What could be more like, and yet more unlike? They are both feelings, and they are both loves.

The uncleanness of our own soul flows downward with the love of worldly care, while the sanctity of Your Spirit raises us upward by the love of release from anxiety. That love enables us to lift our hearts to You where Your Spirit is "moving over the waters." Thus, we have come to that supreme rest where our souls will have passed through the waters that give no standing ground.

CHAPTER 8—LIGHT PENETRATES DARKNESS

The angels fell, and the soul of man fell, thus indicating the deep darkness of the abyss. The abyss would have still held the entire spiritual creation had You not said in the beginning, "Let there be light: and there was light." Every obedient mind in Your heavenly city had to hold fast to You and rest in Your Spirit, which moved unchangeable over all things changeable. Otherwise, even the heaven of heavens would have been a dark shadow, instead of being light in the Lord[484] as it is now.

You clearly show how noble You made the rational creation even in the restless misery of the fallen spirits, who reveal their own darkness when stripped of the garments of Your light. You, O God, will enlighten our darkness, clothe us in garments of light, and make our darkness as the noonday.

Give Your self to me, O my God, restore Yourself to me! I love You, but if my love is too little, let me love You ever more strongly. I can't measure my love so that I know how much is lacking. How much love is required before I can run in to Your embrace and be hidden in "the secret place of Your presence"[485] and not be turned away? Nevertheless, I do know this: My existence is anguish except in You—not only in my outward life, but within my inmost self as well. Any abundance I have that is not God, is poverty.

CHAPTER 9—THE HOLY SPIRIT

Neither the Father nor the Son was "moving over the waters." If we understand this as a motion in space, as a body moves, then not even the Holy Spirit "moved." However, if we understand the changeless preeminence of God being above every changeable thing, then Father, Son, and Holy Spirit "moved over the waters."

Why is this said of Your Spirit alone, as if He had been in a "place" that is not a place? Why is it said of Him, about whom alone it is written, "He is Your gift?" It's in Your gift that we rest, and there we enjoy You. Our rest is our "place," and love lifts us up toward that place. Your good Spirit lifts our lowliness from the gates of death.[486]

Our peace rests in the goodness of will. The body tends toward its own place by its own gravity. A weight does not tend downward only, but moves to its own place. Fire tends upward, while a stone tends downward. They are propelled by their own mass and they seek their own places. Oil poured under the water rises above the water, while water poured on oil sinks beneath. They are moved by their own mass and seek their own place. If they are out of order, they are restless, but when their order is restored, they are at rest. My weight is my love, and by it I'm carried wherever I'm carried.

By Your gift,[487] we are enflamed and carried upward. We burn inwardly and move forward. We ascend Your ladder which is in our heart, and sing a psalm of ascents,[488] causing us to glow inwardly with Your good fire.[489] We go forward because we ascend to the peace of Jerusalem,[490] for "I was glad when they said to me, 'Let us go into the house of the Lord.'"[491] There Your good pleasure will settle us so that we will desire nothing more than to dwell there forever.[492]

Chapter 10—From Darkness into Light

Happy would that creature be who, though it was in itself other than You, still had not known any other state from the time it was made. It was never without Your gift, which moves over everything changeable, and it was lifted up by the call in which You said, "Let there be light: and there was light."[493]

There is a distinction in us between the time when we were darkness and the time when we were made light. However, we're not told what the case would have been with that creature if the light had not been made. The creature is spoken of as though there had been something of flux and darkness in it beforehand so that the cause by which it was made to be otherwise might be evident.

In other words, by being turned to the unfailing Light it might become light.

Let him who is able, understand this, and let him who is not, ask of You. Why trouble me, as if I could "give light to every man that comes into the world"?[494]

Chapter 11—The Trinity

Who can understand the all-powerful Trinity? Yet who doesn't speak about it, if indeed it is of that which he speaks? Rare is the soul who, when he speaks of the Trinity, also knows about what he speaks. Men contend and strive, but no man sees the vision of it without peace.

I could wish that men would consider three things that are within themselves. These three things are quite different from the Trinity, but I mention them so that men may exercise their minds and test themselves, and come to realize how different from it they are.[495]

The three things I speak of are: to be, to know, and to will. I am, and I know, and I will. I am a knowing and a willing being. I know that I am and that I will, and I will to be and to know. Therefore, in these three functions let him who can, see how integral a life is—for there is one life, one mind, one essence. Finally, the distinction does not separate the things, and yet it's a distinction. Surely a man has this distinction before his mind. Let him look into himself and see, and tell me. However, when he discovers and can say anything about any one of these, let him not think that he has thereby discovered what is immutable (unchangeable) above them all, which _is_ immutably and _knows_ immutably and _wills_ immutably.

Who can readily determine whether there is a Trinity because these three functions exist in the one God, or whether all three are in each Person so that they are each threefold, or whether both of these notions are true and, in some mysterious manner, the Infinite is in itself its own Selfsame object—at once one and many, so that by itself it is and knows itself and is sufficient to itself without change, so that the Selfsame is the abundant magnitude of its Unity? Who can in any way express it plainly? Who can in any way make a hasty pronouncement about it?

CHAPTER 12—THE DARKNESS OF IGNORANCE

Go forward in your confession, O my faith. Say to the Lord your God, "Holy, holy, holy, O Lord my God, in Your name we have been baptized, in the name of the Father, Son, and Holy Spirit." In Your name we baptize, in the name of the Father, the Son, and the Holy Spirit. Among us, God in His Christ made "heaven and earth," namely, the spiritual and carnal members of His Church. It's true that before it received "the form of doctrine," our "earth"[496] was "invisible and unformed," and we were covered with the darkness of our ignorance. You correct man for his iniquity,[497] and "Your judgments are a great abyss."[498]

However, because Your Spirit was moving over these waters, Your mercy didn't forsake our wretchedness. You said, "Let there be light; repent, for the kingdom of heaven is at hand."[499] Repent, and let there be light. Because our soul was troubled within us, we remembered You, O Lord, from the land of Jordan, and from the mountain.[500] As we became displeased with our darkness we turned to You, "and there was light." We were in darkness before, but now we are light in the Lord.[501]

Chapter 13—Deep Calls Unto Deep

We live by faith and not by sight. We are saved by hope, but hope that is seen isn't hope. "Deep calls unto deep at the noise of Your waterfalls."[502] The apostle Paul said, "I...could not speak to you as to spiritual *people* but as to carnal, as to babes in Christ"[503] However, even he didn't count himself to have apprehended, but forgetting the things that are behind and reaching forth to the things that are before, he pressed on to those things that are ahead.[504] He groaned under his burden and his soul thirsted after the living God as the stag pants for the water brooks.[505] "Desiring to be further clothed by His house which is from heaven,"[506] he asked, "When shall I come?"[507]

Paul called to the lower deep, saying, "do not be conformed to this world, but be transformed by the renewing of your mind."[508] And "do not be children in understanding; however, in malice be babes, but in understanding be mature."[509] "O foolish Galatians, who has bewitched you?"[510] However, this is not only in Paul's own voice but also in Your voice, who sent Your Spirit from above through Him who both "ascended up on high"[511] and opened the floodgates of His gifts, that the force of His streams might make glad the city of God.[512]

The Bridegroom's friend[513] sighs for that city and for Paul. Now Paul has the first fruits of the Spirit laid up with him, but still groans within himself, waiting for adoption, the redemption of his body.[514] To Christ he sighs, for he is a member of the Bride, the body of Christ. He isn't jealous for himself, but in the voice of Your waterfalls Paul calls upon that other deep, of which he is jealous and in fear. Paul feared that, as the serpent subtlety seduced Eve, his mind would be corrupted from the purity of our Bridegroom, Your only Son.

What a light of beauty that will be when "we shall see Him as He is"![515] And when these tears shall pass away which "have been my food day and night, while they continually say to me, 'Where *is* your God?'"[516]

CHAPTER 14—HOPE IN THE LORD

I declare: "O my God, where are You? See now, where are You?" I catch my breath in You for a little while, when I pour out my soul beyond myself in the voice of joy and praise, in the voice of one that keeps a holy day.[517] Still my soul is cast down because it relapses and becomes an abyss; rather it feels like it's still an abyss. My faith speaks to my soul—the faith that You kindle to light my path in the night. "Why are you cast down, O my soul? And why are you disquieted within me? Hope in God; for I shall yet praise Him, the help of my countenance and my God."[518]

God's word is a lamp to my feet.[519] Therefore, I will hope and persevere until the night—that mother of the wicked—passes. I will persevere until the Lord's wrath subsides, whose children we once were, of whom we were beforehand in darkness, and whose residue we still bear about us in our bodies, dead because of sin.[520] Hope and endure until the day breaks and the shadows flee.[521]

Hope in the Lord: "My voice You shall hear in the morning, O LORD"[522] and I will forever give You praise. I will stand in the morning and see my God, for He is the health of my countenance,[523] and who quickens the mortal body by the Spirit that dwells within.[524]

God, in His mercy, moved over our lightless and restless inner deep. From this we've received a pledge and a guaranty through His Holy Spirit. We are now in the light. We are already saved by hope and are children of the light and children of the day, not children of the night or of the darkness,[525] which we had been before.

Only You, God, can rightly distinguish between the children of the night and us, the children of the day. We are still in this uncertain state of human knowledge, but You test the heart and call the light day, and the darkness night.[526] Who can see us clearly but You? What do we have that we have not received from You? For You made from the same lump some vessels to noble, and others to ignoble, use.[527]

Chapter 15—The Firmament of God's Word

Who but You, O God, made for us the authority of Your divine Scripture to be over us as firmament? For "the heavens shall be rolled up like a scroll,"[528] but are now stretched over us like a skin. Your divine Scripture is of more awe-inspiring authority now that those mortal men through whom You dispensed it to us have departed this life. You know, O Lord, how You clothed Adam and Eve with skins when they became mortal because of sin.[529]

In much the same way, You stretched out the firmament of Your Word as a skin—that is to say, You've spread Your harmonious words over us through the ministry of mortal men. By their very death that solid firmament of authority in Your Word as spoken forth by them, stretches high over all that now drift under it, whereas while they lived on earth their authority was not so widely extended. You had not yet spread out the heaven like a skin, and had not yet spread abroad the fame of their death.

Let us see, O Lord, "the heavens, the work of Your fingers."[530] Clear away from our eyes the fog with which You have covered them. In the heavens—Your Scriptures—is Your testimony that gives wisdom even to the little ones. O my God, out of the mouth of babes and nursing infants You have perfected Your praise.[531] We know of no other books that so utterly destroy man's pride. They break down the adversary and self-defender that resists Your reconciliation in an effort to justify his own sin. O Lord, I know of no other such pure words that persuade me to confess and make my neck submissive to Your yoke. These words invite me to serve You for nothing else than Your own sake.

Let me understand these things, O good Father. Grant this to me, since I'm placed under them. For You have established these things for those placed under them.

Other waters are above this firmament, and I believe that they are immortal and removed from earthly corruption. Let them praise Your name—this super-celestial society, Your angels, who have no need to look up at this firmament or to gain a knowledge of Your Word by reading it. Let them praise You, for they always behold Your face and read in Your expression, with no syllables in time, what Your eternal will intends.

We Will See Him As He Is

These celestial ones read, they choose, and they love. They are always reading, and what they read never passes away. For by choosing and by loving they read the very immutability[532] of Your counsel. Their book is never closed, nor is the scroll folded up, because You are their book, and are so eternally.

You arranged the heavenly host above this firmament. You made it firm over the infirmities of the people below the heavens, so they might look up and learn of Your mercy, which proclaims You, in time, the maker of all times.

"Your mercy, O LORD, *is* in the heavens; Your faithfulness *reaches* to the clouds."[533] The clouds pass away, but the heavens remain. The preachers of Your Word pass away from this life into another, but Your Scripture is spread abroad over the people, even to the end of the world. Indeed, both heaven and earth shall pass away, but Your words shall never pass away.[534] The scroll shall be rolled together, and the "grass" over which it was spread shall, with all its goodliness, pass away; but Your Word remains forever.[535]

Your Word now appears to us in the dark image of the clouds and through the glass of heaven, not as it really is. Even if we are the beloved of Your Son, what we shall be has not yet appeared.[536] He has seen us through the entanglement[537] of our flesh. He is fair speaking and has enflamed our love for Him so that we run after His fragrance.[538] But "when He is revealed, we shall be like Him, for we shall see Him as He is."[539] As He is, O Lord, we shall see Him—although that time isn't yet.

CHAPTER 16—THE FOUNTAIN OF LIFE

Just as You are the utterly Real, You alone fully know, since You are immutably, and You <u>know</u> immutably, and You <u>will</u> immutably. Your Essence knows and wills immutably. Your Knowledge is and wills immutably. Your Will is and knows immutably. It doesn't seem right to You that the immutable Light should be known by the enlightened but mutable creature in the same way as it knows itself. Therefore, to You my soul is as a land where there is no water.[540] For, just as my soul cannot enlighten itself by itself, so my soul cannot satisfy itself by itself. "For with You *is* the fountain of life; In Your light we see light."[541]

Chapter 17—The Fruit of Kindness

Who has gathered the "embittered ones"[542] into a single society? They all have the same end, which is temporal and earthly happiness. This is their motive for doing everything, though they may fluctuate within an innumerable diversity of concerns. Who but You, O Lord, gathered them together thirsting for You? You said, "Let the waters be gathered together into one place and let the dry land appear." The sea is Yours as well, because You made it. Likewise, Your hands formed the dry land.[543] It's not the bitterness of men's wills but the gathering together of the waters which is called "the sea." However, You curb the wicked lusts of men's souls and fix their boundaries—how far they are allowed to advance, and where their waves will be broken against each other. Thus You make it "a sea," by the providence of Your governance over all things.

You water the souls that thirst after You and who appear before You, separated from "the society of the [bitter] sea" by reason of their different ends. You water them by a secret and sweet spring, so that "the earth" may bring forth her fruit, and by commanding it, O Lord, their souls may bud forth in works of mercy after their kind.[544]

Therefore, we show love for our neighbor in ministering to his bodily needs, and our soul has seed in itself after its kind. This seed is found in our own infirmity, when out of our compassion we reach out to the relief of the needy, helping them, as we desire to be helped ourselves. Thus we help, not only in easy problems (as is signified by "the herb yielding its seed") but also in the offering of our best strength in providing them protection (such as "the tree bearing its fruit"). This is to say, that we seek to rescue him who is suffering injury from the hands of the powerful, furnishing him with the sheltering protection that comes from the strong arm of a righteous judgment.[545]

CHAPTER 18—SURROUNDED BY THE FIRMAMENT OF GOD'S WORD

O Lord, I pray, let it happen as You have prepared it, as You give joy and the capacity for joy. Let truth spring up out of the earth, and let righteousness look down from heaven,[546] and let there be lights in the firmament.[547]

Let us break our bread with the hungry, let us bring the homeless poor to our house, let us clothe the naked, and never turn away those of our own flesh.[548] Behold how good it is by the fruits that spring forth from the earth. Let our temporal light break forth, and let us, from even this lower level of fruitful action, come to the joy of contemplation and hold on high the Word of Life. Let us, at length, appear like "lights in the world,"[549] clinging to the firmament of Your Scripture.

Through the Scriptures, You make plain how we may distinguish between things intelligible and things tangible, as if between the day and the night. You also reveal how to distinguish between souls who give themselves to things of the mind and others absorbed in things of sense. Thus it is that You are not alone in the secret of Your judgment as You were before the firmament was made, and before You divided the light and the darkness.

Now, Your spiritual children are placed and ranked in this same firmament, thus manifesting Your grace throughout the world, that it may shed light upon the earth. Again, it will divide between the day and night, and will be for the signs of the times,[550] because old things have passed away, and all things are become new.[551] Our salvation is nearer than when we believed, because "the night is far spent and the day is at hand."[552]

"You crown the year with Your goodness"[553] and send laborers into Your harvest. Others have labored in the sowing and sending as well, to make new sowings whose harvest shall not be until the end of time. Thus You grant the prayers of him who seeks, and bless the years of the righteous man. However, You are always the Selfsame, and in Your years which fail not You prepare a granary for our transient years. By an eternal design You spread the heavenly blessings on the earth in their proper seasons.

Gifts of God Likened to Stars

"To one there is given by Your Spirit the word of wisdom",[554] which resembles the greater light for those whose delight is in the clear light of truth, and as the light which is given for the ruling of the day.[555] To another, the word of knowledge is given by the same Spirit—as it were, the "lesser light." To another, faith; to another, the gift of healing; to another, the power of working miracles; to another, the gift of prophecy; to another, the discerning of spirits; to another, different kinds of tongues. All these gifts may be compared to "the stars." The one and selfsame Spirit is at work in them as He wills, dividing to everyone his own portion and making stars to appear in their bright splendor for the profit of souls.

The word of knowledge contains all the mysteries that change in their seasons like the moon. However, all the other promises of gifts, which when counted are like the stars, fall short of that splendor of Wisdom in which the day rejoices and are only for the ruling of the night. Yet they are necessary for those who are spiritually immature and carnal, to whom Your servant couldn't speak though he could speak wisdom among the mature.[556]

The natural man, when he is a babe in Christ, drinks milk until he is able to eat solid food. Until his eye is able to look into the sun, don't leave him in a lightless night. Instead, let him be satisfied with the light of the moon and the stars. You discuss these things with us wisely, our God, in Your Book, which is Your "firmament." That so we may be able to view all things in admiring contemplation, although till now we must do so through signs and seasons, and in days and years.

CHAPTER 19—LIGHTS IN THE FIRMAMENT

For the "the dry land" to appear, You say: "Wash yourselves, make yourselves clean; put away the evil of your doings from before My eyes. Cease to do evil. Learn to do good; seek justice, rebuke the oppressor; defend the fatherless, plead for the widow."[557] Then the earth will bring forth the green herb for food and fruit-bearing trees. "Come now, and let us reason together, says the Lord,"[558] that there may be lights in the firmament of heaven and that they may shine upon the earth.

A rich man asked Jesus, the good Teacher, what he must do to attain eternal life. The rich man thought Jesus was only a man and nothing more, so let the good Teacher answer—He is good for He is God. Let Jesus answer that, if he would enter into life, he must keep the commandments. Let the man put away from himself the bitterness of malice and all wickedness. Let him not kill, commit adultery, steal, or bear false witness[559] so that "the dry land" may appear and bring forth the honoring of fathers and mothers and the love of neighbor.

"All these I have kept." the man replied.

Where do so many thorns come from, if the earth is really fruitful? Uproot the brier patch of greed.

The Lord said, "Sell what you have and be filled with fruit by giving to the poor, and store up treasure in heaven. Then, follow Me."

Lights in the Heavens

However, you, O elect people, are set in the firmament of the world. You have forsaken all that you may follow the Lord. Therefore, follow Him and confound the mighty! Follow Him, O beautiful feet,[560] and shine in the firmament. Follow Him so that the heavens may declare His glory, dividing the light of the perfect ones[561]—though not yet so perfect as the angels—from the darkness of the little ones, who are nevertheless not utterly despised. Shine over all the earth, and let the day be lighted by the sun, speak the Word of wisdom to the day ("day unto day utters speech"[562]) and let the night, lighted by the moon, display the Word of knowledge to the night. The moon and stars give light for the night, the night does not extinguish them, and they illumine in its proper mode.

It's as if God were saying, "Let there be lights in the firmament of the heaven!" and suddenly a sound came from heaven as if it were a rushing mighty wind, and there appeared flames of fire, which sat on each of them.[563] Then they were made to be lights in the firmament of heaven, having the Word of life.

Run to and fro everywhere, you holy fires, you lovely fires, for you are the light of the world and you are not to be hidden under a basket.[564] He to whom you cling is raised on high, and has raised you on high with Him. Run to and fro and make yourselves known among all the nations!

CHAPTER 20—THE MYSTERIES OF GOD

Let the sea conceive and bring forth our works, and let the waters nurture the moving creatures that have life.[565] By separating the precious from the vile we are made the mouth of God[566] by whom He said, "Let the waters bring forth." This does not refer to the living creatures that the earth brings forth, but to the creeping creatures that have life and the fowls that fly over the earth.

By the ministry of Your holy ones, Your mysteries have overcome the raging waves of the world to instruct the nations in Your name, and Your baptism. Among these things many great and marvelous works have been wrought, which are analogous to the huge whales. The words of Your messengers have flown over the earth, high in the firmament of Your Word that is spread over them as the authority under which they are to fly wherever they go. There is no speech nor language where their voice isn't heard. "Their line has gone out through all the earth, and their words to the end of the world."[567] You, O Lord, have multiplied these things by Your blessing.

Am I speaking falsely? Am I confused and not distinguishing correctly between the knowledge of the firmament of heaven and the physical works in the swelling sea and beneath the firmament of heaven? There are those things, the knowledge of which is solid and defined. It does not increase from generation to generation and so they stand as lights of wisdom and knowledge. However, there are many and varied physical processes that manifest these same principles. Thus one thing growing from another is multiplied by Your blessing. O God, You refresh our easily wearied mortal senses, so that in our mental understanding, one thing may be signified in many different ways and by different bodily motions.

The Soul Has a Higher Life

"The waters" have brought forth these mysteries, but only at Your word. The needs of the people who were alien to the eternity of Your truth have called them forth, but only in Your gospel. It was these "waters" which cast them up, whose stagnant bitterness was the reason why they came forth through Your Word.

Now all the things that You have made are fair, and yet, You are inexpressibly fairer. If Adam had not fallen away from You, that brackish sea—the human race—so deeply prying, so boisterously swelling, so restlessly moving, would never have flowed forth from his belly. Thus, there would have been no need for Your ministers to use physical and tangible signs in the midst of many "waters" in order to show forth their mystical deeds and words. For this is the way I interpret the phrases "creeping creatures" and "flying fowl."

Nevertheless, men who've been instructed, initiated and made dependent on Your physical mysteries would be unable to profit from them if it weren't that their soul has a higher life. Nor would they unless, after the word of its admission, it did not look beyond toward its perfection.

Chapter 21—The Coming Glory

Therefore, in Your Word, it's not the depth of the sea but "the earth,"[568] separated from the brackishness of the water, that brought forth "the living soul" itself![569]

Now, this soul no longer has need of baptism as the heathen, or as it did when it was covered with the waters. There can be no other entrance into the Kingdom of Heaven, since You have appointed that baptism should be the entrance. Nor does it seek great, miraculous works by which to buttress faith. For such a soul does not refuse to believe unless it sees signs and marvels, now that "the faithful earth" is separated from "the waters" of the sea, which have been made bitter by infidelity. Thus, for them, "tongues are for a sign, not to those who believe but to those who do not believe."[570]

The earth, which You founded above the waters, doesn't stand in need of those flying creatures which the waters brought forth at Your word. Send forth Your word into it by the agency of Your messengers. For we only tell of their works, but it is You who does the works in them, so that they may bring forth "a living soul" in the earth.

The earth brings forth "the living soul" because "the earth" is the cause of such things being done by Your messengers, just as the sea caused the production of the creeping creatures having life and the flying fowl under the firmament of heaven. "The earth" no longer needs them, although it feeds on the Fish taken out of the deep,[571] set out on that table which You prepared in the presence of those who believe. To this end He was raised from the deep so that He might feed "the dry land." "The fowl," even though they were produced in the sea, will yet be multiplied on the earth.

Let Your Ministers Do Their Work On Earth

The preaching of the first evangelists was called forth by reason of man's infidelity, but the faithful also are exhorted and blessed by them day-by-day in many ways. "The living soul" has its origin from "the earth," because to the faithful alone is there any profit in restraint from the loves of this world, so that their soul may live to You. This soul was dead while it was living in pleasures, pleasures that bear death in them, whereas You, O Lord, are the living delight of the pure heart.

Therefore, let Your ministers do their work on "the earth." Not as they formerly did in "the waters" of infidelity when they had to preach and speak by miracles, mysteries, and mystical expressions, in which ignorance—the mother of wonder—gives them an attentive ear because of its fear of occult and strange things. This is the entry into faith for the sons of Adam who are forgetful of

You, who hide themselves from Your face, and who have become a darkened abyss. Instead, let Your ministers work even as on "the dry land," safe from the whirlpools of the abyss. Let them be an example unto the faithful by living before them and stirring them up to imitation.

Men will listen in such a setting, not with the mere intent to hear, but also to act. Seek the Lord and your soul will live[572] and "the earth" will bring forth "the living soul." Be not conformed to this world[573] separate yourselves from it. The soul lives by avoiding that which brings death if they are loved. Restrain yourselves from the unbridled wildness of pride, from the lazy passions of luxury, and from what is falsely called knowledge.[574]

Your Word Is A Fountain of Life

This how the wild beast is tamed, the cattle subdued, and the serpent made harmless. For, in allegory, these figures are the motions of our mind. In other words, the haughtiness of pride, the delight of lust, and the poison of curiosity are motions of the dead soul. Not so dead that it has lost all motion, but dead because it has deserted the fountain of life, and so has been taken captive by this transitory world and conformed to it.

Your Word, O God, is a fountain of life eternal, and it does not pass away. Therefore, this desertion is restrained by Your Word when it says, "Be not conformed to this world,"[575] to the end that "the earth" may bring forth a "living soul" in the fountain of life. This soul is disciplined by Your Word, Your evangelists, and by imitating the followers of Your Christ. For this is the meaning of "after his kind." A man tends to follow the example of his friend. Thus, Paul says, "Become as I am, because I have become as you are."[576]

Therefore, in this "living soul" there will be good beasts, acting meekly. You have commanded this, saying: "Do your work in meekness and you shall be loved by all men."[577] The cattle will be good, for if they eat well they'll not suffer, and if they don't eat at all they'll still not lack. The serpents will be good, not poisonous to do harm, but only cunning in their watchfulness. They will explore only as much of this temporal nature as is necessary for the eternal nature to be "clearly seen, being understood by the things that are made."[578] All these animals will obey reason when, having been restrained from their death-dealing ways, they live and become good.

Chapter 22—Created in the Image of God

O Lord God, our Creator, when our affections have been turned from the love of the world, in which we died by living ill, we will be transformed. When we began to be "a living soul" by living well, and when the word, "Be not conformed to this world," which You spoke through Your apostle has been fulfilled in us, then will follow what You said immediately after: "But be transformed by the renewing of your mind."[579] We are transformed so that we may be able to prove what Your will is. This will not be creation "after their kind," as if we were following a neighbor who went before us, nor will it be as if we were living after the example of a better man. You didn't say, "Let man be made after his kind," but rather, "Let Us make man in Our image, according to Our likeness."[580]

This is why Your minister begat children by the gospel, so that he wouldn't always have babes that he would have to nurse. He said, "Be transformed by the renewing of your minds, that you may prove what is the good and acceptable and perfect will of God."[581]

You didn't say, "Let man be made," but rather, "Let Us make man." Nor did You say, "After his kind," but after "Our image" and "likeness." Indeed, it's only when man has been renewed in his mind, and comes to behold and apprehend Your truth, that he doesn't need another man as his director, showing him how to imitate other human examples. Instead, by Your guidance, he proves what is Your good and acceptable and perfect will—and You teach him! Now that he is able to understand, You show him the trinity of the Unity and the unity of the Trinity.

This is explains how the plural statement, "Let Us make man," is also connected with the statement in the singular, "And God made man." It is said in the plural, "After Our likeness," and then in the singular, "After the image of God." Man is thus transformed in the knowledge of God, according to the image of Him who created him. Now, having been made spiritual, man judges all things, that is, all things that are appropriate to be judged, and he is judged of no other man.[582]

CHAPTER 23—MAN AS JUDGE

The phrase, "he judges all things," means that man has dominion over the fish of the sea, the fowl of the air, all cattle and wild beasts, all the earth, and over every creeping thing that creeps on the earth. He does this by the power of reason in his mind by which he perceives "the things of the Spirit of God."[583] However, when man was put in this high office, he didn't understand all that was involved and was reduced to the level of the beasts, becoming like them.[584]

Therefore, O God, by the grace You have given us—since we are Your workmanship, created in good works (not only those who are in spiritual authority but also those who are spiritually subject to them)—You made man male and female. Here everyone is equal in Your spiritual grace where, as far as sex is concerned, there is neither male nor female, just as there is neither Jew nor Greek, bond nor free.

Spiritual Judgment

Spiritual men judge spiritually, whether in authority or subject to authority. They don't judge by the light of the spiritual knowledge that shines in the firmament, for it's inappropriate for them to judge by such an awe-inspiring authority. Nor does it behoove them to judge regarding Your Book itself, although there are some things in it that aren't clear. Instead, we submit our understanding to it and believe with certainty that what is hidden from our sight is still rightly and truly spoken. Even though a man is spiritual and renewed by the knowledge of God according to the image of God who created him, he must be a doer of the Word rather than its judge.[585]

Furthermore, the spiritual man doesn't judge concerning the division between spiritual and carnal men known only to Your eyes, O God, and which may not be made manifest to us by their external works. We may not know them by their fruits, but You, O God, know them and have divided and called them secretly, before the firmament was made. Nor does the spiritual man judge the disordered state of society in this world. For what business is it of his to judge those who are outside Your Church, since he can't know which of them may later come into the sweetness of Your grace? Nor can he know which of them may continue in the perpetual bitterness of their sin.

The Dominion of Man

Man received dominion over the fish of the sea, the fowls of the air, all cattle, all the earth, and over every creeping thing that creeps on the earth. Even though man was made after Your image, he didn't receive the authority of dominion over the...

- lights of heaven.
- secret heaven.
- day and the night which You called forth before the creation of the heaven.
- gathering together of the waters which is the sea.

Man judges and approves what he finds right and disapproves what he finds amiss. This is true whether in celebration of those mysteries that initiate those whom Your mercy has sought out in the midst of many waters, or in that sacrament that exhibits the Fish itself[586] upon which, being raised from the depths, the righteous "earth" (the Church) feeds.

Man judges and approves the use of words as well, which are subject to the authority of Your Book. These words burst forth and sound from the mouth, as if "flying" under the firmament, interpreting, expounding, discoursing, disputing, blessing, invoking You, so that the people answer, "Amen."[587] The reason that these words must be pronounced vocally is because of the abyss of this world and the blindness of our flesh in which thoughts cannot be directly seen,[588] they must be spoken aloud in our ears. Thus, although the flying fowl are multiplied on the earth, they still take their origins from the waters.

The spiritual man also judges by approving what is right and reproving what he finds amiss in the works and morals of the faithful, such as in their almsgiving, which is signified by the phrase, "The earth bringing forth its fruit." Further, he judges the "living soul," which is then made to live by disciplining her affections in purity, fasting, and holy meditation. Man also judges concerning everything perceived by the bodily senses. It can be said that man should judge all matters about which he has the power of correction.

CHAPTER 24—THE MANIFOLD MEANING OF GOD'S WORD

What kind of mystery is this? Behold, O Lord, You bless men so that they may be "fruitful and multiply, and replenish the earth." Are You making a sign for us in this that we may understand something allegorically? Why didn't You also bless the light, which You called "the day," or the firmament of heaven, or the lights, the stars, the earth, or the sea?

I might reply, O God, that by Your creating us after Your image, You willed to bestow this gift of blessing upon man alone. However, You similarly blessed the fishes and the whales so that they would be fruitful and multiply and replenish the waters of the sea. Likewise, You blessed the fowls so that they would be multiplied on the earth. I might say that this blessing properly belonged only to such creatures as are propagated from their own kind, if I could find it given also as a blessing to trees, and plants, and the beasts of the earth. But this "increase and multiply" was not said to plants, trees, beasts or serpents, though all of these, along with fishes and birds and men, do actually increase by propagation and so preserve their species.

What, then, shall I say, O Truth, O my Life? Was this idly and vainly said? Surely not, O Father of piety. Far be it from a servant of Your Word to say anything like this! However, if I don't understand what You meant by that phrase, let those who are more intelligent than I interpret it better, according to the degree that You have given each of us the ability to understand.

God Has Not Spoken In Vain

Let my confession be pleasing in Your eyes as well, for I confess to You that I believe, O Lord, that You have not spoken this in vain. Nor will I be silent as to what my reading has suggested to me. It's valid, and I don't see anything to prevent me from so interpreting the figurative sayings in Your Book. I know that a thing understood only one way in the mind may be expressed in many different ways by the body. I also know that a thing that has only one manner of expression through the body may be understood by the mind in many different ways. For example: The love of God and of our neighbor. How many different mysteries and countless languages, and in each language, by how many different ways of speaking, this love is signified physically!

Likewise, the "young fish" in "the waters" increase and multiply. On the other hand, whomever you are who reads this, observe and behold what Scripture declares and how the voice pronounces it <u>in only one way</u>, "In the beginning God created heaven and earth."[589] Isn't this understood in many different ways by different kinds of true interpretations that don't involve the deceit of error? Thus the offspring of men are fruitful and do multiply.[590]

Be Fruitful and Multiply

If, then, we consider the nature of things in their strictly literal sense and not allegorically, the phrase, "Be fruitful and multiply," applies to all things that are begotten by seed. It cannot be for nothing that this blessing is attributed only to the offspring of marine life and man. Therefore, if we treat these words figuratively, as I judge that the Scripture intended them to be, then we discover that the characteristic of fruitfulness belongs also to…

- the spiritual and physical creations, signified by "heaven and earth"

- the righteous and unrighteous souls, signified by "light and darkness"

- the sacred writers through whom the Law is uttered, signified by "the firmament established between the waters and the waters"

- the earthly commonwealth still steeped in bitterness, signified by "the sea"

- the zeal of holy souls, signified by "the dry land"

- the works of mercy done in this present life, signified by "the seed-bearing herbs and fruit-bearing trees"

- spiritual gifts which shine out for our edification, signified by "the lights of heaven"

- human affections ruled by temperance, signified by "the living soul"

In all these instances we meet with multiplicity, fertility and increase, but the particular way in which "Be fruitful and multiply" is exemplified differs widely. Thus a single category may include many things that we can't discover except through their signs displayed physically, and by the things being thoroughly thought through by the mind.

Therefore, we interpret the phrase, "The generation of the waters," as referring to the physically expressed signs of fruitfulness, since they're made necessary by the degree of our involvement in the flesh. However, the power of human generation refers to the process of mental conception, as seen in the fruitfulness of reason. Therefore, we believe that to both of these two kinds it's been said by You, O Lord, "Be fruitful and multiply." You have granted us, in this blessing, the ability and power, not only to express what we understand by a single idea in many different ways, but also to understand in many ways what we find obscurely expressed in a single statement. Thus the waters of the sea are replenished, and their waves are symbols of diverse meanings. Likewise, the earth is replenished with human offspring. Its dryness is the symbol of its thirst for truth, and of the fact that reason rules over it.

Chapter 25—Mercy Signified by Fruits of the Earth

O my Lord God, I also desire to say what the following Scripture suggests to me. I'll speak without fear, because I speak the truth as You inspire me to know Your will in what I say concerning these words. I don't believe I can speak the truth by any other inspiration than Yours, since You are the Truth, and every man a liar.[591] He that speaks a lie, speaks out of himself. Therefore, if I'm to speak the truth, I must speak of Your truth.

You have given every seed-bearing herb on the face of the earth for our food, and all trees that bear in themselves seed of their own kind. You've given these not to men only, but to all the fowls of the air, the beasts of the field, and all creeping things.[592] However, You've not given these things to the fishes or great whales.

Works of Mercy

We've said, that by these fruits of the earth the works of mercy were signified and figured forth in an allegory. From the fruitful earth, things are provided for the necessities of life. Such an "earth" was the godly Onesiphorus, to whose house You gave mercy because he often refreshed Paul and wasn't ashamed of his bonds.[593]

This was also the way of the brethren from Macedonia, who bore such fruit and supplied to Paul what he lacked. However, notice how Paul grieves for certain "trees," which didn't give him the fruit that was due: "At my first defense no one stood with me, but all forsook me. May it not be charged against them."[594]

We owe "fruits" to those who minister spiritual doctrine to us through their understanding of the divine mysteries. We owe these to them as men. We owe these fruits, also, to "the living souls" since they offer themselves as examples for us in their own self-restraint. Finally, we owe these fruits to "the flying creatures" because of their blessings that are multiplied on the earth, for "Their line has gone out through all the earth, and their words to the end of the world."[595]

Chapter 26—Gifts and Fruits

Those who are fed by these "fruits" find their joy in them, but those whose god is their belly find no joy. For those who offer these fruits, it's not the fruit itself that matters, but the spirit in which they're given. Therefore, he who serves God and not his own belly may rejoice in these fruits, and I plainly see why. I see it, and rejoice with him greatly.

Paul had received from the Philippians the things they had sent by Epaphroditus, and I can see why he rejoiced. He was fed by what his joy was found in. Speaking truly, Paul said, "I rejoice in the Lord greatly, that now at the last your care of me has flourished again, in which you were once so careful, but it had become a weariness to you."[596]

The Philippians, in their extended period of weariness in well doing, had become weak and were, so to say, dried up—they were no longer bringing forth the fruits of good works. Paul began rejoicing in them, because they were again flourishing in ministering to his needs. Therefore he added:

> Not that I speak in regard to need, for I have learned in whatever state I am, to be content: I know how to be abased, and I know how to abound. Everywhere and in all things I have learned both to be full and to be hungry, both to abound and to suffer need. I can do all things through Christ who strengthens me.[597]

Finding Joy

Where do you find joy in all things, O great Paul? What is the cause of your joy? On what do you feed, O man, renewed now in the knowledge of God after the image of Him who created you? What food is owed such creatures? What feeds you? It is joy! Listen to what follows: "Nevertheless you have done well that you shared in my distress."[598] This is what Paul found his joy in and what he fed upon.

The Philippians had done well, not merely because Paul's need had been relieved, but because he knew both how to abound and how to suffer need, in You who strengthened him. Therefore, he said:

> Now you Philippians know also that in the beginning of the gospel, when I departed from Macedonia, no church shared with me concerning giving and receiving

but you only. For even in Thessalonica you sent aid once
and again for my necessities. Not that I seek the gift, but
I seek the fruit that abounds to your account.[599]

Paul finds his joy in the fact that the Philippians have returned
once again to these good works. He's glad that they're flourishing
again, as a fruitful field when it recovers its fertility.

Was it because of his needs alone that Paul said, "You have sent
me gifts according to my needs?" Does he find joy in that? No. Not
for that alone. But how do we know this? We know it because he
adds, "Not that I seek the gift, but I seek the fruit."[600]

Distinguishing Between Gift and Fruit

I've learned from You, O my God, how to distinguish between
the terms "gift" and "fruit." A "gift" is the thing itself, given by one
who bestows life's necessities on another, such as money, food,
drink, clothing, shelter, and aid. However, the "fruit" is the good
and right will of the giver. The good Teacher, Jesus, not only said,
"He that receives a prophet," but added, "In the name of a
prophet." Likewise, He didn't just say, "He who receives a
righteous man," but added, "In the name of a righteous man."[601]
Therefore, the former shall receive the reward of a prophet and the
latter, that of a righteous man.

Jesus also declared, "Whoever shall give a cup of cold water to
one of these little ones to drink," and then added, "In the name of
a disciple," concluding, "Truly I tell you he shall not lose his
reward." The "gift" involves receiving a prophet, receiving a
righteous man, handing a cup of cold water to a disciple. However,
the "fruit" is to do all this in the name of a prophet, in the name
of a righteous man, and in the name of a disciple.

The widow fed Elijah with "fruit." She knew that she was feeding a man of God and this is why she did so. However, the raven fed Elijah with a "gift." The inner man of Elijah was not fed by this "gift," but only the outer man, which otherwise would have perished for lack of food.

CHAPTER 27—FISHES AND GREAT WHALES

Therefore I will speak before You, O Lord, what is true. I believe that the phrase, "fishes and great whales," signifies the mysteries of initiation and great works of miracles. The uninstructed[602] and the infidel require these before they can successfully be led to the Church after providing refreshment or otherwise aiding Your servants. These folk don't really know why this kindness should be done, and to what end.

Therefore, the pagan doesn't feed the saint, and the saint doesn't feed the pagan. The pagans don't offer their "gifts" through a holy and right intent, nor do the saints rejoice in the gifts of those who don't yet see the "fruit." The "fruit" is what feeds the mind and the same gladdens the mind. Therefore, fishes and whales are not fed on such food as what the earth alone brings forth, when they've been separated and divided from the bitterness of "the waters" of the sea.

CHAPTER 28—GOD DECLARED CREATION "VERY GOOD"

You, O God, looked upon everything You had made and declared that it was very good.[603] We see the entire creation as well, and it's all very good. When, in each separate kind of Your work, You said, "Let them be made," and they were made, You saw that it was good. I've counted seven times where it is written that You saw what You had made was "good." Then, there is the eighth time when You saw <u>all</u> things that You had made and they were not only good, but <u>very</u> good. They were now seen as a totality. Individually things were only good, but taken as a totality they were both good and very good.

Beautiful bodies express this truth. A body consists of several parts, each of which is beautiful. The body itself is far more beautiful than any of its individual parts separately, even though the parts are separately beautiful.

CHAPTER 29—TIME HAS NO EFFECT ON GOD'S WORD

I looked attentively to find whether it was seven or eight times that You saw Your works were good and when they were pleasing to You. However, I discovered that there was no "time" in Your seeing which would help me to understand in what sense You had looked so many "times" at what You had made. So I said: "O Lord, isn't Your Scripture true? You are true, and Your truth sets it forth. Why, then, do You say that in Your seeing there are no times, while Scripture tells me that what You made each day You saw to be good, and when I counted them found how many 'times'?"

You answered me because You are my God. You speak to Your servant with a strong voice in his inner ear, saying: "O man, what my Scripture says, I say. Though it speaks in terms of time, My Word is not affected by time. It exists coeternally with My Self. Thus the things you see through my Spirit, I see. Just as what you say through my Spirit, I say. Nevertheless, while you see those things in time, I don't, and while you speak those things in time, I don't."

CHAPTER 30—CONFRONTING FALSE DOCTRINES

I heard this, O Lord my God, and drank of the sweetness of Your truth. I understood that to some men Your works are displeasing. These men say that You made many of Your works under the compulsion of necessity—such as the pattern of the heavens and the courses of the stars—and that You didn't make them out of what was Yours. They say that these works were already created elsewhere and from other sources. These unbelievers say that You collected, fashioned and wove these other works together, as if they were plundered from Your conquered enemies.

Of other things, these blasphemers say that You neither made them nor arranged them, all flesh, for example, and the very small living creatures, and everything held to the earth by roots. They say a hostile mind and an alien nature, not created by You and in every way contrary to You, fashioned and framed all these things in the nether parts of the world.[604] They who speak thus are insane. They neither see Your works through Your Spirit, nor recognize You in them.

CHAPTER 31—SEEING THINGS AS THEY ARE

For those who see these things through Your Spirit, it is You who sees them in them. Therefore, when they see that these things are good, it's You who sees that they are good. Whatsoever things are pleasing because of You, it's You who gives us pleasure in those things. Those things that please us through Your Spirit are pleasing to You in us.

For what man knows the things of a man except the spirit of the man which is in him? Even so no one knows the things of God except the Spirit of God. Now we have

received, not the spirit of the world, but the Spirit who is
from God, that we might know the things that have been
freely given to us by God.[605]

I'm admonished to say: "Yes, truly. No man knows the things of
God, but the Spirit of God. But how do we also know what things
are given us by God?" The answer given is... "Because we know
these things by his Spirit; for no one knows but the Spirit of God."

As it's truly said to those who speak through the Spirit of God,
"It is not you who speak," so it's also said to these who know
through the Spirit of God, "It is not you yourselves who know."
Likewise, it may be said to those who perceive through the Spirit
of God that a thing is good, "It is not they who see, but God who
sees that it is good."

Therefore, it's one thing to think like the men who judge
something to be bad when it is good, as do those whom we have
already mentioned, yet quite another that a man should see as
good what is good. This is the case with many whom Your creation
pleases because it is good, yet what pleases them in it is not You so
they prefer to find their joy in Your creatures rather than to find it
in You.

It's yet another thing that when a man sees something to be
good, God should see in him that it's good. Then, God may be
truly loved in what He has made. God can't be loved except
through the Holy Spirit, because "the love of God has been poured
out in our hearts by the Holy Spirit who was given to us."[606] It's
by Him that we see whatever we see to be good in any degree, since
it's from Him, who doesn't exist in any particular degree but who
simply is what He is.

Chapter 32—We See Your Very Good Creation

Thank You, O Lord! We see the heaven and the earth, either the physical part, higher and lower, or the spiritual and physical creation. We see the light made and divided from the darkness for the adornment of these parts, from which the universal mass of the world or the universal creation is constituted.

We see the firmament of heaven, either the original "body" of the world between the spiritual (higher) waters and the physical (lower) waters[607] or the expanse of air (heaven) through which the fowls of heaven wander. They wander between the waters that move in clouds above them, dropping down in dew on clear nights, and those waters that are heavy and flow along the earth.

We see the waters gathered together in the vast plains of the sea. We see the dry land, first bare and then formed, so as to be visible and well-ordered, and the soil of herbs and trees.

We see the light shining from above, the sun to serve the day, the moon and the stars to bring cheer in the night. We see by all these that the intervals of time are marked and noted.

We see on every side the watery elements, fruitful with fishes, beasts, and birds, and we notice that the density of the atmosphere that supports the flight of birds is increased by the evaporation of the waters.

We see the face of the earth, complete with earthly creatures. We see man, created in Your image and likeness, in the very image and likeness of You. We see that Your likeness is having the power of reason and understanding, by virtue of which man has been set over all irrational creatures. Just as there is in his soul one element that controls by its power of reflection and another that is made subject so that it should obey. Likewise, physically, the woman was made for the man. Although she had a like nature of rational intelligence in the mind, still in the sex of her body she should be similarly subject to the sex of her husband. For the appetite of action is subjected to the deliberation of the mind in order to conceive the rules of right action.

These things we see, and each of them is good; and the whole is very good!

CHAPTER 33—GOD'S WORKS PRAISE HIM

Let Your works praise You, that we may love You, and let us love You that Your works may praise You. Your works have a beginning in time and an end, a rising and a setting, a growth and a decay, a form and a privation. Thus, these works have their successions of morning and evening, partly hidden and partly plain. For they were made from nothing by You, and not from You. Neither were they made from any matter that is not Yours, or that was created beforehand. They were created from matter that was created by You at the same time that You formed its formlessness, with no interval of time.

However, since the matter of heaven and earth is one thing and the form of heaven and earth is another, You created matter out of absolutely nothing, but the form of the world You formed from formless matter. But both were done at the same time, so that form followed matter with no delaying interval.

CHAPTER 34—THE ORDER OF CREATION

We've also explored the question of what You desired to figure forth, both in the creation and in the description of things in this particular order. We've seen that things taken separately are good and all things taken together are very good, both in heaven and earth.

We've seen that creation was wrought through Your Word, Your only Son, the Head and the Body of the Church, and signifies Your predestination before all times, without morning and evening. But when, in time, You began to unfold the things destined before time, to make hidden things manifest and reorder our disorders—since our sins were over us and we had sunk into profound darkness away from You—You justified the ungodly and divided them from the wicked.

You made the authority of Your Book a firmament between those above who would be open to to You and those beneath who would be subject to those above. You gathered the society of unbelievers into a conspiracy so that the zeal of the faithful would become manifest. Also, that the unbelievers might bring forth works of mercy unto You by giving their earthly riches to the poor to obtain heavenly riches.

Kindling the Lights in the Firmament

You then kindled the lights in the firmament, which are Your holy ones who have the Word of Life and who shine with an exalted authority, warranted to them by their spiritual gifts. Then, for the instruction of the unbelieving nations, out of physical matter You produced the mysteries and the visible miracles and the sounds of words in harmony with the firmament of Your Book, through which the faithful should be blessed.

After this You formed "the living soul" of the faithful, through the ordering of their passions by the strength of self-restraint. You renewed, after Your image and likeness, the mind which is faithful to You alone and that needs to imitate no human authority. Thus,

You subordinated rational action to the higher excellence of intelligence, as the woman is subordinate to the man.

Finally, in all Your ministries, which were needed to perfect the faithful in this life, You willed that these same faithful ones should themselves bring forth good things, profitable for their temporal use and fruitful for the life to come.

We see all these things, and they are very good, because You see them "very good" in us. You have given us Your Spirit, by which we may see them "very good" and love You in them.

CHAPTER 35—THE SABBATH OF LIFE ETERNAL

O Lord God, grant us Your peace, for You have given us all things. Grant us the peace of quietness, the peace of the Sabbath, the peace without an evening. All this most beautiful array of things, all so very good, will pass away when all their courses are finished, for in them there is both morning and evening.

However, the seventh day is without an evening and it has no setting, for You have sanctified it with an everlasting duration. After all Your works of creation, which were very good, You rested on the seventh day. You created them all in unbroken rest so that the voice of Your Book might speak to us with the prior assurance that after our works, which also are very good because You have given them to us, we may find our rest in You, in the Sabbath of life eternal.

CHAPTER 36—THE WORK OF GOD—THE REST OF GOD

You will rest in us then, as now You work in us. That will be Your rest through us, as these are Your works through us. But You,

O Lord, work evermore and are always at rest. You see not in time, You move not in time, You rest not in time. Yet You made all those things which are seen in time—indeed, the very times themselves—and everything that proceeds in and from time.

CHAPTER 37—ASK, SEEK, KNOCK

We can see all those things that You've made because they are. However, they are because You see them.[608] We see with our eyes that they are, and we see with our minds that they are good. But You saw them as made when You saw that they would be made.

In this present time, we've been moved to do well. Your Spirit has quickened our heart, but in the former time, having forsaken You, we were moved to do evil. Nevertheless, You, O the one good God, have never ceased to do good!

We have accomplished certain good works by Your good gifts, and even though they are not eternal, we still hope after these things here, to find our rest in Your great sanctification. However, You are the Good, and need no rest. You are always at rest, because You are Your own rest.

What man will teach men to understand this? And what angel will teach the angels? Or what angels will teach men? We must ask it of You; we must seek it in You; we must knock for it at Your door. Only thus shall we receive; only thus shall we find; only thus shall Your door be opened.

Endnotes

Retraction Notes

[1] Gen. 1:1 (NKJV)

[2] Gen. 2:2

[3] Notice here the echo of Acts 9:1.

[4] Psalms 100:3

Book One Notes

[5] Psalms 145:3

[6] Psalms 147:5

[7] Romans 10:14

[8] Psalms 22:26

[9] Matt. 7:7-8

[10] A reference to Bishop Ambrose of Milan; see Book 5, Ch. 13; Book 8, Ch. 11.

[11] Psalms 139:8

[12] Jer. 23:24

[13] Cf. Psalms 18:31

[14] Psalms 35:3

[15] Psalms 19:12

[16] Psalms 19:13 (NLT)

[17] Psalms 116:10

[18] Cf. Psalms 32:5

[19] Cf. Job 9:2

[20] Psalms 130:3

21 Psalms 102:27

22 Psalms 102:27

23 Cf. Psalms 92:1

24 Cf. Psalms 51:5

25 Augustine believed that the rite of baptism established the image of Christ in the person.

26 Psalms 78:39

27 Cf. Psalms 72:27

28 Aeneid, VI, 457

29 Aeneid, II

30 *Lignum* is a common metaphor for the cross; and it was often joined to the figure of Noah's ark, as the means of safe transport from earth to heaven.

31 This apostrophe to "the torrent of human custom" now switches its focus to the poets who celebrated the philanderings of the gods; see *De civ. Dei*, II, vii-xi; IV, xxvi-xxviii.

32 Probably a contemporary disciple of Cicero (or the Academics) whom Augustine had heard levy a rather common philosopher's complaint against Olympian religion and the poetic myths about it. Cf. De Labriolle, I, 21 (see Bibl.).

33 Terence, *Eunuch.*, 584-591; quoted again in *De civ. Dei*, II, vii.

34 *Aeneid*, I, 38.

35 Cf. Ps. 103:8 and Ps. 86:15.

36 Psalms 27:8

37 An interesting mixed reminiscence of *Enneads*, I, 5:8 and the story of the prodigal son found in Luke 15:13-24.

38 Psalms 123:1

39 Matthew 19:14

40 Another Plotinian echo; cf. *Enneads*, III, 8:10.

Book Two Notes

41 Another Plotinian phrase; cf. *Enneads*, I, 6, 9:1-2.

42 Cf. Gen. 3:18 and *De bono conjugali*, 8-9, 39-35 (*N-PNF*, III, 396-413).

43 1 Cor. 7:28.

[44] 1 Cor. 7:1.

[45] 1 Cor. 7:32, 33.

[46] Cf. Matt. 19:12.

[47] Twenty miles from Tagaste, famed as the birthplace of Apuleius, the only notable classical author produced by the province of Africa.

[48] Another echo of Psalms 130:1, and the most explicit statement we have from Augustine of his motive and aim in writing these "confessions."

[49] Cf. 1 Cor. 3:9.

[50] Ps. 116:16.

[51] Cf. Jer. 51:6; 50:8.

[52] Cf. Ps. 73:7.

[53] Cicero, *De Catiline*, 16.

[54] *Avertitur*, the opposite of *convertitur*: the evil will turns the soul *away* from God; this is sin. By grace it is turned *to* God; this is *conversion*.

[55] Psalms 116:12.

[56] Psalms 19:12.

[57] Cf. Matt. 25:21.

Book Three Notes

[58] Cf. Job 2:7, 8.

[59] 2 Cor. 2:16.

[60] *Eversores*, "over turners," from *overtere*, to overthrow or ruin. This was the nickname of a gang of young hoodlums in Carthage, made up largely of students in the schools.

[61] A minor essay now lost. Its existence is known from other writers, but the only fragments that remain are in Augustine's works: *Contra Academicos*, III, 14:31; *De beata vita*, X; *Soliloquia*, I, 17; *De civitate Dei*, III, 15; *Contra Julianum*, IV, 15:78; *De Trinitate*, XIII, 4:7, 5:8; XIV, 9:12, 19:26; *Epist.* CXXX, 10.

62 Note this merely parenthetical reference to his father's death and contrast it with the account of his mother's death in Book. 9, Chs. 10-12.

63 Col. 2:8, 9.

64 I.e., Marcus Tullius Cicero.

65 This refers to the Manicheans, a pseudo-Christian sect founded by a Persian religious teacher, Mani (c. A.D. 216-277). They professed a highly eclectic religious system chiefly distinguished by its radical dualism and its elaborate cosmogony in which good was co-coordinated with light, and evil with darkness. There was, in the sect, an esoteric minority called *perfecti*, who were supposed to obey the strict rules of an ascetic ethic. The rest were *auditores*, who followed, at a distance, the doctrines of the *perfecti* but not their rules. The chief attraction of Manicheism lay in the fact that it appeared to offer a straightforward, apparently profound and rational solution to the problem of evil, both in nature and in human experience. Cf. H.C. Puech, *Le Manich_isme, son fondateur—sa doctrine* (Paris, 1949); F.C. Burkitt, *The Religion of the Manichees* (Cambridge, 1925); and Steven Runciman, *The Medieval Manichee* (Cambridge, 1947).

66 James 1:17.

67 Cf. Plotinus, *Enneads*, V, 3:14.

68 Cf. Luke 15:16.

69 Cf. Ovid, *Metamorphoses*, VII, 219-224.

70 For the details of the Manichean cosmogony, see Burkitt, *op. cit.*, ch. 4.

71 Prov. 9:18.

72 Prov. 9:17.

73 Cf. *Enchiridion*, IV.

74 Cf. Matt. 22:37-39.

75 Cf. 1 John 2:16. See also Bk. 10, Chs. 30ff, for a more elaborate analysis.

76 Cf. Ex. 20:3-8; Ps. 144:9. Augustine, in his *Sermon* 9, points out that in the Ten Commandments, *three* pertain to God and *seven* to men.

77 Acts 9:5.

78 An example of this, which Augustine doubtless had in mind, is God's command to Abraham to offer up his son, Isaac, as a human sacrifice. Cf. Gen. 22:1, 2.

79 *Electi sancti.* Another Manichean term for the *perfecti*, the elite and "perfect" among them.

80 Ps. 144:7.

Book Four Notes

81 Ps. 50:14.

82 Cf. John 6:27.

83 Ps. 74:21.

84 Cf. Ps. 4:2.

85 This refers to the rites of soothsayers, in which animals were killed for divination and to appease the gods.

86 Cf. Hos. 12:1.

87 Ps. 41:4.

88 John 5:14.

89 Ps. 51:17.

90 Vindicianus; see below, Bk. 7, Ch. 6.

91 James 4:6; 1 Peter 5:5.

92 Rom. 5:5.

93 Cf. Ps. 106:2.

94 Cf. Ps. 42:5; 43:5.

95 *Ibid.*

96 Cf. Ovid, *Tristia*, IV, 4:74.

97 Cf. Horace, Ode I, 3:8, where he speaks of Virgil. Augustine's memory alters the text slightly here.

98 2 Tim. 4:3.

99 Ps. 119:142.

100 Ps. 80:3.

101 Ps. 19:5.

[102] John 1:10.

[103] *De pulchro et apto*; a lost essay with no other record except echoes in the rest of Augustine's aesthetic theories. Cf. *The Nature of the Good Against the Manicheans*, 8-15; *City of God*, 11, 18; *De ordine*, 1, 7:18; 2, 19:51; *Enchiridion*, 3, 10; 1, 5.

[104] Eph. 4:14.

[105] Ps. 72:18.

[106] Ps. 18:28.

[107] John 1:16.

[108] John 1:9.

[109] Cf. James 1:17.

[110] Cf. James 4:6; 1 Peter 5:5.

[111] Ps. 78:39.

[112] Cf. Jer. 25:10; 33:11; John 3:29; Rev. 18:23.

[113] Cf. Ps. 51:8.

[114] The first section of the *Organon*, which analyzes the problem of predication and develops "the ten categories" of *essence* and the nine "accidents." This existed in a Latin translation by Victorinus, who also translated the *Enneads* of Plotinus, to which Augustine refers in Bk. 8, Ch. 2.

[115] Cf. Gen. 3:18.

[116] Again, the Prodigal Son theme; cf. Luke 15:13.

[117] Cf. Ps. 17:8.

Book Five Notes

[118] Ps. 35:10.

[119] Cf. Ps. 19:6.

[120] Cf. Rev. 21:4.

[121] Cf. Ps. 138:6.

[122] Ps. 8:7.

[123] Heb. 12:29.

[124] An echo of the opening sentence of Book 1, Ch. 1.

[125] Cf. 1 Cor. 1:30.

[126] Cf. Matt. 22:21.

[127] Cf. Rom. 1:21ff.

128 Cf. Rom. 1:23.

129 Cf. Rom. 1:25.

130 Wisdom of Solomon 11:20 (The Apocrypha).

131 Cf. Job 28:28.

132 Eph. 4:13, 14.

133 Ps. 37:23.

134 Ps. 142:5.

135 Cf. Gen. 3:16.

136 Cf. Eph. 2:15.

137 Bk. 1, Ch. 11.

138 Cf. Ps. 51:17.

139 A constant theme in The Psalms and elsewhere; cf. Ps. 136.

140 Cf. Ps. 41:4.

141 Cf. Ps 141:3ff.

142 Followers of the skeptical tradition established in the Platonic Academy by Arcesilaus and Carneades in the third century B.C. They taught the necessity of suspended judgment in all questions of truth, and would allow nothing more than the consent of probability. This tradition was known in Augustine's time chiefly through the writings of Cicero; cf. his *Academica*. This kind of skepticism shook Augustine's complacency severely, and he wrote one of his first dialogues, *Contra Academicos*, in an effort to clear up the problem it posed.

143 The Manicheans were officially banned in Rome.

144 Ps. 139:22.

145 A mixed figure here, put together from Ps. 4:7; 45:7; 104:15; the phrase *sober intoxication of Your wine* is almost certainly the echo of a stanza of one of Ambrose's own hymns, *Splendor paternae gloriae*, which Augustine had doubtless learned in Milan: "*Bibamus sobriam ebrietatem spiritus.*" Cf. W.I. Merrill, *Latin Hymns* (Boston, 1904), pp. 4, 5.

146 Ps. 119:155.

147 Cf. 2 Cor. 3:6. Augustine's discovery of the allegorical method of interpretation opened new horizons for him in

Biblical interpretation, which he adopted as a settled principle in his sermons and commentaries.

Book Six Notes

[148] Cf. Ps. 71:5.

[149] Cf. Ps. 10:1.

[150] Cf. Luke 7:11-17.

[151] Cf. John 4:14.

[152] Rom. 12:11.

[153] 2 Tim. 2:15.

[154] Cf. Gen. 1:26ff.

[155] 2 Cor. 3:6.

[156] Another reference to the Academic doctrine of *suspendium*; cf. Bk. 5, Ch. 10.

[157] This is the basic assumption of Augustine's philosophy of the nature of knowledge.

[158] Cf. Heb. 11:6.

[159] Cf. Plato, *Politicus*, 273 D.

[160] Alypius was more than Augustine's close friend; he became bishop of Tagaste and was prominent in local Church affairs in the province of Africa.

[161] Prov. 9:8.

[162] Cf. Luke 16:10.

[163] Luke 16:11, 12.

[164] Cf. Ps. 145:15.

[165] Here a long soliloquy begins summing up his turmoil over the past decade and his present plight of confusion and indecision.

[166] Isa. 28:15.

[167] Sirach 3:26 (the Apocrypha). Also known as "Ecclesiasticus", or the "Wisdom of Jesus the Son of Sirach".

[168] The normal minimum legal age for marriage was twelve! Cf. Justinian, *Institutiones*, 1, 10:22.

[169] Cf. Ps. 33:11.

[170] Cf. Ps. 145:15, 16.

171 A variation on "restless is our heart until it comes to find rest in You," Bk. 1, Ch. 1.

172 Cf. Isa. 46:4.

Book Seven Notes

173 Thirty years old; although the term "youth" normally included the years twenty to forty.

174 *Phantasmata*, mental constructs, which may be internally coherent but correspond to no reality outside the mind.

175 This echoes of Plato's *Timaeus* and Plotinus' *Enneads*, although with no effort to recall the sources or elaborate the ontological theory.

176 Cf. the famous "definition" of God in Anselm's metaphysical argument: "that being than whom no greater can be conceived." Cf. *Proslogium*, II-V.

177 This simile is Augustine's apparently original improvement on Plotinus' similar figure of the net in the sea; *Enneads*, IV, 3:9.

178 Gen. 25:21 to 33:20.

179 Job 15:26.

180 Cf. Ps. 103:9-14.

181 James 4:6.

182 Cf. John 1:14.

183 Cf. John 1:1-3

184 Cf. John 1:4

185 Cf. John 1:4-10.

186 John 1:11, 12

187 John 1:13.

188 John 1:14.

189 Phil. 2:6.

190 Phil. 2:7-11.

191 Rom. 5:6; 8:32.

192 Luke 10:21.

193 Cf. Matt. 11:28, 29.

194 Cf. Ps. 25:9, 18.

[195] Matt. 11:29.

[196] Rom. 1:21, 22.

[197] Rom. 1:23.

[198] The allegorical interpretation of the Israelites' plundering the Egyptians (Ex. 12:35, 36) made it refer to the liberty of Christian thinkers in appropriating whatever was good and true from the pagan philosophers of the Greco-Roman world.

[199] Cf. Acts 17:28.

[200] Cf. Rom. 1:25.

[201] Cf. Ps. 39:11.

[202] Exodus 3:14

[203] Rom. 1:20.

[204] A classic discussion of the negative character of evil and the positive character of good, a fundamental premise in Augustine's metaphysics. This doctrine of the goodness of all creation is taken up into the scholastic metaphysics; cf. *Confessions*, Bks. 12-13, and Thomas Aquinas, *Summa contra gentes*, II: 45.

[205] Ps. 148:7-13.

[206] Ps. 148:1-5.

[207] "The evil which overtakes us has its source in self-will, in the entry into the sphere of process and in the primal assertion of the desire for self-ownership" (Plotinus, *Enneads*, V, 1:1).

[208] Rom. 1:20.

[209] This is a very candid and plain account of a Plotinian ecstasy, the pilgrimage of the soul from its absorption in things to its rapturous but momentary vision of the One. This is one of two ecstatic visions reported in the *Confessions*; the other is, of course, the last great moment with his mother at Ostia (Bk. 9, Ch. 10). One comes before the "conversion" in the Milanese garden (Bk. 8, Ch. 12), the other, after. They ought to be compared with particular interest in their *similarities* as well as their significant differences. Cf. also K.E. Kirk, *The Vision of God* (London, 1932), pp. 319-346.

[210] 1 Tim. 2:5.

211 Rom. 9:5.

212 John 14:6.

213 An interesting reminder that the Apollinarian heresy was condemned but not extinct.

214 It is worth remembering that both Augustine and Alypius were new believers and were presumably receiving doctrinal instruction in preparation for their eventual baptism and full membership in the Catholic Church. That their ideas on the incarnation were in such confusion at this stage raises an interesting problem.

215 Cf. 1 Cor. 11:19.

216 Cf. 1 Cor. 3:11f.

217 Rom. 7:22, 23.

218 Rom. 7:24, 25.

219 Cf. Prov. 8:22 and Col. 1:15. Augustine is here identifying the figure of Wisdom in Proverbs with the figure of the Logos in the Prologue to the Fourth Gospel. In the Arian controversy both these references to God's Wisdom and Word as "created" caused great difficulty for the orthodox, for the Arians triumphantly appealed to them as proof that Jesus Christ was a "creature" of God. But Augustine was a Chalcedonian before Chalcedon, and there is no doubt that he is here quoting familiar Scripture and filling it with the interpretation achieved by the long struggle of the Church to affirm the coeternity and consubstantiality of Jesus Christ and God the Father.

220 Cf. Ps. 62:1, 2, 5, 6.

221 Cf. Ps. 91:13.

222 A figure that compares the dangers of the solitary traveler in a bandit-infested land and the safety of an imperial convoy on a main highway to the capital city.

223 Cf. 1 Cor. 15:9.

Book Eight Notes

224 Ps. 35:10.

[225] Cf. Ps. 116:16, 17.

[226] Cf. Ps. 8:1.

[227] 1 Cor. 13:12 (KJV).

[228] Matt. 19:12.

[229] Rom. 1:21.

[230] Job 28:28.

[231] Prov. 3:7.

[232] Rom. 1:22.

[233] Col. 2:8.

[234] Virgil, *Aeneid*, VIII, 698.

[235] Ps. 144:5.

[236] Luke 15:4-5.

[237] Cf. Luke, ch. 15.

[238] Cf. Luke, ch. 15.

[239] 1 Cor. 1:27.

[240] A garbled reference to the story of the conversion of Sergius Paulus, proconsul of Cyprus, in Acts 13:4-12.

[241] 2 Tim. 2:21.

[242] Gal. 5:17.

[243] Eph. 5:14.

[244] Rom. 7:22-25.

[245] These were the last obstacles that remained for Augustine. His intellectual difficulties had been cleared away and his intention to become a Christian had become strong. But his unrestrained sexual desire and immersion in his career were too firmly fixed in habit to be overcome by an act of conscious resolution.

[246] Trier, an important imperial town on the Moselle; the emperor referred to here was probably Gratian. Cf. E.A. Freeman, "Augusta Trevororum," in the *British Quarterly Review* (1875), 62, pp. 1-45.

[247] These men were government agents whose duties ranged from postal inspection and tax collection to espionage and secret police work. They seemingly were everywhere, and were generally dreaded by the populace; cf. J.S. Reid,

"Reorganization of the Empire," in *Cambridge Medieval History*, Vol. I, pp. 36-38.

248 The inner circle of imperial advisers; usually rather informally appointed and usually with precarious tenure.

249 Cf. Luke 14:28-33.

250 Eph. 5:8.

251 Cf. Ps. 34:5.

252 Compare to Paul's remarks in Rom. 7:15-17.

253 Cf. Ps. 6:3; 79:5,8.

254 Doubtless from Ponticianus, in their earlier conversation.

255 Matt. 19:21.

256 Rom. 13:13.

257 Note the parallels here to the conversion of Anthony.

258 Rom. 14:1.

259 Eph. 3:20.

Book Nine Notes

260 Ps. 116:16, 17.

261 An imperial holiday season, from late August to the middle of October.

262 Cf. Ps. 46:10.

263 Luke 14:14.

264 Cf. Ps. 125:3.

265 The heresy of Docetism, one of the earliest and most persistent of all Christological errors.

266 Cf. Ps. 27:8.

267 The group included Monica, Adeodatus (Augustine's fifteen-year-old son), Navigius (Augustine's brother), Rusticus and Fastidianus (relatives), Alypius, Trygetius, and Licentius (former pupils).

268 A roundabout acknowledgment that none of Augustine's Cassiciacum works have any distinctive or substantial Christian content. This has often been pointed to as evidence that Augustine's conversion thus far had brought him no farther than to a kind of Christian Platonism; cf. P.

Alfaric, *L'fvolution intellectuelle de Saint Augustin* (Paris, 1918).

269 Cf. *Epistles* II and III.

270 A symbolic reference to the "cedars of Lebanon"; cf. Isa. 2:12-14; Ps. 29:5.

271 There is perhaps a remote connection here with Luke 10:18-20.

272 Ever since the time of Ignatius of Antioch who referred to the Eucharist as "the medicine of immortality," this had been a popular metaphor to refer to the sacraments; cf. Ignatius, *Ephesians* 20:2.

273 Ps. 4:1.

274 John 7:39.

275 Ps. 4:2,3.

276 Ps. 4:4.

277 *Idipsum*—the oneness and immutability of God.

278 Ps. 4:8.

279 1 Cor. 15:54.

280 *Concerning the Teacher.*

281 This was apparently the first introduction into the West of antiphonal chanting, which was already widespread in the East. Ambrose brought it in, and Gregory brought it to perfection.

282 Cf. S. of Sol. 1:3, 4.

283 "All flesh is grass." Cf. Isa. 40:6 & 1 Peter 1:24. See also Bk. 11, Ch. 2.

284 The Apocrypha: Ecclesiasticus 19:1 (also known as the *Wisdom of Jesus the Son of Sirach* or simply *Sirach*).

285 1 Tim. 5:9.

286 Phil. 3:13.

287 Cf. 1 Cor. 2:9.

288 Ps. 36:9.

289 Cf. Compare this report of a "Christian ecstasy" with the Plotinian ecstasy related in Bk. 7, Ch. 17.

290 The Apocrypha: Cf. The Wisdom of Solomon 7:21-30; see especially v. 27: "Though she is but one, she [Wisdom] can do all things, and while remaining in herself, she renews all things."

291 Matt. 25:21.

292 1 Cor. 15:51.

293 Navigius, who had joined them in Milan, but about whom Augustine is curiously silent except for brief and unrevealing references.

294 A.D. 387.

295 1 Tim. 1:5.

296 This passage compares, as Augustine doubtless intended, with the story of his morbid grief at the death of his boyhood friend, above, Bk. 4, Chs. 4-7.

297 Ps. 101:1.

298 Ps. 68:5.

299 Sir Tobie Matthew (adapted). For Augustine's own analysis of the scansion and structure of this hymn, see *De musica*, VI, 2:2-3; for a brief commentary on the Latin text, see A. S. Walpole, *Early Latin Hymns* (Cambridge, 1922), pp. 44-49.

300 1 Cor. 15:22.

301 Matt. 5:22.

302 2 Cor. 10:17.

303 Rom. 8:34. See also, Heb. 7:25.

304 Cf. Matt. 6:12.

305 Ps. 143:2.

306 Matt. 5:7.

307 Cf. Rom. 9:15.

308 Ps. 119:108.

Book Ten Notes

309 Cf. 1 Cor. 13:12.

310 Eph. 5:27.

311 Ps. 51:6.

312 John 3:21.

313 1 Cor. 2:11.

314 1 Cor. 13:7.

315 Ps. 32:1.

316 Ps. 144:7, 8.

317 Cf. Rev. 8:3-5. "And the smoke of the incense with the prayers of the saints went up before God out of the angel's hand" (v. 4).

318 See Phil. 1:6.

319 1 Cor. 2:11.

320 1 Cor. 13:12.

321 Isa. 58:10.

322 Rom. 1:20.

323 Cf. Rom. 9:15.

324 A pre-Socratic "physiologer" who taught that the air is God.

325 An important text for Augustine's conception of sensation and the relation of body and mind.

326 Rom. 1:20.

327 Ps. 32:9.

328 The notion of the soul's immediate self-knowledge is a basic conception in Augustine's psychology and epistemology.

329 The mind-body dualism typical of the Augustinian tradition.

330 Luke 15:8.

331 Cf. Isa. 55:3.

332 Gal. 5:17.

333 Ps. 42:11.

334 When he is known at all, God is known as the Self-evident. This is, of course, not a doctrine of innate ideas but rather of the necessity, and reality, of divine illumination as the *dynamic source* of all our knowledge of divine reality. Cf. Coplestone, *op. cit.*, ch. IV, and Cushman, *op. cit.*

335 The Apocrypha: Cf. Wisdom of Solomon 8:21.

336 1 John 2:16.

337 Eph. 3:20.

338 1 Cor. 15:54.

339 Cf. Matt. 6:34.

340 1 Cor. 9:27.

341 Cf. Luke 21:34.

342 *See note 27.* Cf. Wis. 8:21.

343 The Apocrypha: Ecclesiasticus 18:30, (also known as the Wisdom of Jesus the Son of Sirach, or simply Sirach).

344 1 Cor. 8:8.

345 Phil. 4:11-13.

346 Ps. 103:14.

347 Cf. Gen. 2:7; 3:19.

348 Luke 15:24.

349 The Apocrypha: Ecclesiasticus 23:6, (also known as the Wisdom of Jesus the Son of Sirach, or simply Sirach).

350 Titus 1:15.

351 Rom. 14:20.

352 1 Tim. 4:4.

353 1 Cor. 8:8.

354 Cf. Col. 2:16.

355 Rom. 14:3.

356 Luke 5:8.

357 John 16:33.

358 Cf. Ps. 139:16.

359 Cf. 2 Cor. 5:2.

360 Cf. Tobit, chs. 2 to 4.

361 Gen. 27:1; cf. Augustine's *Sermon* IV, 20:21f.

362 Cf. Gen., ch. 48.

363 Again, Ambrose, *Deus, creator omnium,* an obvious favorite of Augustine's. See above, Bk. 9, Ch. 12.

364 Ps. 25:15.

365 Ps. 121:4.

366 Ps. 26:3.

367 1 John 2:16.

368 Cf. Ps. 103:3-5.

369 Cf. Matt. 11:30.

370 1 Peter 5:5.

371 Cf. Ps. 18:7, 13.

[372] Cf. Isa. 14:12-14.

[373] Cf. Prov. 27:21.

[374] Cf. Ps. 19:12.

[375] Ps. 109:22.

[376] Ps. 31:22.

[377] Cf. the parable of the Pharisee and the Publican, Luke 18:9-14.

[378] Cf. Eph. 2:2.

[379] 2 Cor. 11:14.

[380] Rom. 6:23.

[381] Cf. 1 Tim. 2:5.

[382] Cf. Rom. 8:32.

[383] Phil. 2:6-8.

[384] Cf. Ps. 88:5; see Ps. 87:6 (Vulgate).

[385] Ps. 103:3.

[386] Cf. Rom. 8:34.

[387] John 1:14.

[388] 2 Cor. 5:15.

[389] Ps. 119:18.

[390] Col. 2:3.

[391] Ps. 21:27.

Book Eleven Notes

[392] Matt. 6:8.

[393] The "virtues" of the Beatitudes, the reward for which is blessedness; cf. Matt. 5:1-11.

[394] Ps. 118:1; cf. Ps. 136.

[395] An interesting symbol of time's ceaseless passage; the reference is to a water clock (*clepsydra*).

[396] Cf. Ps. 130:1.

[397] Ps. 74:16.

[398] A repetition of the metaphor above, Bk. 9, Ch. 7.

[399] Ps. 26:7.

[400] Ps. 119:18.

[401] Cf. Matt. 6:33.

402 Col. 2:3.

403 Augustine was profoundly stirred in mind and heart, by the great mystery of creation and the Scriptural testimony about it. In addition to this long and involved analysis of time and creation which follows here, he returned to the story in Genesis repeatedly in other works written after *Confessions*.

404 The final test of truth for Augustine, is self-evidence and the final source of truth is the indwelling Logos.

405 Cf. the notion of creation in Plato's *Timaeus* (29D-30C; 48E-50C), in which the Demiurgos (craftsman) fashions the universe from pre-existent matter and imposes as much form as the Receptacle will receive. The notion of the world fashioned from pre-existent matter of some sort was a universal idea in Greco-Roman cosmology.

406 Cf. Ps. 33:9.

407 Matt. 3:17.

408 Cf. John 1:1-3.

409 Cf. Augustine's emphasis on Christ as true Teacher in *De Magistro*.

410 Cf. John 3:29.

411 Cf. Ps. 103:4, 5.

412 Ps. 104:24.

413 The notion of the eternity of this world was widely held in different versions in Greek philosophy, and was incorporated into the Manichean rejection of the Christian doctrine of *creatio ex nihilo* (creation out of nothing), which Augustine is citing here.

414 Cf. Ps. 102:27.

415 Ps. 2:7.

416 *Spatium*, which means extension either in space or time.

417 Cf. Ps. 139:6.

418 *Memory, experience,* and *expectation*: a pattern that corresponds vaguely to the *movement* of Augustine's thought in the *Confessions*: from direct experience back to the supporting

memories and forward to the outreach of hope and confidence in God's provident grace.

[419] Cf. Ps. 116:10.

[420] Cf. Matt. 25:21, 23.

[421] The universal principles of "common sense." This idea became a basic category in scholastic epistemology.

[422] Gen. 1:14.

[423] Cf. Josh. 10:12-14.

[424] Cf. Ps. 18:28.

[425] Literally the distance between the elbow and the tip of the middle finger, in the imperial system of weights and measures it was 17.5 inches.

[426] *Distentionem*, "spread-out-ness"; cf. Descartes' notion of *res extensae*, and its relation to time.

[427] Ps. 100:3.

[428] Here Augustine begins to summarize his own answers to the questions he has raised in his analysis of time.

[429] The same hymn of Ambrose quoted above, Bk. 9, Ch. 12.

[430] This theory of time is worth comparing with its most notable restatement in modern poetry, in T.S. Eliot's *Four Quartets*.

[431] Ps. 63:3.

[432] Cf. Phil. 3:12-14.

[433] Cf. Ps. 31:10.

[434] This marks the preparation for the transition from this analysis of time to the exploration of the mystery of creation in Bks. 12 and 13.

Book Twelve Notes

[435] Rom. 8:31.

[436] Matt. 7:7, 8.

[437] Vulgate: Ps. 113:16 (compares to Ps. 115:16, KJV; see also Ps. 148:4 KJV): Augustine finds a distinction here that the Hebrew text does not support. The Hebrew is a typical nominal sentence and means simply "The heavens are the heavens of Yahweh". The reading Augustine uses seems to

rest on a variant Hebrew text. This idiomatic construction does not mean "the heavens of the heavens," but rather "highest heaven." This is a familiar way of emphasizing a superlative in Hebrew (e.g., "King of kings," "Song of songs"). The singular thing can be described superlatively only in terms of itself!

438 It's interesting that Augustine seemed to prefer the *invisibilis et incomposita* of the Old Latin version of Gen. 1:2 over the *inanis et vacua* of the Vulgate, which was surely accessible to him. Since this is to be a key phrase in the succeeding exegesis this reading can hardly have been the casual citation of an old and familiar version. Is it possible that Augustine may have had the sensibilities and associations of his readers in mind—for many of them may have not known Jerome's version or, at least, not very well?

439 *Abyssus*, literally, the unplumbed depths of the sea, and as a constant meaning here, "the depths beyond measure."

440 Gen. 1:2.

441 Augustine may not have known the Platonic doctrine of nonbeing (cf. *Sophist*, 236C-237B), but he clearly is deeply influenced here by Plotinus; cf. *Enneads*, II, 4:8f., where matter is analyzed as a substratum without quantity or quality; and 4:15: "Matter, then, must be described as the indefinite...Matter is indeterminateness and nothing else." In short, *materia informis* is sheer possibility; not anything and not nothing!

442 The opposite of "invisible and unformed."

443 Isa. 6:3; Rev. 4:8.

444 *Ex nihilo*.

445 Cf. Gen. 1:6.

446 The created earth really exists but never is self-sufficient.

447 1 Cor. 13:12.

448 The Apocrypha: Cf. Ecclesiasticus 1:4 (also known as the Wisdom of Jesus the Son of Sirach, or simply Sirach).

449 2 Cor. 5:21.

450 Cf. Gal. 4:26.

451 2 Cor. 5:1.

452 Ps. 26:8.

453 Ps. 119:176.

454 Cf. Ps. 28:1.

455 Cf. Rom. 8:26.

456 The heavenly Jerusalem of Gal. 4:26, which had become a favorite Christian symbol of the peace and blessedness of heaven.

457 Cf. 2 Tim. 2:14.

458 1 Tim. 1:5.

459 Matt. 22:35-40.

460 This is the basis of Augustine's defense of allegory as both legitimate and profitable in the interpretation of Scripture. He didn't mean that there is a plurality of literal truths in Scripture but a multiplicity of perspectives on truth, which amounted to different levels and interpretations of truth. This gave Augustine the basis for a positive tolerance of varying interpretations that held fast to the essential common premises about God's primacy as Creator.

461 In this chapter, Augustine summarizes what he takes to be the Christian consensus on the questions he has explored about the relation of the intellectual and physical creations.

462 Cf. 1 Cor. 8:6.

463 Cf. Col. 1:16.

464 Gen. 1:9.

465 Note how this reiterates a constant theme in the *Confessions* as a whole, which is a further indication that Bk. 12 is an integral part of the single whole.

466 Cf. John 8:44.

467 The essential thesis of the *De Magistro*; it has important implications both for Augustine's epistemology and for his theory of Christian nurture; cf. the *De catechizandis rudibus*.

468 Cf. 1 Cor. 4:6.

469 Cf. Deut. 6:5; Lev. 19:18; see also Matt. 22:37, 39.

470 An echo of Job 39:13-16.

471 The thicket residents mentioned above.

472 Cf. Ps. 143:10.

473 Something of an understatement! It is interesting to note that Augustine devotes more time and space to these opening verses of Genesis than to any other passage in the entire Bible—and he never commented on the *full* text of Genesis.

474 Transition, in preparation for the concluding book (13), which undertakes a constructive resolution to the problem of the analysis of the mode of creation made here in Bk. 12.

Book Thirteen Notes

475 Cf. 2 Cor. 5:21.

476 Cf. Ps. 36:6. Augustine said elsewhere that "the great preachers [receivers of God's illumination] are the mountains of God," because they first catch the light on their summits. The abyss he called "the depth of sin" into which the evil and unfaithful fall.

477 Cf. *Timaeus*, 29D-30A, "He [the Demiurge-Creator] was good: and in the good no jealousy...can ever arise. So, being without jealousy, he desired that all things should come as near as possible to being like himself...He took over all that is visible...and brought it from order to order, since he judged that order was in every way better" (F. M. Cornford, *Plato's Cosmology*, New York, 1937, p. 33). Cf. *Enneads*, V, 4:1, and Athanasius, *On the Incarnation*, III, 3.

478 Cf. Gen. 1:2.

479 Cf. Ps. 36:9.

480 Cf. Gen. 1:6.

481 Rom. 5:5.

482 1 Cor. 12:1.

483 Cf. Eph. 3:14, 19.

484 Cf. Eph. 5:8.

485 Cf. Ps. 31:20.

486 Cf. Ps. 9:13.

[487] The Holy Spirit.

[488] Psalms 120-134 were regarded as a single series of ascending steps by which the soul moves up toward heaven. These psalms are still sub-titled "A Song of Ascents" and can be used to draw the worshiper closer into the heart of God.

[489] Tongues of fire, symbol of the descent of the Holy Spirit; cf. Acts 2:3, 4.

[490] Cf. Ps. 122:6.

[491] Ps. 122:1.

[492] Cf. Ps. 23:6.

[493] Gen. 1:3.

[494] John 1:9.

[495] Cf. the detailed analogy from self to Trinity in *De Trinitate*, IX-XII.

[496] I.e., the Church.

[497] Cf. Ps. 39:11.

[498] Ps. 36:6.

[499] Gen. 1:3 and Matt. 4:17; 3:2.

[500] Cf. Ps. 42:5, 6.

[501] Cf. Eph. 5:8.

[502] Ps. 42:7.

[503] Cf. 1 Cor. 3:1.

[504] Cf. Phil. 3:13.

[505] Cf. Ps. 42:1.

[506] Cf. 2 Cor. 5:1-4.

[507] Ps. 42:2.

[508] Rom. 12:2.

[509] 1 Cor. 14:20.

[510] Gal. 3:1.

[511] Eph. 4:8, 9.

[512] Cf. Ps. 46:4.

[513] Cf. John 3:29.

[514] Cf. Rom. 8:23.

[515] 1 John 3:2.

[516] Ps. 42:3.

517 Cf. Ps. 42:4.

518 Ps. 43:5.

519 Cf. Ps. 119:105.

520 Cf. Rom. 8:10.

521 Cf. S. of Sol. 2:17.

522 Cf. Ps. 5:3.

523 Ps. 43:5.

524 Cf. Rom. 8:11.

525 1 Thess. 5:5.

526 Cf. Gen. 1:5.

527 Cf. Rom. 9:21.

528 Isa. 34:4.

529 Cf. Gen. 3:21.

530 Ps. 8:3.

531 Cf. Ps. 8:2.

532 Unchangeable nature.

533 Ps. 36:5.

534 Cf. Matt. 24:35.

535 Cf. Isa. 40:6-8.

536 Cf. 1 John 3:2.

537 *Retia*, literally "a net"; such as those used by the gladiators who used nets to entangle their opponents.

538 Cf. S. of Sol. 1:3, 4.

539 1 John 3:2.

540 Cf. Ps. 63:1.

541 Ps. 36:9.

542 *Amaricantes*, a figure which Augustine develops both in the *Exposition of the Psalms* and *The City of God*. Commenting on Ps. 65, Augustine says: "For the sea, by a figure, is used to indicate this world, with its bitter saltiness and troubled storms, where men with perverse and depraved appetites have become like fishes devouring one another." In *The City of God*, he speaks of the bitterness of life in the *civitas terrena*; cf. XIX, 5.

543 Cf. Ps. 95:5.

544 Cf. Gen. 1:10f.

545 Augustine sees an analogy between the good earth bearing its fruits and the ethical "fruit-bearing" of the Christian love of neighbor.

546 Cf. Ps. 85:11.

547 Cf. Gen. 1:14.

548 Cf. Isa. 58:7.

549 Cf. Phil. 2:15.

550 Cf. Gen. 1:19.

551 Cf. 2 Cor. 5:17.

552 Cf. Rom. 13:11, 12.

553 Ps. 65:11.

554 For this entire passage, cf. the parallel developed here with 1 Cor. 12:7-11.

555 Cf. Gen. 1:16.

556 Cf. 1 Cor. 3:1; 2:6.

557 Isa. 1:16-17.

558 Isa. 1:18.

559 Cf. Matt. 19:16-22 and Ex. 20:13-16.

560 Cf. Isa. 52:7.

561 *Perfectorum*. Is this a conscious use, in a Christian context, of the distinction he had known so well among the Manicheans—between the *perfecti* and the *auditores?*

562 Ps. 19:2.

563 Cf. Acts 2:2, 3.

564 Cf. Matt. 5:14, 15.

565 Cf. Gen. 1:20.

566 Cf. Jer. 15:19.

567 Ps. 19:4.

568 That is, the Church.

569 An allegorical ideal type of the *perfecti* in the Church.

570 1 Cor. 14:22.

571 The fish was an early Christian symbol for "Jesus Christ."

572 Cf. Ps. 69:32.

573 Cf. Rom. 12:2.

574 Cf. 1 Tim. 6:20.

575 Cf. Rom. 12:2.

576 Gal. 4:12.

577 The Apocrypha: Cf. Ecclesiasticus 3:19 (also known as the Wisdom of Jesus the Son of Sirach, or simply Sirach).

578 Cf. Rom. 1:20.

579 Rom. 12:2.

580 Gen. 1:26.

581 Rom. 12:2 (mixed text).

582 Cf. 1 Cor. 2:15.

583 1 Cor. 2:13.

584 Cf. Ps. 49:20.

585 Cf. James 4:11.

586 See above, Ch. 21.

587 Cf. 1 Cor. 14:16.

588 Another reminder that, ideally, knowledge is immediate and direct.

589 Here, again, as in an ending summary, Augustine restates his central theme and motif in the whole of his *Confessions*: the primacy of God, His constant creativity, His mysterious, unwearied, and un-frustrated redemptive love. All are summed up in this mystery of creation in which the purposes of God are announced and from which all Christian hope takes its premise.

590 That is, from basic and essentially simple ideas, they proliferate multiple—and valid—implications and corollaries.

591 Cf. Rom. 3:4.

592 Cf. Gen. 1:29, 30.

593 Cf. 2 Tim. 1:16.

594 2 Tim. 4:16.

595 Cf. Ps. 19:4.

596 Phil. 4:10 (mixed text).

597 Phil. 4:11-13.

598 Phil. 4:14.

599 Phil. 4:15-17.

600 Phil. 4:17.

601 Cf. Matt. 10:41, 42.

602 *Idiotae*: there is some evidence that this term was used to designate pagans (unbelievers) who had a nominal connection with the Christian community but were not formally enrolled to study the beliefs of the Catholic Church.

603 Gen. 1:31.

604 A reference to the Manichean cosmogony and similar dualistic doctrines of "creation."

605 1 Cor. 2:11, 12.

606 Rom. 5:5.

607 Augustine himself had misgivings about this passage. He said in the *Retractions*, that this statement was made "without sufficient thought." He then added, with great justice: "Whatever the case, the matter is very obscure."

608 Cf. *The City of God*, XI, 10, on Augustine's notion that the world exists as a thought in the mind of God.

Topic Index

CLASSICS IN MODERN ENGLISH

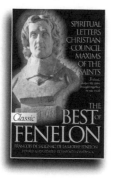

SPIRITUAL
LETTERS
CHRISTIAN
COUNCIL
MAXIMS
OF THE
SAINTS

THE
BEST OF
FENELON

FRANÇOIS DE SALIGNAC DE LA MOTHE-FENELON

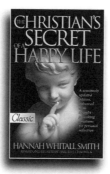

THE CHRISTIAN'S
SECRET
OF A
HAPPY LIFE

HANNAH WHITALL SMITH

E M BOUNDS
THE CLASSIC COLLECTION
ON
PRAYER

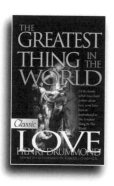

THE
GREATEST
THING IN THE
WORLD

LOVE
HENRY DRUMMOND

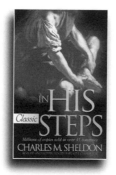

IN HIS
STEPS

CHARLES M. SHELDON

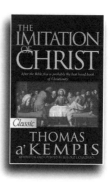

THE
IMITATION
OF
CHRIST

THOMAS
a' KEMPIS

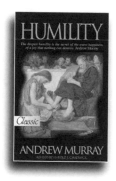

HUMILITY

ANDREW MURRAY

MADAME
JEANNE
GUYON

EXPERIENCING UNION WITH GOD
THROUGH INNER PRAYER
& THE WAY AND RESULTS OF
UNION WITH GOD

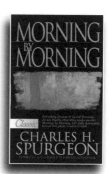

MORNING
BY
MORNING

CHARLES H.
SPURGEON

THE CLASSICS COLLECTION

CLASSICS IN MODERN ENGLISH

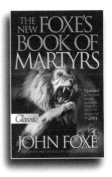

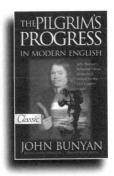

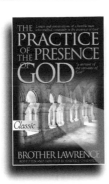

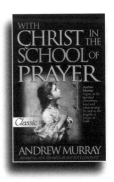

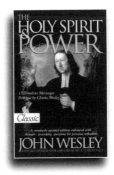

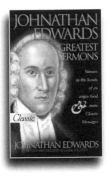

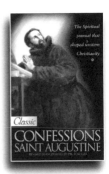

7 Point Advantage

Color timeline
Detailed indexes
Author biographies
Beautifully illustrated
One of a fabulous collection
Each title is an in-depth Bible study
Sensitively revised in modern English

THE CLASSICS COLLECTION